D0843563

FEE MINING
AND
ROCKHOUNDING
ADVENTURES
IN THE
WEST

By

James Martin Monaco
&
Jeannette Hathaway Monaco

Published by:
Gem Guides Book Co.
1275 W. 9th Street
Upland, CA 91786

Copyright © 2007
Gem Guides Book Co.

Second revised Edition

Printed and bound in the United States of America

Cover Design: Scott Roberts

Library of Congress Control Number: 2007929285
ISBN: 978-1-889786-38-4

DISCLAIMER:
Due to the possibility of personal error, typographical error, misinterpretation of information and the many changes due to man or nature, *Fee Mining and Rockhounding Adventures in the West*, its publisher and all other persons directly or indirectly associated with this publication assume no responsibility for accidents, injury or any losses by individuals or groups using this publication.

In rough terrain and hazardous areas all persons are advised to be aware of possible changes due to man or nature that occur at the various collecting sites.

"There is something about treasure that fastens itself upon a man's mind. He will pray and blaspheme and still persevere, and will curse the day he heard of it, and will let his last hour come upon him unawares, still believing that he missed it by only a foot."

— Joseph Conrad —

Good luck hunting for your treasure. May this book be a resource to aid your search.

— Jenny & Jim Monaco —

TABLE OF CONTENTS

8

WYOMING

We have always enjoyed traveling and treasure hunting. We have panned for gold, dug for precious stones and searched beaches for Spanish treasure–meeting great people everywhere we go. However, there have been many times after a trip when we discovered that we were within minutes of a place to mine and unaware it existed. It frustrated us to no end to miss opportunities to enjoy our hobby. Another frustration was to travel to a gold-bearing area of California, only to find that every square inch of territory was covered with mining claim posters. We decided to search for a source book that would help us find places to treasure hunt and rock collect. To date, we have not found that book. So, we did the next best thing–we wrote one ourselves. Now you and your family won't miss a collecting opportunity that is only a few miles away, just because you never knew of its existence.

There are over a hundred places for you to go and try your luck on your own adventure. We are certain that we have only scratched the surface. At the end of this book there is a page for you to help us make additions to a future edition. If you know of a mineral site or mine we have left out, drop us a note and we'll add it to the next edition.

Some places listed are best suited for beginners. They have instructors, equipment rentals and help for you when you need it. They are established mines with reliable, helpful and experienced staffs. We like these places because you can go and get help if you need it. They are well suited to families. There are people around with whom you can swap stories and specimens.

Some of the places listed are wild and isolated. These locations are better suited to prospectors with experience and their own equipment. They are off the beaten path and offer opportunities to enjoy the outdoors undisturbed.

This book is intended as a resource for your next trip. Pack up your car or mobile home and plan an adventure. Many places allow you to camp right at the site. Mining and collecting sites are organized to give you a good idea of what each establishment has to offer. Choose the ones that best fit your level of hunting. We have included brief information and what equipment you need to bring. PLEASE CALL AHEAD TO BE SURE THE ESTABLISHMENT WILL BE OPEN DURING THE TIME YOU PLAN TO VISIT.

Anyone who plans to visit any of these locations for the purpose of collecting or mining is advised to call ahead to make reservations and verify that the site or mine is open. Phone numbers, websites and other contact information changes constantly, but every effort for this edition was made to give the most current information possible. Some locations open and close based on the weather or snow cover. It is always a good idea to check before you make the trip.

We hope this guidebook will become a valuable resource to you, and that you and your family will have wonderful adventures together. We are planning a trip across North America in the near future. We will be using our own book as a reference. Maybe we will see you at some of the collecting and prospecting areas. Best of luck in your search.

TIPS AND RULES TO FOLLOW:

1. Let a friend know exactly where you plan to go and when you plan to return.

2. Be sure to check in when you get back. This is always a good idea and an especially important practice when searching in a remote area of the country.

3. If your search takes you off the beaten path or into an area of the country with which you are unfamiliar, do your research.

4. Don't travel alone.

5. If you need a permit or to gain permission to mine on private land, get it before you venture out. There is nothing as frustrating as getting to your destination without proper permits.

6. Be sure to bring a stocked first aid kit with you to care for cuts and bruises. In some areas of the country a snake bite kit is recommended.

7. As with any form of exercise, it is wise to check with your physician before undertaking a strenuous outing.

8. Be familiar with local plants and animals, weather conditions and climate. All this information will help you to be better prepared and insure a safe, productive expedition.

9. Check that you have packed the proper tools and equipment for your adventure.

   a. Include eye protection for mining that requires the use of hammers or chisels.

   b. Pack work gloves to keep your hands from blistering.

   c. The clothes you choose to pack will depend on the season, climate and terrain in which you will mine.

10. There are some items that are needed for most trips:

   a. Bring a hat, sturdy boots and comfortable clothes.

   b. Long pants will protect your legs from brush and other hazards.

   c. Take bug spray and sun screen with you.

   d. Bring clothing for changes in temperature and weather. Dress in layers so you can remove your windbreaker, sweater, sweatshirt or vest as the day or you heat up. Older clothing is preferable since it may get stained.

   e. A rain poncho should be in your standard equipment, as well as a clean change of clothing, socks and a towel. Dry, clean clothes cheer the spirit, soothe the soul and make the ride home more bearable.

   f. Some locations require only a swimsuit and towel, while other locations may require a wet suit and scuba tank, so check with your destination or details.

   g. Many sites provide food and drink. Others do not. It is wise to always carry drinking water with you, especially if you are traveling in desert areas. Pack plenty of food. Physical labor builds a big appetite!

The following commandments were taken from the website of the Museum of the City of San Francisco who credits its origin with a man named James M. Hutchings. He wrote them in 1853 and first published them in a newspaper called the *Placerville Herald*. They were so popular, that he self-published them on letter sheets and sold them individually.[1]

A man spake these words, and said: I am a miner, wandering "from away down east," to sojourn in a strange land. And behold I've seen the elephant, yea, verily, I saw him, and bear witness, that from the key of his trunk to the end of his tail, his whole body hath passed before me; and I followed him until his huge feet stood before a clapboard shanty; then with his trunk extended he pointed to a candle-card tacked upon a shingle, as though he would say Read, and I read the:

MINER'S TEN COMMANDMENTS

I. Thou shalt have no other claim than one.

II. Thou shalt not make unto thyself any false claim, nor any likeness to a mean man, by jumping one: for I, a miner, am a just one, and will visit the miners around about, and they will judge thee; and when they shall decide, thou shalt take thy pick, thy pan, thy shovel and thy blankets with all thou hast and shall depart seeking other good diggings, but thou shalt find none. Then when thou hast paid out all thy dust, worn out thy boots and garments so that there is nothing good about them but the pockets, and thy patience is like unto thy garments, then in sorrow shall thou return to find thy claim worked out, and yet thou hath no pile to hide in the ground, or in the old boot beneath thy bunk, or in buckskin or in bottle beneath thy cabin, and at last thou shalt hire thy body out to make thy board and save thy bacon.

III. Thou shalt not go prospecting before thy claim gives out. Neither shalt thou take thy money, nor thy gold dust, nor thy good name, to the gaming table in vain; for monte, twenty-one, roulette, faro, lansquenet and poker, will prove to thee that the more thou puttest down the less thou shalt take up; and when thou thinkest of thy wife and children, thou shalt not hold thyself guiltless—but insane.

IV. Thou shalt not remember what thy friends do at home on the Sabbath day, lest the remembrance may not compare favorably with what thou doest here. Six days thou mayst dig or pick; but the other day is Sunday; yet thou washest all thy dirty shirts, darnest all thy stockings, tap thy boots, mend thy clothing, chop the whole week's firewood, make up and bake thy bread, and boil thy pork and beans, that thou wait not when thou returnest from thy long-tom weary. For in six days' labor only though canst do it in six months; and though, and thy morals and thy conscience, be none the better for it; but reproach thee, shouldst thou ever return with thy worn-out body to thy mother's fireside.

V. Though shalt not think more of all thy gold, and how thou canst make it fastest, than how thou will enjoy it after thou hast ridden rough-shod over thy good old parents' precepts and examples, that thou mayest have nothing to reproach thee, when left ALONE in the land where thy father's blessing and thy mother's love hath sent thee.

VI. Thou shalt not kill; neither thy body by working in the rain, even though thou shalt make enough to buy physic and attendance with; nor thy neighbor's body in a duel, or in anger, for by "keeping cool,"thou canst save his life and thy conscience. Neither shalt thou destroy thyself by getting "tight," nor "stewed," nor "high," nor "corned," nor "half- seas over," nor "three sheets in the wind," by drinking smoothing down—"brandy slings," "gin cocktails," "whiskey punches," "rum toddies," nor "egg-noggs." Neither shalt thou suck "mint juleps," nor "sherry- cobblers," through a straw, nor gurgle from a bottle the "raw material," nor take "it straight" from a decanter; for, while thou art swallowing down thy purse, and the coat from off thy back thou art burning the coat from off thy stomach; and if thou couldst see the houses and lands, and gold dust, and home comforts already lying there—"a huge pile"—thou shouldst feel a choking in thy throat; and when to that thou addest thy crooked walkings thou wilt feel disgusted with thyself, and inquire "Is thy servant a dog that he doeth these things!" Verily, thou shalt say, "Farewell, old bottle, I will kiss thy gurgling lips no more; slings, cocktails, punches, smashes, cobblers, nogs, toddies, sangarees and juleps, forever farewell. Thy remembrance shames one; henceforth, I cut thy acquaintance, and headaches, tremblings, heart-burnings, blue devils, and all the unholy catalogue of evils that follow in thy train. My wife's smiles and my children's merry-hearted laugh, shall charm and reward me for having the manly firmness and courage to say NO. I wish thee an eternal farewell."

VII. Thou shalt not grow discouraged, nor think of going home before thou hast made thy "pile," because thou hast not "struck a lead," nor found a "rich crevice," nor sunk a hole upon a "pocket," lest in going home thou shalt leave four dollars a day, and going to work, ashamed, at fifty cents, and serve thee right; for thou knowest by staying here, thou mightst strike a lead and fifty dollars a day, and keep thy manly self respect, and then go home with enough to make thyself and others happy.

VIII. Thou shalt not steal a pick, or a shovel, or a pan from thy fellow-miner; nor take away his tools without his leave; nor borrow those he cannot spare; nor return them broken, nor trouble him to fetch them back again, nor talk with him while his water rent is running on, nor remove his stake to enlarge thy claim, nor undermine his bank in following a lead, nor pan out gold from his "riffle box," nor wash the "tailings" from his sluice's mouth. Neither shalt thou pick out specimens from the company's pan to put them in thy mouth or pocket; nor cheat thy partner of his share; nor steal from thy cabin-mate his gold dust, to add to thine, for he will be sure to discover what thou hast done, and will straightaway call his fellow miners together, and if the law hinder them not, will hang thee, or give thy fifty lashes, or shave thy head and brand thee, like a horse thief, with "R" upon thy cheek, to be known and read of all men, Californians in particular.

IX. Thou shalt not tell any false tales about "good diggings in the mountains," to thy neighbor that thou mayest benefit a friend who had mules, and provisions, and tools and blankets he cannot sell,—lest in deceiving thy neighbor, when he returneth through the snow, with naught save his rifle, he present thee with the contents thereof, and like a dog, thou shalt fall down and die.

X. Thou shalt not commit unsuitable matrimony, nor covet "single blessedness;" nor forget absent maidens; nor neglect thy "first love;"—but thou shalt consider how faithfully and patiently she awaiteth thy return; yea and covereth each epistle that thou sendest with kisses of kindly welcome—until she hath thyself. Neither shalt thou cove thy neighbor's wife, nor trifle with the affections of his daughter; yet, if thy heart be free, and thou dost love and covet each other, thou shalt "pop the question" like a man.

A new Commandment give I unto thee—if thou has a wife and little ones, that thou lovest dearer than life,—that thou keep them continually before thee, to cheer and urge thee onward, until thou canst say, "I have enough—God bless them—I will return." Then from thy much-loved home, with open arms shall thy come forth to welcome thee, with weeping tears of unutterable joy that thou art come; then in the fullness of thy heart's gratitude, thou shalt kneel together before thy Heavenly Father, to thank him for thy safe return. AMEN— So mote it be.

FORTY-NINER[1]

Footnote
[1] http://www.sfmuseum.org/hist7/tencom.html, Gladys Hansen, Museum of the City of San Francisco, 2001.

Now you need to pack your tools. The following list consists of the standard tools you will need for almost all of your adventures. This list is meant to help you get organized.

STANDARD TOOLS:
- 5-gallon Bucket
- Chisels
- Closable Plastic Container (Film Canister)
- Collecting Bag
- Crowbar/Pry Bar
- Eye Protection (Goggles)
- First-Aid Kit
- Gads
- Screwdriver
- Rock Hammer
- Pencil and Notepad
- Pick
- Proper Clothing
- Rags
- Shovel
- Sledgehammer
- Small Trowel and Hand Garden Tools
- Snacks
- Water
- Work Gloves
- Ziplock Bags

Some mines require specialized equipment. Whenever possible we have tried to include that information with the listing for the individual mine.

ADDITIONAL EQUIPMENT FOR SAPPHIRE / DIAMOND / OPAL MINING:
- Plastic Spray Bottle
- 1/8-, 1/4- and 1/2-inch Sifting Screens
- Tweezers
- Washtub
- Whisk Broom or Brush

GOLD MINING TOOLS:
- Collecting Bottles
- Gold Pan
- Snuffer Bottle

ADDITIONAL EQUIPMENT FOR EXPERIENCED GOLD MINERS:
- Dredge
- Highbanker
- Metal Detector
- Sluice Box

If you plan to do any metal detecting, you need to pack your detector, a pouch to hold your finds and some kind of scoop or shovel. Many mines can provide all the tools that you will need. Some rent equipment, while still others provide very little. We suggest that you check with the individual mine if you are uncertain of what to bring along.

To make the most out of your adventure once you get there you need to observe the following words to the wise to give you a leg up on the greenhorns.

1. When swinging rock hammers, sledgehammers or a pick, make sure everyone is clear of your work area, and that you have adequate footing.

2. Never enter caves or old mining tunnels. Snakes love caves for their cool shade. Caves are also frequented by other animals including mountain lions and bears. Old shafts are extremely dangerous and unstable. They are not worth the risk. Never tunnel into banks with overhangs or on cliffs.

3. If you are searching for gold for the first time, try to get a panning lesson. Many mines teach gold panning. You can teach yourself of course, but, in our opinion, nothing compares to watching an expert and gaining some real experience.

4. Stay out of fast-moving water. Do not damage or prospect in the riverbank or disturb plant life while mining. Be sure you are not in a flash flood area. Heavy rains upstream can flood downstream in minutes and under a clear blue sky.

5. Check out the plant life on the banks to avoid poison ivy or other harmful plants.

6. Contain all camp fires in a fire pit.

7. If you are working a dredge, clear all large rocks away from the hole you are working to prevent cave-ins or rock slides. Be careful when digging into a bank that the hole does not collapse. Never work in a hole deeper than you are tall if you are alone.

8. Remember to fill in the holes you dig. Holes are dangerous and unsightly.

9. Watch over children and inexperienced miners. Instruct children on how to use tools. Point out hazards and take frequent breaks.

The scales used for precious metals and gemstones are different than those to weigh zucchini. Gold miners speak on pennyweight and jewelers talk in terms of carats and grams.

Gems are weighed in carats, not to be confused with karats used to distinguish the purity of gold. The word carat comes from ancient India where carob seed were used as small consistent weights.

The word pennyweight comes from the Gold Rush days when a miner would compare the weight of his gold dust in comparison to the weight of a penny. The size of a penny in 1849 was somewhat larger than the flimsy zinc versions minted now.

The size of gemstones is measured in millimeters.

Here is some conversions to help you see what is what.

PENNYWEIGHT CONVERSIONS:
- 1 Pennyweight (dwt) = 7.776 Carats
- 1 Pennyweight (dwt) = 1.55 Grams
- 1 Pennyweight (dwt) = 24 Grains
- 1 Pennyweight (dwt) = 0.05 Troy Ounces

CARAT CONVERSIONS:
- 1 Carat = 0.20 Grams
- 1 Carat = 0.1287 Pennyweight
- 1 Carat = 0.0064 Troy Ounce
- 1 Gram = 5 Carats
- 1 Pennyweight = 7.776 Carats
- 1 Troy Ounce = 155.5 Carats

TROY WEIGHT
- 24 Grains = 1 Pennyweight
- 20 Pennyweight = 1 Troy Ounce
- 12 Troy Ounces = 1 Troy Pound
- 1 Millimeter = 0.03937 Inches
- 1 Inch = 25.4 Millimeters

MOHS TABLE OF HARDNESS

Friedrich Mohs devised the scale of mineral hardness in 1822. He picked ten minerals and rated them in terms of their strength with ten being the hardest. A Mohs criterion for a mineral to be listed with a higher number was that it could scratch the specimen in the category below it. Mohs original representative minerals are underlined in the list below.

MOHS SCALE

1	<u>Talc</u>
2	<u>Gypsum</u>, Pearl
3	<u>Calcite</u>, Malachite
4	<u>Fluorite</u>, Opal
5	<u>Apatite</u>, Glass, Lapis
6	<u>Orthoclase</u>, Jade, Hematite, Onyx, Peridot, Zircon
7	<u>Quartz</u>, Garnet, Emerald, Amethyst, Aquamarine, Citrine, Tourmaline
8	<u>Topaz</u>, Chrysoberyl, Cubic Zirconia
9	<u>Corundum</u>, Ruby, Sapphire
10	<u>Diamond</u>

The Reed Gold Mine reported the first gold find in the United States. As the story goes, in 1799, Reed's son, Conrad, found a large yellow rock in Little Meadow Creek while playing hooky from church. A silversmith in Concord was unable to identify the rock, but measured its weight at seventeen pounds. The Reeds used it as a door stop until a jeweler bought it for $3.50 in 1802, less than one-tenth of its value. Later Reed discovered his mistake and "convinced" the jeweler to compensate him. Mining later began by Reed and others and a twenty-eight-pound nugget was found. A total of $100,000 worth of gold was unearthed by 1824. North Carolina was the first gold producing state in the United States

Gold was discovered in 1806 near Spotsylvania County, Virginia. Several mines were in operation by 1825. Mining ceased in 1849 when the Virginia miners left the state to head for the gold rush in California. In 1850, the production of gold in Virginia was reduced by half because of a labor shortage. Gold was last mined commercially in Virginia in 1947 as a by-product of lead mining.

Gold was also discovered in South Carolina in the early 1800s. Lancaster County was shipping gold to the U.S. Mint in 1829. Mining, interrupted by several wars, continued throughout the 1800s.

Georgia had a gold rush in 1828 which lasted to 1850 with over four thousand miners working the hills. Gold was first discovered in Georgia in 1818 by Mr. Benjamin Hicks. He made the discovery by kicking over a rock to expose a lump of gold the color and size of an egg's yolk. Miners deserted this area as their counterparts in Virginia had, when gold was discovered in California, but they came back when California gold ran out in 1855. Mining was again interrupted, this time by the Civil War, to be resumed after the end of the war. Commercial mining of gold continued until World War II.

New Mexico gave the cry of gold in the Ortiz Mountains, south of Santa Fe, in 1828. This was not the first gold rush in this area. Spanish conquistadors discovered and mined gold here after searching throughout South America and Mexico. Prior to that Native Americans mined gold here for unknown periods of time.

Alabama had its own gold rush beginning in the 1830s. Gold was discovered in Tennessee in 1831 on the Ococee Land District, which belonged to the Cherokees. The land was taken along with the gold. The most famous area here was Cokercreek, which is still producing gold today.

In 1838, gold was found in Ohio where it was deposited fourteen thousand years earlier during the glacier's retreat. The origin of this gold was probably somewhere in northern Canada.

The largest gold rush in North America occurred in 1849 in California. Gold had been discovered a year earlier at Sutter's Sawmill by a worker named James W. Marshall. In January of 1848, a dam was built on the American River. Water was channeled to the dam to remove the loose dirt and gravel and then turned off again.

On Monday, January 24, 1848, James Marshall walked in the channel and spotted grains of shiny metal the size of wheat. Suspecting this was gold he rushed to tell his fellow workers that he had found a gold mine. Captain John Sutter was informed of the potential find and did all within his power to prevent this story from leaking out, while buying as much surrounding land from the Native Americans as possible. The remoteness of the area slowed the speed of the discovery.

In March of 1848, gold was mined and the discovery reported in the San Francisco newspapers. Soon men from around the world began to migrate to Coloma, California to establish the first mining camp. John Sutter was there to sell supplies, food, tools and claims to the would-be miners.

In the fall of 1849, the number of miners in California had forever changed the population distribution in the United States. Men worked in groups, mining an area until the gold disappeared. The miners then moved up the creeks and rivers to search for other gold deposits. Camp towns sprang up overnight, to disappear just as quickly. Many of these towns are well preserved and still exist along Highway 49. Their names create vivid images; Fiddletown, Rough and Ready, Chinese Camp, Sutters Creek, Placerville and Gold Run—to name a few. In 1853, at least $65 million worth of gold was taken from California mines. Mining in California continued until the surface gold played out in 1855.

During the same time period, gold was discovered in Alaska at the Kenai River in 1848 by a Russian mining engineer. Alaska did not become a U.S. territory until March 30, 1867. Alaska had a series of strikes or rushes in Anchorage, Nome and Fairbanks. Gold continues to be discovered today in Alaska.

Nevada was found to have gold in 1849. During the gold mining process, much blue clay was uncovered and discarded. This clay was later found to be rich in silver. Silver became the true treasure of Nevada.

The western states were searched for gold and silver. It was found in 1852 in Idaho, Montana and Oregon, in Washington in 1853 and Utah in 1858. That same year gold miners in Arizona were earning $4 to $150 a day.

In 1859, the slogan "Pike's Peak or Bust" became the cry of gold miners heading for Colorado. Gold production in Colorado reached forty million troy ounces.

Montana, which had shown some gold in 1852, became the next rush site in 1863, when large quantities of gold were found near Virginia City.

The Black Hills of South Dakota, in and around Rapid City, experienced their own influx of miners for gold between 1876 and 1878.

Gold is still mined commercially in the U.S. and small scale miners are still out there, even as you read this, with picks, shovels, dredges and sluice boxes looking for that precious metal.

 Interstate Highway

 U.S. Highway

 State Highway

 City

 State Capital

 River

 National Park, Monument, Forest, Wilderness, Wildlife Refuge

 Site Number Marker

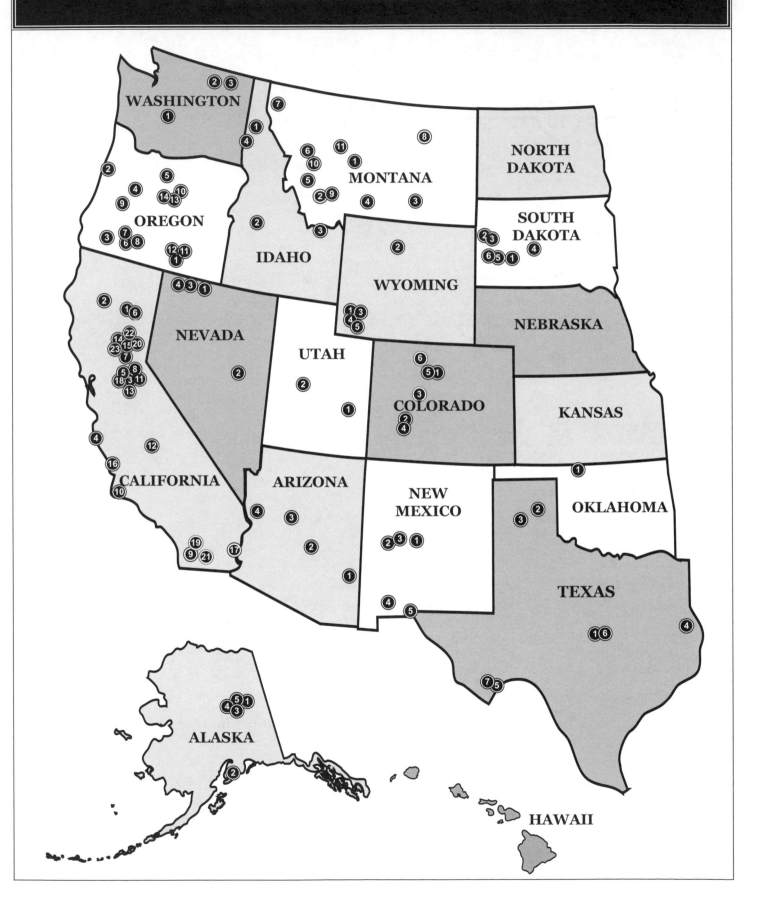

ALASKA
- (1) Chena Hot Springs Resort
- (2) Crow Creek Mine
- (3) El Dorado Gold Mine
- (4) Nome Creek
- (5) Paradise Valley

ARIZONA
- (1) Black Hills Rockhounding Area
- (2) Goldfield Ghost Town & Mine Tours
- (3) Prescott National Forest Lynx Creek
- (4) Gold Road Mine Tour

CALIFORNIA
- (1) Butte Recreation Area
- (2) Big Flat Recreation Area
- (3) California Gold
- (4) Cape San Martin
- (5) Gold Prospecting Adventures, LLC
- (6) Golden Caribou Mining Association
- (7) Hangtown's Gold Bug Park
- (8) Hidden Treasure Gold Mine
- (9) Himalaya Tourmaline Tours
- (10) Jalama Beach Park
- (11) Kennedy Gold Mine
- (12) Keyesville Recreation Area
- (13) Little Valley Inn & Gold Prospecting
- (14) Malakoff Diggins State Historic Park
- (15) Marshall Gold Discovery State Historic Park
- (16) Moonstone Beach
- (17) Opal Hill Mine
- (18) Roaring Camp Mining Company
- (19) The Oceanview Mine
- (20) The Sixteen to One Mine
- (21) The Stewart Mine
- (22) Union Flat Casual Mining Area
- (23) Wild West Gold Mining Adventures

COLORADO
- (1) Argo Gold Mine & Mill
- (2) Bachelor-Syracuse Mine Tour
- (3) Country Boy Mine
- (4) Old Hundred Gold Mine Tour
- (5) Phoenix Gold Mine
- (6) Vic's Gold Panning

IDAHO
- (1) Emerald Creek Garnet Area
- (2) Idaho Gold Prospecting Adventures
- (3) Spencer Opal Mine
- (4) 3-D Panhandle Gems/Garnet Queen Mine

MONTANA
- (1) Confederate Gulch Adventures
- (2) Crystal Park
- (3) Custer Country
- (4) Gallatin National Forest
- (5) Gem Mountain Sapphire Mine
- (6) L◆E Ranch
- (7) Libby Creek Panning Area
- (8) Paleo Prospectors
- (9) Red Rock Mine
- (10) Sapphire Gallery
- (11) Spokane Bar Sapphire Mine

NEVADA
- (1) Bonanza Opal Mines
- (2) Garnet Fields Rockhound Area
- (3) Rainbow Ridge Opal Mine
- (4) Royal Peacock Opal Mines

NEW MEXICO
- (1) Blanchard Rock Shop
- (2) Kelly Mine
- (3) Nitt Mine & North Graphic Mine
- (4) Rockhound State Park
- (5) The Kilbourne Hole Volcanic Center

OKLAHOMA
- (1) Salt Plains National Wildlife Refuge

OREGON
- (1) Dust Devil Mining Company
- (2) Oregon's Ocean Beaches
- (3) Oregon Gold Trips, LLC
- (4) Quartzville Recreational Corridor
- (5) Richardsons Rock Ranch
- (6) Rogue River National Forest–Little Applegate Recreation Area
- (7) Rogue River National Forest – Golden Nugget Recreation Area
- (8) Rogue River National Forest–Tunnel Ridge Recreation Area
- (9) Sharps Creek Recreation Area
- (10) Lucky Strike Mine
- (11) Spectrum Sunstone Mines
- (12) Spectrum Sunstone Mines Gem Tours
- (13) Whistler Springs
- (14) White Fir Springs

SOUTH DAKOTA
- (1) Big Thunder Gold Mine
- (2) Black Hills Mining Museum
- (3) Broken Boot Gold Mine
- (4) Buffalo Gap National Grassland
- (5) Glory Hunters Gold Mine
- (6) Wade's Gold Mill

TEXAS
- (1) Garner Seaquist Ranch
- (2) Lake McClellan Recreation Area
- (3) Lake Mackenzie Reservoir
- (4) Lake Sam Rayburn Reservoir
- (5) Stillwell Ranch & RV Park
- (6) Wayne Hofmann Ranch
- (7) Woodward Ranch/Bird Mine/Needle Peak

UTAH
- (1) Lin Ottinger's Tours
- (2) U-Dig Fossils

WASHINGTON
- (1) Geology Adventures
- (2) Stonerose Interpretive Center
- (3) Sullivan Creek/Colville National Forest

WYOMING
- (1) Severns Studio & Fossil Company
- (2) The Wyoming Dinosaur Center
- (3) Tynsky's Fossil Fish Tours
- (4) Ulrich's Fossil Gallery
- (5) Warfield Fossil Quarries

"A ton of gold."

The U.S. purchased Alaska from Russia in 1867. At the time the territory was mainly known by fur trappers and, of course, the indigenous people. During the 1880s the U.S. experienced the worst economic depression ever known. Silver prices crashed, placer deposits disappeared and for the majority gold grew increasingly difficult to find in California. Prospectors moved on. By the 1870s some miners arrived at the edge of the Yukon and Alaska. In 1896, oil was discovered in Alaska but the public took little notice. Desperate people longed for a chance to strike it rich, and tales were told of the good old days of the 1849 Gold Rush. In 1886 it happened again in one of the most inhospitable places on earth.

Rich deposits of placer gold were discovered and mined. Two ships sailed from Alaska, the *Portland* bound for Seattle and the *Excelsior* bound for San Francisco. The ships arrived within three days of each other. A Seattle newsman named Beriah Brown decided that printing the weight of the shipment would be more sensational than printing the monetary value. He was right. News flashed around the world–a ton of gold was discovered in Alaska. The rush was on.

Among the first to sail north was a young Jack London who took only twelve days to gather supplies before sailing from California with his cousin. It took his cousin only two days of travel in Alaska before throwing in the towel and sailing for home. But Jack had "Klondike fever" and remained for two years when a bad case of scurvy, a disease common in Alaska at the time, forced him to quit. He left no richer in gold, but with a wealth of experience which he later translated into his stories.

Back in the lower forty-eight states, desperate "stampeders" tried to gain passage on ships loaded to capacity. Those who arrived late in the season were stranded until the ice broke the following May.

Many could not afford the cost of passage or rightly assumed that the overland route was shorter. This mistake cost many their fortune and some their lives. Although less lengthy than sea routes, the overland trip was grueling and dangerous. The trail forced a choice–White Pass or Chilkoot Pass. Both were arduous. White Pass later became Dead Horse Pass as the route was littered with the carcasses of hundreds of frozen horses worked and starved to death. The Chilkoot Pass was shorter but rose two thousand feet, one thousand of that in the last half-mile. This became known as "the Golden Stairs". Eager men thought to cross to the Yukon, strike it rich and be home before winter hit. Those who did make it over the pass carried their several hundred pounds over one trip at a time. The path up the Golden Stairs was made single file, with a few places carved from the snow for men to step aside. The route was littered with a variety of discarded items, including food, that would be desperately missed come winter. The Royal Canadian Mounted Police set up a border crossing and insisted prospectors carry a years worth of supplies, enough to survive the winter or turn back. This stipulation saved countless lives. The weight of this gear was ponderous. Some of the provisions required included one hundred pounds of navy beans, twenty pounds of coffee, seventy-five pounds of fruit and one pound of citric acid (to prevent scurvy) and four hundred pounds of flour. It took forty trips to get a ton of gear up over the mountain. In 1898 on a Palm Sunday, sixty-five people died in an avalanche here.

Those who made it over the pass faced accidents, epidemics of spinal meningitis, small pox and scurvy. The bitter cold, endless nights and a long winter was more than many could stand. The term "cabin fever" became part of the national consciousness. Many died, many turned back. But a few "cheechakos", newcomers, did survive long enough to see the river ice break in the spring and claim the title "sourdoughs."

Once again, mining miners or swindling them became the surest way to strike it rich. Flour and eggs, if you could find them, sold for ridiculous sums of gold. Female singers and dance hall girls received a percentage of the drinks they sold or shared with lonely miners. The number of ways to relieve men of their gold was as limitless as men's imagination.

The Alaska Gold Rush faded as the placer deposits grew scarce. Some hard rock miners remained. Silver was found in 1919. Coal and tin were mined with other lesser minerals. Visitors to Alaska still search for gold, and many find impressive nuggets. But there is always more money to be made mining miners. Some Alaskan cities still make their living relieving Cheechakos of their grubstake, as anyone who has taken a cruise to northern waters can attest.

ALASKA SITE MAP

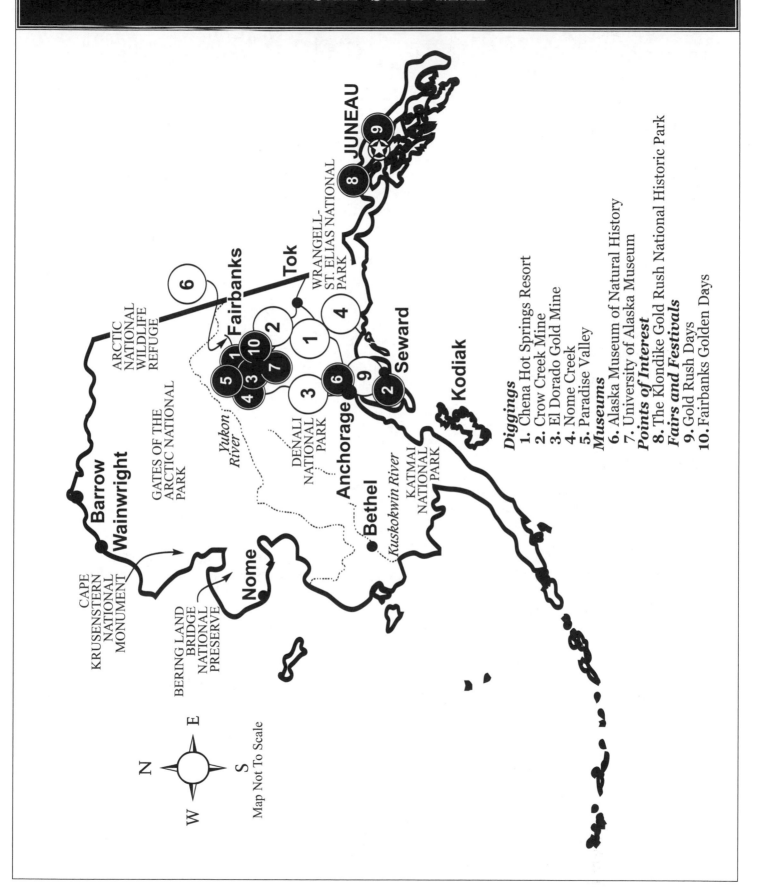

JUNEAU ⑨

⑧

Tok

Fairbanks

⑥

WRANGELL-
ST. ELIAS NATIONAL
PARK

② ④

① ⑩

⑤ ③ ④ ⑦ ③ ⑥ ⑨ ② Seward

Anchorage

Kodiak

ARCTIC
NATIONAL
WILDLIFE
REFUGE

GATES OF THE
ARCTIC NATIONAL
PARK

Yukon
River

DENALI
NATIONAL
PARK

Bethel

Kuskokwin River

KATMAI
NATIONAL
PARK

Barrow

Wainwright

CAPE
KRUSENSTERN
NATIONAL
MONUMENT

BERING LAND
BRIDGE
NATIONAL
PRESERVE

Nome

N
W — E
S

Map Not To Scale

Diggings
1. Chena Hot Springs Resort
2. Crow Creek Mine
3. El Dorado Gold Mine
4. Nome Creek
5. Paradise Valley
Museums
6. Alaska Museum of Natural History
7. University of Alaska Museum
Points of Interest
8. The Klondike Gold Rush National Historic Park
Fairs and Festivals
9. Gold Rush Days
10. Fairbanks Golden Days

ADDRESS:
Chena Hot Springs Resort
P.O. Box 58740
Fairbanks, AK 99711
(907) 451-8104 or (800) 478-4681
http://www.chenahotsprings.com

DIRECTIONS:
Chena Hot Springs is fifty-six miles east of Fairbanks on paved roads. From Fairbanks, take the Steese Expressway south to Richardson Highway. Turn left onto Badger Road. Take a right onto Nordale Road then a left onto Chena Hot Springs Road and follow the signs to the resort.

SEASON:
Open year-round

HOURS:
Contact the resort for when panning is available.

COST:
$20—Fee for panning

WHAT TO BRING:
Pack a suitcase if you are planning to stay, and don't forget your swimsuit.

INFORMATION:
Now if you were a prospector in Alaska would you walk fifty-six miles from Fairbanks to soak your cold, aching bones in a hot spring? That is just what many men did as early as 1905. Chena Hot Springs grew in reputation as a place with healing waters, treating everything from weak lungs to rheumatism. The waters contain sulfate, chloride and bicarbonate of sodium along with other trace elements. By 1911 the resort had a stable, bathhouse and TWO CABINS.

Facilities are much improved making this spot a favorite for Alaskans in the winter, and tourists in the summer months. Chena Hot Springs has indoor and outdoor pools that stay at a constant 100°F. The resort has hotel rooms, cabins, a campground, restaurant, bar and even an airstrip. Popular activities at the resort include: gold panning, aurora watching, dogsled rides, horseback riding, ice fishing and snowmobile riding.

ADDRESS:
Crow Creek Mine
P.O. Box 113
Girdwood, AK 99587
(907) 278-8060
http://www.akmining.com/mine/crow.htm

DIRECTIONS:
Drive south from Anchorage forty-two miles on the Seward Highway to Girdwood-Alyeska Recreation Area. Turn left onto Alyeska Highway. Drive two miles, turn left onto Crow Creek Road. Drive three to five miles to Crow Creek Mine.

SEASON:
May 15 through October 1 weather permitting

HOURS:
9:00 a.m. to 6:00 p.m. daily

COST:
Panning
$8–Adult fee for panning
$4–Children ages 12 and under fee for panning
$3–Sightseers and camera buffs fee for panning
$5 per unit–Fee for camping (no water or electricity)

WHAT TO BRING:
The owners will supply you with pans and shovels.

INFORMATION:
Crow Creek Mine was built in 1898 as a mining camp which includes a mess hall, blacksmith's shop, bunkhouse, barn, ice house and meat cache. During the period between 1898 to 1940, the mine produced an average of seven hundred ounces of gold per month. But who knows what they left behind?

Visitors will get a demonstration on how to pan for gold and then can try their luck finding "a little color" in the creek.

This historic mine is located at the site of the original mining camp in the Chugach National Forest. A gift shop is available if you'd like to beef up your own cache with a pair of nugget earrings, jewelry or memorabilia.

ADDRESS:
El Dorado Gold Mine
1975 Discovery Drive
Fairbanks, AK 99709
(866) 479-6673
orders@eldoradogoldmine.com
http://www.eldoradogoldmine.com/

DIRECTIONS:
Daily tours depart from the old train station, one and three-tenths miles north of Fox, Alaska on the Elliott Highway, located just nine miles north of Fairbanks.

SEASON:
Mid-May through mid-September

HOURS:
Morning and afternoon tours most days.

COST:
$27.95–Adult fee
$19.95–Children's fee

WHAT TO BRING:
Equipment is provided.

INFORMATION:
    El Dorado is Spanish for "place of gold," and if you are looking for gold, this is the place. In Alaska's interior the gold rush began over one hundred years ago. This site offers an authentic gold extraction experience. Your visit begins with a ride on the Tanana Valley Railroad into the gold fields, including a permafrost tunnel and a walking tour of a mining camp. Alaskan miners teach you about mining methods and the area history. The tour takes about two hours and ends with a mining lesson. Next you're at work at the sluice box filled with warm water, extracting your own gold. The guides help greenhorns find their first flash in the pan and everyone hits pay dirt. Have your poke weighed in the cook shack. Have a complimentary cup of coffee and home-made cookie while you wait. The original stampeders never had it this good!

ADDRESS:
Bureau of Land Management
White Mountain District Office
1150 University Avenue
Fairbanks, AK 99709
(907) 474-2200
http://www.blm.gov/ak/whitemountains/nomecrvalley.htm#

DIRECTIONS:
From Fairbanks, Alaska, take Steese Highway (State Highway 6) northeast fifty-seven and three-tenths miles. Then travel north for six miles on U.S. Creek Road. Large white signs mark the specific four-mile stretch of Nome Creek open to public mining.

SEASON:
May through October

HOURS:
Daylight
(summer daylight is twenty-four hours a day)

COST:
Free

WHAT TO BRING:
Only hand tools such as gold pans, pry bars, picks, shovels, manually-fed sluice boxes and rocker boxes are permitted.

INFORMATION:
There is a four-mile section along Nome Creek that is open to gold panning. Access to the public claim area requires one ford of Nome Creek. Call the Public Lands Information Center at the above number for current road conditions. The public claim area is clearly marked with large white signs located along the creek. Stay within this area to insure that you do not trespass on private claims.

Gold panning and prospecting are permitted, with some restrictions, on most public land in Alaska. These lands include national forests, wildlife refuges and some state parks. You can get information on additional areas to prospect in Alaska by contacting the Alaska Public Lands Information Center at (907) 456-0527.

ADDRESS:
3350 Thomas Street, #165
Fairbanks, AK 99709
(907) 479-5704
http://www.akpub.com/aktt/parad.html

DIRECTIONS:
Arrival may be by car or plane. By plane you will fly to Fairbanks, Alaska, then fly from Fairbanks to Paradise Valley. Paradise Valley is two hundred thirty miles north/northwest of Fairbanks. By car, you will travel through Yukon Territory, Canada, and then to Alaska. There are several route options. Paradise Valley will help you with your route.

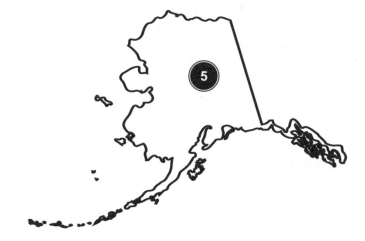

SEASON:
Mid-May through September

HOURS:
Daylight
(summer daylight is twenty-four hours a day)

COST:
$130–Fee for metal detecting
$90–Fee for gold panning
$100–Fee for sluicing
$150–Fee for dredging (2 1/2-inch dredge)
$170–Fee for dredging (3-inch dredge)

WHAT TO BRING:
Prospecting equipment is available to rent or, you can bring your own. Paradise Valley will provide you with a list of clothing, food and other supplies needed for your trip.

INFORMATION:
 Paradise Valley produces some of the largest gold nuggets found today. They are a full-service wilderness recreation company with twenty years of experience. You are lodged in a twelve foot by twenty-four foot, or larger wood cabin. Send your own food prior to your trip. Usually people stop at the grocery store in Fairbanks to pick up their food prior to arrival. Food can be arranged for an additional charge of $50 per day.
 You must book ahead to visit Paradise Valley. No dogs are allowed, and no hunting. If you are not prospecting but visiting with a prospector, the cost is $90 per day. This is a trip of a lifetime.

MUSEUMS

SITE 6.
Alaska Museum of Natural History
> 201 N. Bragaw
> Anchorage, AK 99508
> (907) 274-2400
> webcontact@alaskamuseum.org
> www.alaskamuseum.org/
> • This museum displays the largest number of Alaskan rocks, minerals and fossils in the state. Exhibits on the Alaskan Gold Rush include minerals, tools and historic artifacts.

SITE 7.
University of Alaska Museum
> P.O. Box 756960
> 907 Yukon Drive
> Fairbanks, AK 99775-6960
> (907) 474-7505
> http://www.uaf.edu/museum/
> • The Geology Collection includes examples of minerals and gems from Alaska and the Pacific Rim; ore samples from Alaska and arctic Canada; placer gold; gold nuggets; and meteorites.

POINTS OF INTEREST

SITE 8.
The Klondike Gold Rush National Historic Park
> Box 517
> Skagway, AK 99840
> (907) 983-2921
> http://www.nps.gov/archive/klgo/home.htm
> • Visit the historic buildings and trails of the 1898 Alaskan Gold Rush.

FAIRS AND FESTIVALS

SITE 9.
Gold Rush Days
> Alaska Division of Tourism
> P.O. Box 110801
> Juneau, AK 99811
> (907) 463-5706
> http://www.juneaugoldrush.com/
> • This is a three-day festival, held in June of each year, full of fun events for the family to enjoy. Come and celebrate Juneau's gold rush history.

SITE 10.
Fairbanks Golden Days
> The Greater Fairbanks Chamber of Commerce
> 250 Cushman Street, Suite 2-D
> Fairbanks, AK 99701
> (907) 452-1105
> http://fairbanks-alaska.com/golden-days-schedule.htm
> • This event celebrates the discovery of gold in Fairbanks with a ten-day festival. Every July, the town celebrates by donning period costumes for this street festival of dancing, treasure hunts and other fun events. Save room for the sourdough pancake feast.

All you will find in that desert is your tombstone.

As far back as 1000 BC, native peoples used stone tools, fire and water to crack and shatter rock to extract turquoise, coal, hematite, clay, copper and cinnabar (mercury sulfide). The cinnabar was used as bright body paint. Copper and turquoise were fashioned into decorative items and jewelry.

Spaniards arrived in Arizona as early as 1526 in search of gold. Hopeful of discovering a wealth of precious metals as great as the Incas, rumors of cities of gold spread like prairie fire. Years of searching yielded no such cities, but the rumors remain. Rich strikes were finally found in 1535, some of which were Native American mines with the shafts and ladders still in place. Spanish settlement of what is now Arizona began.

A rich silver vein was discovered at a mission called Arizonac. This area gave the state its name. The word was a corruption by the Spanish of the local people. The root word is either the Papago's word Arizonac, meaning "place of little spring" or the Aztec word Arizuma meaning "silver-bearing."

The Spanish encountered great difficulty settling and mining in this region due to the resistance of the Apaches and Navajos who did not approve of the Spanish appearance in their territory. Conflict continued until the land became part of the United States territories in 1848.

Gold was discovered in California in 1848 by James Marshall, and the southwest became inundated with prospectors looking for the next great strike.

Over the following twenty-five years gold was heavily mined. Prospectors scoured the land looking for fabled mines like the Lost Dutchman. Theories, treasure maps and rumors increased as the gold grew scarce.

Gradually gold mining became less profitable, and silver mining replaced gold. In 1877 a man named Edward Schieffelin headed into the desert, despite warnings by soldiers that the only thing he'd find there were Indians and his own tombstone. What he found was a rich vein of silver. Three years later over ten thousand people lived in his boomtown that he named Tombstone. Famous for silver and the gunfight at the OK Coral, the town suffered hard times when silver prices plummeted and mines flooded with groundwater.

When the federal government stopped coining silver, silver prices dropped and many mines in the west closed for good. The silver is still there, but economics make the mining unprofitable.

Fortunately for Arizona, a new metal came into sharp demand at the same time silver went bust. At the World Exposition in 1893, Thomas Edison demonstrated his alternating current using copper wire. Electricity sparked the national need for copper and Arizona had plenty. Just as silver replaced gold, now copper replaced silver.

Modern miners of Arizona dig for uranium, pumice, lead, copper, zinc, tungsten, gypsum, vanadium, silver and, oh yes, gold! Visitors to Arizona will find many opportunities to search for gold at digging sites.

ARIZONA SITE MAP

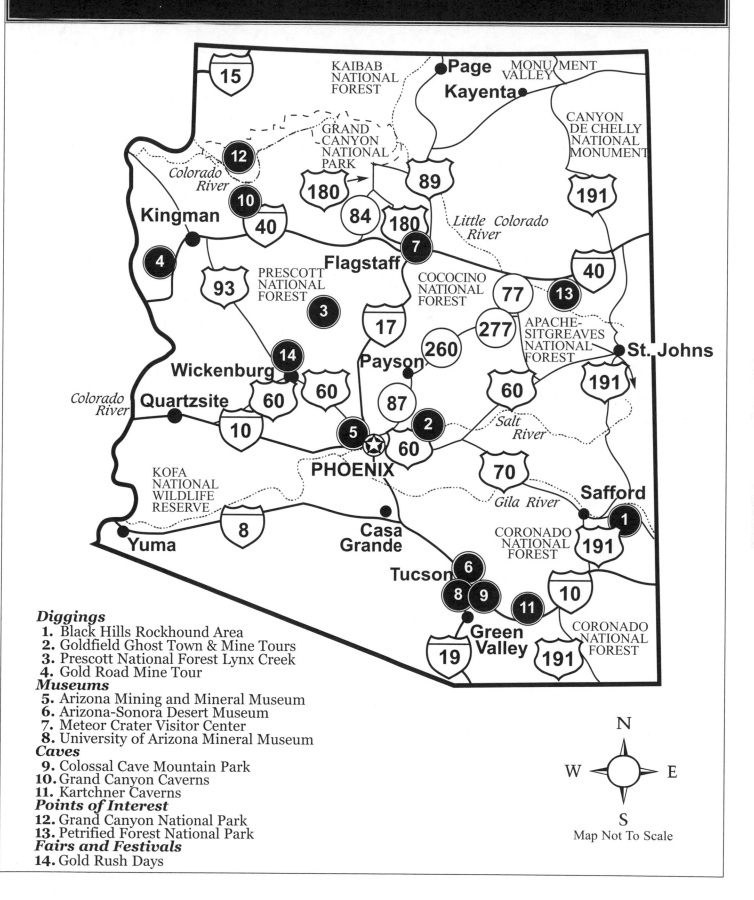

Diggings
1. Black Hills Rockhound Area
2. Goldfield Ghost Town & Mine Tours
3. Prescott National Forest Lynx Creek
4. Gold Road Mine Tour

Museums
5. Arizona Mining and Mineral Museum
6. Arizona-Sonora Desert Museum
7. Meteor Crater Visitor Center
8. University of Arizona Mineral Museum

Caves
9. Colossal Cave Mountain Park
10. Grand Canyon Caverns
11. Kartchner Caverns

Points of Interest
12. Grand Canyon National Park
13. Petrified Forest National Park

Fairs and Festivals
14. Gold Rush Days

Map Not To Scale

ADDRESS:
Bureau of Land Management
Safford Field Office
711 14th Avenue
Safford, AZ 85546-3321
(928) 348-4400
www.blm.gov/az/sfo/rec/bhillrock.htm

DIRECTION:
The Black Hills Rockhound Area is located due east of Phoenix, near the New Mexico border, between Safford and Clifton, Arizona. From Safford take U.S. Highway 70 east to U.S. Highway 191. Travel northeast ten and five-tenths miles to Milepost 141. Just past the marker take BLM Road 3829 to the left, approximately one mile to the register site.

SEASON:
Open year-round

HOURS:
Daylight

COST:
Free

WHAT TO BRING:
You will need standard mining equipment, and a 1/4-inch mesh sifting screen. Bring food and all drinking water.

INFORMATION:
Fire agate is considered a gemstone because of its unique color and fire similar to the luster of a pearl. Fire agates are less costly than fire opals, have a superior hardness and will not fade. Stop at the BLM office to register and obtain directions and rules. Fire agates can be found on the surface, while more superior specimens require some digging. Digging and sifting dirt is the technique used. Fire agates are reddish brown in color and found with fire sometimes visible.

The access road is rough and not appropriate for trailers or passenger cars. Like all southwest areas, rattlesnakes can be found here, especially in the summer months. Rock slides, ledges and old buildings present hazards. Be sure to fill all your digging holes before you leave. If camping in primitive areas, be certain to control and thoroughly extinguish all fires.

ADDRESS:
Goldfield Ghost Town & Mine Tours
4650 North Mammoth Mine Road
Goldfield, AZ 85219
(480) 983-0333
info@apachejunctioncoc.com
http://www.goldfieldghosttown.com/

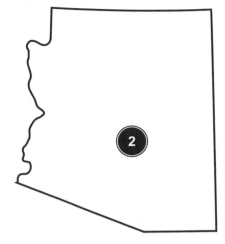

DIRECTIONS:
Apache Junction is located east of Phoenix just north of U.S. Highway 60.

SEASON:
Open year-round

HOURS:
10:00 a.m. to 5:00 p.m.

COST:
Varies depending on the attraction you choose.

WHAT TO BRING:
Bring a camera, sunscreen and a wide-brimmed hat.

INFORMATION:
     Situated at the base of the Superstition Mountains, this town offers many activities to amateur prospectors and history buffs. The town is an 1890s gold mining town now turned into a tourist attraction. This has the advantage of once being the real thing. In 1892, a rich gold vein was discovered here and a town of four thousand appeared in just over a year. When the gold vein disappeared, the town did the same. Today visitors can explore many shops, ride a historic narrow gauge railroad, pan for gold, or tour the Superstition Mountains.
     The Goldfield Ghost Town and Mine tours telephone is (480) 983-0333. This mine offers tours of a reconstructed portion of the Mammoth Mine, an authentic 1890s gold mine. Finish your tour with a chance to pan for gold. The Superstition Mountain Museum relates the history and legends of the Superstitions and includes exhibits of the twenty-three maps of the famous Lost Dutchman Mine. The phone number for the museum is (480) 983-4888. Afterward, take a jeep tour of the Superstition Mountains and see if you can find the Lost Dutchman Mine with Apache Trail Tours at (480) 982-7661. Goldfield also sponsors several yearly events including the Superstition Mountain Mule Rendezvous and the Lost Dutchman Stew Cook-off.

ADDRESS:
Bradshaw Ranger District
344 South Cortez Street
Prescott, AZ 86303
(928) 433-8000
http://www.fs.fed.us/r3/prescott/recreation/propect.shtml

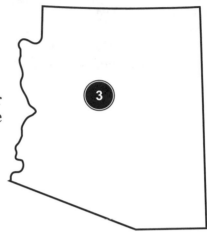

DIRECTIONS:
From Prescott, Arizona take State Highway 69 east to Walker Road. Then take Walker Road south to the Lynx Lake Recreation Area.

SEASON:
Open year-round

HOURS:
Daylight

COST:
Free–Recreational miners

WHAT TO BRING:
You may bring hand tools, non-motorized gold mining equipment, and a metal detector.

INFORMATION:
This area is a good place to search for gold nuggets. You can pan for gold in the creek, or search the land for nuggets. The district is supervised by the U.S. Forest Service. Only gold pans, metal detectors and hand tools are permitted in your search. Do not disturb the natural features of this land.

Pick and shovel excavations may only be done in conjunction with gold panning and metal detecting, and must be done below the high water mark of the stream channels. Excavations must not damage roots or live vegetation. Specific rules and maps are available from the address above.

Camping is primitive. You may camp at this site for up to fourteen days. The following regulations apply to camping here: pack out what you bring in; do not wash dishes or yourself in Lynx Creek; no toilets are available (bury your waste a hundred feet from the creek); and control your campfires.

ADDRESS:
Gold Road Mine Tours
P.O. Box 869
Oatman, AZ 86433
(928) 768-1600
http://www.goldroadmine.com
goldroad@goldroadmine.com

DIRECTIONS:
Located between Oatman and Kingman, Arizona, the Gold Road Mine is two and one-half miles east of Oatman on Route 66. Visit their website for driving directions from your location.

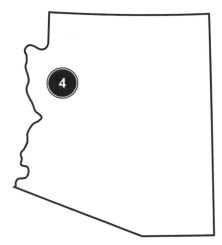

SEASON:
Open all year round

HOURS:
Call for hours of operation

COST:
$12.50–Gold Mining Tour Adult
$6.00–Gold Mining Tour Child
$5.00–Gold Panning

WHAT TO BRING:
Comfortable clothing and a camera or camcorder are recommended.

INFORMATION:
Gold was discovered on this site by a Mexican prospector named Jose Jerez, who came across a chunk of quartz laced with gold while searching for his lost burro.

Today visitors have a chance to tour the circa 1900 mine. Guided tours are conducted through a real underground gold mine. Tours take one hour and are scheduled every thirty minutes. This is an easy walking tour of approximately one-eighth of a mile, and transportation is available for the physically challenged.

After visiting the mine, try your hand at panning for gold. You are guaranteed to find color.

MUSEUMS

SITE 5.
Arizona Mining and Mineral Museum
>   Arizona Department of Mines & Mineral Resources
>   1502 West Washington
>   Phoenix, AZ 85007
>   (602) 255-3795
>   http://www.mines.az.gov/General/museum.html
>   • There are over three thousand minerals on exhibit including: an eight-foot piece of native Arizona copper; a large quartz geode weighing almost five hundred pounds; a two hundred six pound meteor; and a display on lapidary arts including gemstones and carved semiprecious artwork. Mining equipment is also on view.

SITE 6.
Arizona-Sonora Desert Museum
>   2021 North Kinney Road
>   Tucson, AZ 86743
>   (520) 883-2702
>   http://www.desertmuseum.org/
>   • Exhibits include collections of regional minerals and gemstones, moon rock, meteorites, archaeological, paleontological and geologic history of the earth. A limestone cave, complete with stalagmites, stalactites, ponds and salamanders should not be missed.

SITE 7.
Meteor Crater Visitor Center
>   P.O. Box 30940
>   Flagstaff, AZ 86003-0940
>   (928) 289-5898
>   http://www.meteorcrater.com/
>   • The remodeled Visitor Center sits on the lip of a crater five hundred seventy feet deep, and more than four thousand feet wide. The crater was made by a meteor weighing several hundred tons, which hit the earth over fifty thousand years ago. In the 1960's, NASA used this area for practice moon landings. Displayed here is the largest meteorite found in the area and the American Astronaut Wall of Fame. Explore the Interactive Learning Center, go on a guided hike of the crater, and don't miss the movie describing meteor impacts.

Site 8.
University of Arizona Mineral Museum
>   University of Arizona, Flandrau Science Center
>   Tucson, AZ 85721
>   (520) 621-4227
>   http://www.geo.arizona.edu/minmus/
>   • The museum has over seventeen thousand minerals, over seven thousand micromounts, and two displays of meteorites. Minerals from Arizona are featured, but specimens from around the world are also on display.

CAVES

Site 9.
Colossal Cave Mountain Park
>   16721 East Old Spanish Trail
>   Vail, AZ 84641
>   (520) 647-PARK (7275)
>   http://www.colossalcave.com/welcome.html

• This cavern is dry, which means the formations are dormant. Early Native American tribes used the clay in this cave to grind into pigment for paint. The first tours of this cave began in the 1920s and involved a rope and lantern. Modern visitors will be pleased with the flagstone paths and electric lighting. This site has two gift shops.

Site 10.
Grand Canyon Caverns
P.O. Box 180 / Peach Springs, AZ 86434
(520) 422-3223
http://www.gccaverns.com/
• This limestone cave, formed by an inland sea, includes fossils and bones of extinct animals. Grand Canyon Cavern has not been in business for over seventy-five years for nothing.

Site 11.
Kartchner Caverns State Park
2980 State Highway 90 / Benson, AZ 85602
(520) 586-2283
http://www.pr.state.az.us/Parks/parkhtml/kartchner.html
• This cave was only discovered in 1974. The state of Arizona now runs this area as a state park, which includes unique and fragile formations. The park includes hiking trails, picnic facilities, a campground, discovery center and a gift shop.

POINTS OF INTEREST

Site 12.
Grand Canyon National Park
P.O. Box 129 / Grand Canyon, AZ 86023
(928) 638-7888
http://www.nps.gov/grca/
• The canyon averages a mile deep and is ten miles wide at the popular central section. It is a must see.

Site 13.
Petrified Forest National Park
P.O. Box 2217 / Petrified Forest National Park, AZ 86028
(928) 524-6228
http://www.petrified.forest.national-park.com/
• One of the largest collections of agatized and petrified wood is located here on the trails, clay hills and exposed cliff faces. This park, established to protect the largest and most spectacular preserved concentrations of petrified wood in the world, also contains the most diverse and complete fossil record of the Triassic period. The colorful sedimentary layers of the exposed rock formations are part of the Chinle Formation which was brought to the surface about sixty million years ago by the uplifting of the Colorado Plateau and thousands of years of erosion.

FAIRS AND FESTIVALS

Site 14.
Gold Rush Days
Wickenburg Chamber of Commerce
216 West Frontier Street / Wickenburg, AZ 85390
(928) 684-5479
http://www.wickenburgchamber.com/events.asp
• This three-day event has been held in Wickenburg since 1986 and is full of fun events for all. The mining and ranching heritage of this town is celebrated with a rodeo, parade, craft exhibits, a dance, stage entertainment, and drilling and mucking contests using ore carts. Of course, there is a gold panning contest. Keep an eye out for saloon girls distributing garter belts to the crowd.

Seeing the elephant.

For centuries, Native American tribes lived and worked in what is now California. Spanish explorers appeared in the 1500s searching for legendary cities of gold. They never knew how close they came. The Spanish empire discovered safe harbors and used them to resupply their ships traveling to and from Asia. Spain later colonized California and large rancheros of cattle filled the fertile fields for the next three centuries until Mexico won independence from Spain. The first arrivals from the United States came by ship and were sea otter hunters and sailors. Next came the trappers overland and finally the first wagon train arrived in 1841. The route was treacherous as witnessed by the Donner party stranded in the Sierra Nevada Mountains of California in 1846. Also in 1846, America went to war with Mexico for territory including California. American troops rushed in, and the United States took and kept control of the area.

Two years later a carpenter named James Marshall discovered gold in the American River at Sutter's Mill. The discovery made in January, was reported in March in two of San Francisco's newspapers. The Mexican-American War ended one month later. Approximately six thousand men lucky enough to be in California got a year jump on the rest of the country, reaching the gold fields first. The country followed and then came the world. Prospectors arrived by the dangerous sea route of Cape Horn where the Atlantic and Pacific Oceans clash with terrifying force. This route took five to eight months. A faster route overland at the Panamanian Isthmus was discovered, shortening the trip to eight weeks. Travelers on this journey faced the dangers of contracting malaria, yellow fever and other dreaded tropical diseases. The Overland Trail by wagon took three to four months. As the sea routes were expensive and overbooked, many took to the trails, where the hazards included disease, most commonly cholera, typhus and dysentery. Accidents, like drowning while fording rivers, also took many lives. The journey became a race to reach California before the snow reached the mountains.

San Francisco's population ballooned from six hundred in 1848 to twenty-five thousand in 1849. Abandoned ships rotted in her harbors as men left their current way of life, and a lot of work was left undone in a rush to get to the gold fields. One of the most profitable endeavors of this time was "mining miners" or selling products to them. Food stuffs, picks and shovels sold for exorbitant prices. Innovative men made millions. A dry goods merchant arrived in California with canvas to sell for tents. Instead he made heavy-duty pants for miners, and the company of Levi Strauss was born. Philip Armour, of Armour Hot dogs, made millions selling sliced meat in Placerville and John Studebaker first sold wheelbarrows, then buggies and wagons and later automobiles.

Eager miners talked about "seeing the elephant" a phrase which typified the gold rush experience. The tale tells of a farmer who took a wagon full of produce to market with the specific aim of seeing a circus elephant. When he encountered the elephant, his horse bolted, his wagon overturned and he lost his vegetables. He is reported to have said, "I don't give a hang, for I have seen the elephant." Many went to California to see the elephant, but some caught only a glimpse. Only one in twenty returned richer than when they left. But all had seen the "elephant."

Others not only saw the elephant, they got to touch it. The largest gold nugget ever found in America was unearthed at the Carson Hill Mine in November of 1854, and it weighed an astonishing two hundred fourteen pounds. But this was now the exception. The placer gold was gone. Miners moved underground, or they moved on.

After all, they'd found gold in other hills. From 1851 to 1858, strikes were made in Oregon, Montana, Idaho and Nevada. In 1873, gold was discovered in South Dakota's Black Hills. News of the last great strike in the lower forty-eight states arrived in 1891. And men flocked to Cripple Creek, Colorado. Miners poured out of California nearly as fast as they'd arrived.

Today California offers visitors a huge variety of opportunities to search for gold and share in the state's rich history. Rockhounds will also enjoy collecting moonstones, agates and jaspers along the Pacific beaches.

CALIFORNIA SITE MAP

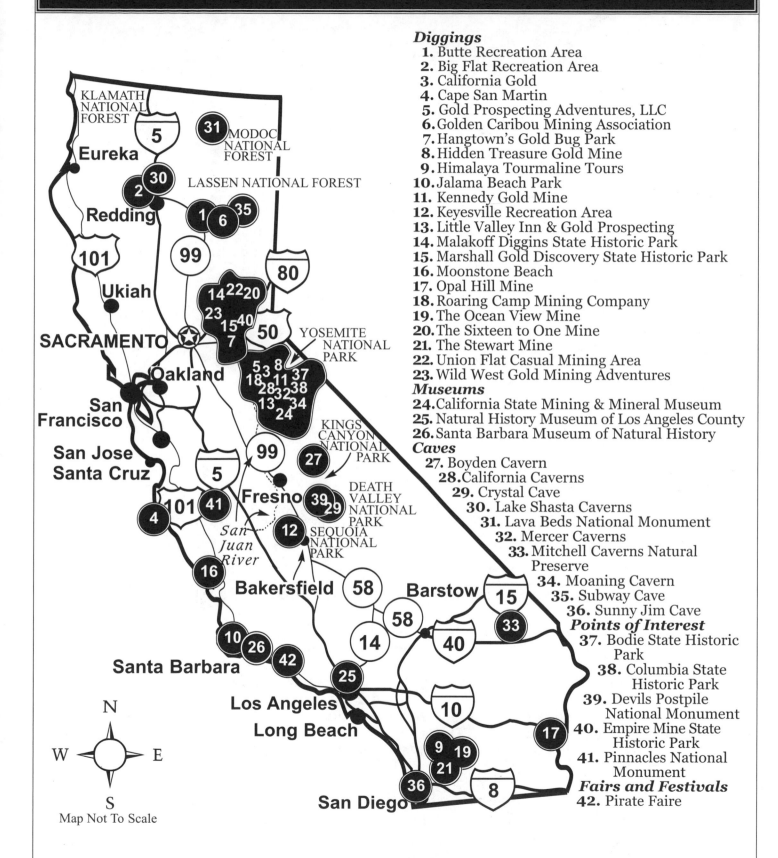

Diggings
1. Butte Recreation Area
2. Big Flat Recreation Area
3. California Gold
4. Cape San Martin
5. Gold Prospecting Adventures, LLC
6. Golden Caribou Mining Association
7. Hangtown's Gold Bug Park
8. Hidden Treasure Gold Mine
9. Himalaya Tourmaline Tours
10. Jalama Beach Park
11. Kennedy Gold Mine
12. Keyesville Recreation Area
13. Little Valley Inn & Gold Prospecting
14. Malakoff Diggins State Historic Park
15. Marshall Gold Discovery State Historic Park
16. Moonstone Beach
17. Opal Hill Mine
18. Roaring Camp Mining Company
19. The Ocean View Mine
20. The Sixteen to One Mine
21. The Stewart Mine
22. Union Flat Casual Mining Area
23. Wild West Gold Mining Adventures

Museums
24. California State Mining & Mineral Museum
25. Natural History Museum of Los Angeles County
26. Santa Barbara Museum of Natural History

Caves
27. Boyden Cavern
28. California Caverns
29. Crystal Cave
30. Lake Shasta Caverns
31. Lava Beds National Monument
32. Mercer Caverns
33. Mitchell Caverns Natural Preserve
34. Moaning Cavern
35. Subway Cave
36. Sunny Jim Cave

Points of Interest
37. Bodie State Historic Park
38. Columbia State Historic Park
39. Devils Postpile National Monument
40. Empire Mine State Historic Park
41. Pinnacles National Monument

Fairs and Festivals
42. Pirate Faire

43

ADDRESS:
Bureau of Land Management–Redding Resource
355 Hemsted Drive
Redding, CA 96002
(530) 224-2100
www.blm.gov/ca/redding/ReddingrecreationButte.html

DIRECTIONS:
From Chico, take State Highway 32 north towards Chester. Drive past Forest Ranch and turn right on Garland Road. Follow Garland Road to Doe Mill Road (210C) to Butte Creek Bridge. Park here to access Sites 12 to 30. To reach Sites 5 to 11, cross the bridge and head east, turning left at Ditch Creek Road (210-C2) which is just west of the creek.

SEASON:
Open year-round–Gold panning
Limited schedule–Dredging

HOURS:
Daylight

COST:
$5 per day per site–Fee for prospecting

WHAT TO BRING:
Bring standard mining and gold mining equipment. Sluice boxes and dredges up to four inches are permitted. Bring your own food, camping supplies and drinking water. This is a national forest and camping is primitive.

INFORMATION:
Butte Creek is a good place to try your panning skills and find some placer gold. Butte Creek has two individual places to prospect. The area has thirty sites. Sites 1 to 4 are not recommended to prospect because it requires crossing private land. Sites 5 to 11 are the most popular because they are flat to allow easy access to camping nearby. Sites numbered 12 to 30 are also available for prospecting.

A BLM permit is required at this unique site for all forms of intrusive mineral collecting such as dredging, pumping, sluicing and extensive panning. You can download the BLM Special Recreation Permit Application from the Butte Recreation Area website (www.blm.gov/ca/redding/ReddingrecreationButte.html). Dredging also requires a California Dredge Permit available from the California Department of Fish and Game at (530) 225-2300.

ADDRESS:
Big Bar Ranger District
Route 1
Box 10
Big Bar, CA 96010
(530) 623-6106

DIRECTIONS:
From Weaverville, take State Highway 299 west for twenty-two miles to the Big Flat Recreation Area.

SEASON:
Open year-round

HOURS:
Daylight

COST:
Free

WHAT TO BRING:
Bring standard mining and gold mining equipment. Sluice boxes and dredges up to four inches are permitted. Bring your own food and drinking water.

INFORMATION:
   The Big Flat Recreation Area is located in Shasta-Trinity National Forest. This is the only area in the forest which is open to the public for gold panning and dredging. No permit is needed for panning in this area. If you are dredging, you do need a California State Fish & Game Dredge permit. The permits can be obtained by calling (530) 225-2300. This area has good access for prospecting and good gold potential.
   Camping is not permitted in this primitive area, but there is an RV park half a mile east of the Big Flat Recreation Area. The RV park has showers, and supplies are available.

ADDRESS:
California Gold
P.O. Box 1132
Jamestown, CA 95327
(209) 984-4914
joshuaj@goldrush.com
http://www.goldfun.com

DIRECTIONS:
California Gold's mining trips are on Woods Creek, between Jamestown and Sonora, California on State Highway 108. California Gold's group panning tours are done at the Marble Quarry Campground in Columbia on State Highway 49.

SEASON:
April through October

HOURS:
Gold Mining Trips–five hours
Group Panning Tour–one hour (call for reservations)

COST:
$79 per person–Adult fee for gold mining trips
Free–Children ages 12 and under free for mining trips
$10 per person–Group fee for gold panning tours

WHAT TO BRING:
Pack a lunch and wear proper attire for prospecting.

INFORMATION:
California Gold has two types of adventures for guests–guided gold mining trips and gold panning tours. On the gold mining trip you will dig, sluice and pan for gold on the richest creek in California. This adventure includes gold mining, time to enjoy your picnic lunch, rock collecting and a visit to a waterfall. Bring your camera on this five-hour excursion and get ready to find some gold.

The gold panning tours are great fun for scouts, school children or any tour group. Your guide is gold geologist Joshua Vick, who was seen on *The Learning Channel's* "Hunt for Amazing Treasures." He will teach you how to pan, educate you about gold, and share stories of California's Gold Rush.

Overnights are now available. When you get back to the Marble Quarry Campground, there is a lot more to do. They have swimming, volleyball, horseback riding and hiking trails available. Nearby you will find Moaning Caverns, river rafting trips, and a scenic railroad.

ADDRESS:
Off Pacific Coast Highway (State Highway 1)
California
No phone

DIRECTIONS:
California Pacific coastal beaches around Cape San
Martin, Jade Cove and Sand Dollar Beach on State
Highway 1.

SEASON:
Open year-round

HOURS:
Daylight

COST:
Free

WHAT TO BRING:
Bring a bucket or other carrying container. The water is cold and the beaches are rugged, rocky
and beautiful. Wear clothing appropriate for the windy northern California beaches.

INFORMATION:
  Green jade and serpentine can be found in these areas: Cape San Martin, Jade Cove and
Sand Dollar Beach. The Cape San Martin Beach access is from State Highway 1 to Willow Creek
Bridge. The best area for searching is from the north side of the point to the Willow Creek
Bridge. Another site is less than two miles north of Cape San Martin at Jade Cove. Access is
marked by a small sign. The turnoff is narrow but can accommodate two or three cars. Within
Jade Cove, about fifty yards offshore is a large, wash rock called Cave Rock. Within the face of
the cave, natural polished jade, nephrite, can be found. Pure nephrite is white, but impurities
give this local type of jade shades varying from green and deep, rich green to lightly tinted and
nearly transparent. Small pebbles of jade can also be found in the gravel beds within the cove.
  An area one-half mile north has the best marked access and the best amenities including
restrooms and picnic tables. This is Sand Dollar Beach. Note the cliffs next to the access steps.
The cliffs are composed of green serpentine laced with gold-colored flakes. There is a campground
across State Highway 1 called Plaskett Creek.
  Please note that Federal law allows the collection of loose jade from the seabed from the west-
ernmost top of Cape San Martin to the stairway at Sand Dollar Beach. No tools may be used to
collect jade, except: a hand tool no greater than thirty-six inches in length which has no moving
parts to maneuver or lift the jade or scratch the surface of a stone as necessary to determine if it
is jade; a lift bag or multiple lift bag with a combined lift capacity of no more than two hundred
pounds; or a vessel to provide access to the authorized areas. You can only collect what you can
carry. California law requires a permit to collect jade, but normally does not enforce this rule if
the jade is collected for personal use. Jade may not be collected above the mean high tide mark.

ADDRESS:
18170 Main Street
P.O. Box 1040
Jamestown, CA 95327
(209) 984-4653 or (800) 596-0009 (reservations)
info@goldprospecting.com
http://www.goldprospecting.com

DIRECTIONS:
Located between Sonora and Oakdale on State
Highway 49 in Jamestown.

SEASON:
Open 364 days a year (closed Christmas day)

HOURS:
Daylight

COST:
$15 per hour–Adults fee for gold panning
$25 per hour–Adults with children fee for gold panning
(trips and courses cost extra)

WHAT TO BRING:
All supplies are provided.

INFORMATION:
   The Gold Prospecting Adventures is just what it claims to be and more. They have an 1849 gold mining camp set up as a living history exhibit. There is a costumed prospector who will explain and demonstrate the workings of the gold pans, cradles and long toms. He will also tell you all about the miner's lifestyle back in 1849. The proprietors ask you to keep a sharp eye out for claim jumpers. Bring a carrot for Molly, the camp mule.
   They run educational school trips, family outings, courses, helicopter trips and white water rafting trips. Course topics include a three-day placer prospecting class, a highbanking class, a one-day dredging trip, and an electronic prospecting class. They even arrange weddings.
   If you want to prospect or you are looking for adventure, this is the place to find some gold. You will find something for everyone from the beginning miner to the expert prospector.

ADDRESS:
Caribou Corner Campground
P.O. Box 300
Belden, CA 95915
(650) 692-1932
www.golden-caribou.com/index.htm
gemc2002@aol.com

INFORMATION:
From Belden, take State Highway 70 to Caribou Road. The Golden Caribou claims are approximately one mile north up the road.

SEASON:
Open year-round

HOURS:
Daylight

COST:
Free–Fee for recreational miners
15% Royalty–Fee for professional miners
$10 per person per day–Fee for some claims

WHAT TO BRING:
Bring standard mining and gold mining equipment, sluice boxes, dredges and highbankers. Some supplies are available for rent.

INFORMATION:
Caribou Corner has many claims that are available for beginners to experts. In 1993, the largest nugget found was a six and one-half ounce nugget of gold. All claims contain fine gold. Most claims have also produced some nuggets. Caribou Corner Campground guarantees that you will find gold.

They offer full-day training sessions, which will teach you the basics of searching for gold and how to use dredges and highbankers. Sessions cost $50, other training is also available.

Caribou Corner Campground has twenty campsites with full hookups. The campground has a shower facility, laundry room, camp store and cafe. Rates are $14 for camping. Cabins are $50 per night.

ADDRESS:
Hangtown's Gold Bug Park
City of Placerville
Parks & Recreation Department
2635 Gold Bug Lane
Placerville CA 95667
(530) 642-5207
http://www.goldbugpark.org/

DIRECTIONS: Located one mile north of Bedford Avenue from U.S. Highway 50 and downtown Placerville.

SEASON:
Open daily April through October and weekends the rest of the year.

HOURS:
Hours vary, so please call ahead

COST:
$4–Adults
$2–Children ages 7 to 16
$1–Rental fee for hand-held audiocassette, self-guided tour
$2–per hour fee for gold panning

WHAT TO BRING:
Bring a flashlight. Wear comfortable clothing, walking shoes and a sweatshirt. The temperature inside the Gold Bug Mine is around 50°F.

INFORMATION:
　　In January of 1848, gold was discovered in the area now known as Placerville and the area was forever changed. The Gold Bug is the only mine in California located on public land. This mine area is listed on the National Register of Historic Places and is owned and operated by the city of Placerville. This location is actually two mines, a small museum, gift shop and stamp mill all in one trip. Guided tours are available for an additional charge. The park has two main attractions, the Gold Bug and Priest Mines.
　　Gold Bug Mine was originally called the Hattie. It opened in 1888 and is an excellent example of hardrock mining. This mine has wooden floors, artificial lighting throughout and an air shaft. Some ground water occasionally accumulates in the wet season. Hendy Stamp Mill is located in a stamp mill building in its original location. When in operation, the mill could be heard over a mile away in Placerville. The Hendy Mill provides a full explanation of the process of extracting ore from quartz.
　　Priest Mine is at the top of the hill above the Gold Bug Mine. This original 1849 mine was the first in the area and is named for the Welsh priest who worked and lived here. There is no lighting and the floor is dirt. Tool marks made by the miners are prominent as well as "rooms" created for living. Hard hats are provided.
　　Other amenities include parking, picnic tables, trails and restrooms.

ADDRESS:
Hidden Treasure Gold Mine Tours
P.O. Box 28
Washington and Main Streets
Columbia, CA 95310
(209) 532-9693
http://www.columbiacalifornia.com/matelot.html

DIRECTIONS:
The Hidden Treasure Gold Mine is located on the corner of Main and Washington Streets in Columbia State Historic Park.

SEASON:
Open year-round
Call for winter hours (shortened hours)
March 1 through September 1 (regular hours)

HOURS:
10:00 a.m. to 5:00 p.m.–Seven days a week

COST:
$10–Adults fee for tour only
$8–Children and Seniors fee for tour only
$3–Fee for panning all day
$5–Fee for a panning plus a lesson using a "guaranteed find" gold pan

WHAT TO BRING:
All tools are supplied by the mine. The mine does have a supply store.

INFORMATION:
The Hidden Treasure Gold Mine is the only active working gold mine open to the public. Discovered in 1879, it still produces gold today. The mine offers several panning opportunities. Don't miss out. Try your luck!

Guided tours leave from the Matelot Gold Mine Supply Store. The office opens at 10:00 a.m. and tours begin at 11:00 a.m. You will travel through eight hundred feet of tunnel to see what a working mine looks like. During your tour of this hardrock mine you can see veins of gold and quartz in the mine walls. The mine temperature is 54°F, so bring a coat.

ADDRESS:
Himalaya Tourmaline Tour
The owners prefer to be contacted by phone or via the internet
(619) 444-3731
info@highdesertgemsandminerals.com
http://www.highdesertgemsandminerals.com/html/himalaya_tourmaline_mine.htm

DIRECTIONS:
Located in Mesa Grande. Call the mine for
reservations and directions

SEASON:
Open year-round

HOURS:
By appointment only

COST:
$50 per person per day–Fee

WHAT TO BRING:
The mine has standing water, so rubber boots are
highly recommended. Work boots are better suited for the tailing piles. Bring your personal gear,
food, water, sunscreen and a flashlight for the
mine tour.

INFORMATION:
 This site offers a rare opportunity to visit a privately-owned, working tourmaline mine.
Located in San Diego County, the Himalaya Tourmaline Mine is an underground mine of five
miles with steep passageways that have been mined for the last 100 years. Visitors will drive to
the site, following your hosts. The road can be rough and four-wheel drive is recommended. The
mine tour takes about 30 minutes, and is followed by an opportunity to search the mine's tailing piles.
 The Himalaya is known for its beautiful gem quality pink and green tourmalines. Bi-colored
and tri-colored gems are also unearthed, along with watermelon colored crystals.
 Other minerals often found here include: quartz, apatite, morganite, cleavelandite, calcite,
lepidolite, feldspar, topaz and spessartine garnet.
 The entrance fee allows visitors access to the mine's dumps for gem screening all day. Space
is limited at this popular site, so reservations are available.
 The same folks that run the Spectrum Sunstone Tours and Spectrum Sunstone Mine in
Oregon now own this mine.

ADDRESS:
Jalama Beach County Park
Star Route
Jalama Road
Lompoc, CA 93436
(805) 736-6316 or (805) 736-3504
http://www.sbparks.org/docs/jalama.html
or http://www.jalamabeach.com

DIRECTIONS:
From Santa Barbara take U.S. Route 101 to U.S Route 1 and drive toward Lompoc for four and five-tenths miles. Turn onto Jalama Road. Drive fourteen miles to the park entrance on the right.

SEASON:
Open year-round

HOURS:
8:00 a.m. daily–Gates and park store

COST:
$6–Fee for day use
There is an additional fee for camping

WHAT TO BRING:
Camping gear, collecting bucket, camera, sunscreen and a beach chair.

INFORMATION:
This oceanfront park has a beach of treasures waiting for rockhounds. Visitors with sharp eyes will find banded and solid onyx, agates of all variety, striped and colorful jasper and even an occasional fossil. The onyx comes from a large deposit north of the parking area that juts into the ocean and is clearly visible from the beach.

Other popular activities at this beach are bird-watching, whale-watching, fishing, surfing, camping and hiking. The park maintains a store and grill, which opens at 8:00 a.m. daily.

Jalama has many amenities including picnic areas, shower facilities, restrooms, BBQ pits and nearly one hundred campsites overlooking the ocean. Twenty-nine sites have full hookups. Camping sites go quickly and are assigned on a first come, first served basis. Checkout is at 2:00 p.m. Where else can you get a beachfront view for $18 a night?

ADDRESS:
Kennedy Mine Foundation
P.O. Box 684
Jackson CA 95642
(209) 223-9542
http://www.kennedygoldmine.com
info@kennedygoldmine.com

DIRECTIONS: The Kennedy Gold Mine is located in Jackson on Highway 49/88.

SEASON:
March through October

HOURS:
9:00 a.m. to 5:00 p.m.

COST:
$9–Adults
$5–Children
(special tours can be arranged for large groups)

WHAT TO BRING:
Comfortable walking or hiking shoes are recommended.

INFORMATION:

This historic mine was claimed in 1860 by Andrew Kennedy, and is one of the two deepest mines on the continent with a vertical depth of 5,912 feet. The mine produced over $34.2 million in gold, making it one of the richest gold mines in the world. The Kennedy and Argonaut Mines of Jackson produced over half of the gold mined in California. But don't worry, they left a little for you.

The mine tours are guided by volunteers and take visitors up and down the hills on the property where they will first notice the one hundred twenty-five-foot metal head frame towering above the mine area and then tour several buildings on site. Mining equipment displays help visitors understand the mining process. After your tour try your luck at panning for gold in the mine's troughs–instruction is available.

ADDRESS:
Bureau of Land Management
3801 Pegasus Drive
Bakersfield, CA 93308-6837
(661) 391-6000
http://www.blm.gov/ca/bakersfield/recmining.html#RecreationalMining

DIRECTIONS:
From Los Angeles go north on Interstate Highway 5 to
Kern County. Take State Highway 99 north. At Bakersfield,
take State Highway 178 to Lake Isabella. Turn left on State
Highway 155. The Keyesville Recreation Area is approxi-
mately one-half mile away.

SEASON:
Open year-round

HOURS:
Daylight

COST:
Free

WHAT TO BRING:
Bring standard mining and gold mining equipment. Sluice boxes and dredges (up to three inches)
are permitted. You must have a permit to use a dredge. Bring your own food, camping supplies
and drinking water.

INFORMATION:
   The Keyesville Recreation Area is located on the Kern River, and is open to the public for
placer mining. Please be aware of private claims and do not trespass. Placer gold is found in this
river. The river is rocky, with some steep grades and dangerous currents. Use of metal detectors
is allowed. Highbanking is not allowed. Best results have been made by searching the cracks and
crevices in the river bedrock.
   This site is popular in the summer, especially on weekends because of its proximity to Los
Angeles. Camping is primitive, but portable toilets are provided in the summer. Camping is limited
to fourteen days per month, and twenty-eight days per year.

ADDRESS:
Little Valley Inn at the Creek
3483 Brooks Road
Mariposa, CA 95338
(800) 889-5444 or (209) 742-6204
innkeeper@littlevalley.com
http://www.littlevalley.com

DIRECTIONS:
Mariposa is located on State Highway 140, southwest of Yosemite.

SEASON:
Open year-round
(prospecting is better done in the warmer months)

HOURS:
This is a country inn with check-in after 3:00 p.m.
and check-out by 11:00 a.m.

COST:
$104 to $130 per night—Room rates
(rooms, suites and cabins available)

WHAT TO BRING:
The Little Valley Inn will provide you with all the equipment you need to pan for gold.

INFORMATION:
    Little Valley Inn has a private mining claim on a gold-bearing creek where guests can learn to prospect like the forty-niners. Instruction is free to guests, as is the use of equipment. This claim is one thousand feet of creek on bedrock.
    Mariposa, California is the site of the southernmost mother lode. There is both placer and hardrock mining still taking place in the area.
    Kit Carson discovered gold here in 1849. The creek was so bountiful that they built the town right next to the water. The town is a history lesson in itself, with historic buildings and a working stamp mill where rock is crushed to extract the gold. Nearby you can visit Bagby Recreational Area where dredging is permitted. Don't forget to visit the California State Mining & Mineral Museum, just four miles from the Inn.

ADDRESS:
Malakoff Diggins State Historic Park
23579 N. Bloomfield Road
Nevada City, CA 95959
(530) 273-4667
State Park Office: (530) 265-2740
http://www.parks.ca.gov/default.asp?page_id=494

DIRECTIONS:
From Nevada City take Highway 49 north for eleven miles to Downieville. Turn right onto Tyler Foote Road and follow the paved area to the park. The road name changes from Curzon Grade Road to Back Bone Road to Der Bec Road and finally to North Bloomfield Road. The last mile on Bloomfield road is unpaved. Total distance from Nevada City is twenty-six miles.

SEASON:
Open year-round

HOURS:
Open until dusk

COST:
Free

WHAT TO BRING:
Bring your gold mining equipment including; gold pan, sluice box, shovel, buckets and classifying screens.

INFORMATION:
The town of North Bloomfield and the Malakoff Mine are both within the three thousand-acre Malakoff Diggins State Historic Park.

Malakoff Diggins, north of Nevada City shows the devastation hydraulic mining caused during the 1849 Gold Rush. High-pressure hoses washed about fifty thousand tons of gravel PER DAY of gold and earth from the mountains! By 1884, the farmers downstream had enough. Folks as far away as San Francisco complained about the mess. The hydraulics were shut down permanently, but not before changing the landscape forever.

There are many hiking trails around the digging area. The park also contains picnic, camping areas, lakes, streams and diggings.

A small museum is open in the summer, which documents the history of this area. Gold panning is offered nearby, but you can't use a hose!

ADDRESS:
Marshall Gold Discovery State Historic Park
P.O. Box 265
310 Back Street
Coloma, CA 95613
(530) 622-3470
http://www.parks.ca.gov/?page_id=484

DIRECTIONS:
Coloma is located east of Sacramento. From Interstate Highway 80, exit at Auburn and take State Highway 49 south twenty miles to Coloma.

SEASON:
Open year-round

HOURS:
8:00 a.m. to dusk

COST:
$5 per vehicle—Fee

WHAT TO BRING:
Bring standard gold mining equipment.
Sluicing and dredging are not permitted here.

INFORMATION:
This is the site of Sutter's Mill, where James Marshall found gold and started the California Gold Rush. On this site in 1848, James W. Marshall found shining gold nuggets in the American River. Now a state historic park is located here. Within the park is a gold museum and replicas of buildings including Sutter's Sawmill, a blacksmith shop, a Chinese store and much more.

The mining exhibit contains examples of the equipment used by the forty-niners and depicts gold mining methods such as placer, hardrock and hydraulic mining. This area was so gold laden that the business district of Coloma was torn down so the area could be mined for gold.

A forty-five minute walking tour will take you by all of the sites and to the spot where James Marshall discovered gold. Activities include four walking tours that are one-third to one-half mile in length. Gold panning is available here on the streambed.

Be sure to visit Sutter's Mill within the park, where in 1839, John Sutter received a land grant from Mexico and established a settlement in Sacramento. In 1847, Sutter sent aid to the Donner Party trapped in the Sierra Nevada Mountains.

ADDRESS:
Cambria Chamber of Commerce
767 Main Street
Cambria, CA 93428
(805) 927-3624

DIRECTIONS:
Moonstone Beach is in Cambria. From State Highway 1, take Exit State Road 1 at Windsor Boulevard. Take Moonstone Beach Drive to the beach.

SEASON:
Open year-round

HOURS:
Daylight

COST:
Free

WHAT TO BRING:
You'll want a pail or another collecting container to hold your moonstones.

INFORMATION:
   Rock hunting and beach-combing are popular pastimes here. A variety of stones can be found on the beach, including California "jade," agates and moonstones. Moonstones are a cloudy, milky quartz. When polished, moonstones are clear with an internal fiery glow. Agates have a translucent look and the stone may have an orange-peel texture. Expect the beach to be somewhat rocky, and the water is often chilly.
   For day use there are two parks: Leffingwell Landings and Shamel Park. Both parks offer restrooms, picnic areas and beach access. The area has numerous hotels. This beach town has much to do, including shopping, whale watching and visiting Hearst Castle.

ADDRESS:
Nancy Hill
Opal Hill Mine
P.O. Box 497
Palo Verde, CA 92266
(760) 854-3093
http://www.desertusa.com/magjan98/stories/opal.html

DIRECTIONS:
Blythe is located off of Interstate Highway 10 in southeast California, near the Arizona border. From Blythe, take State Highway 78 south to Palo Verde. Continue on State Highway 78 to Fourth Street and travel west through town for about one mile. Continue on Fourth Street as it curves to the right, heads out of town and towards the mountains, traveling approximately nine miles to the mine. Take a left turn into the mine office.

SEASON:
October 1 through May 1

HOURS:
Daylight

COST:
$15 per person per day–Fee

WHAT TO BRING:
Take a rock hammer, chisel, whisk broom, gloves, goggles and a long-handled screwdriver. Bring plenty of drinking water for this arid climate.

INFORMATION:
This is a wonderful place to find quality fire agates and is certainly a bargain for the price of admission. The fire agates appear somewhat orange in color and resemble opals with flashes of internal color. In addition to the fire agates, you can find chalcedony, quartz crystals, apatite, barite and various other minerals.

Some hardrock mining is necessary. The mine owners are very helpful, and will make sure you get the most out of your efforts. It does take effort to remove the fiery gemstones from the tough host rock.

Camping is available at the mine. There are also some trailers here for your use. No reservations are required. Dogs are welcome as well, so bring your whole family.

ADDRESS:
P.O. Box 278
Pine Grove, CA 95665
(209) 296-4100
roaringcamp@volcano.net
http://www.roaringcampgold.com

DIRECTIONS:
From Sacramento take U.S. Highway 50 to State Highway 16 (Jackson Highway). Take a right on State Highway 49, continuing south to Jackson for about two miles. From that point, take State Highway 88 east for about nine miles until you come to Pine Grove. Follow the road to the camp.

SEASON:
May 1 through September 30

HOURS:
Tours begin at 8:30 a.m., 10:00 a.m. and 2:30 p.m.
Tours are four hours in length

COST:
$550 per week–Fee for one to two people
(includes a cabin and use of the facilities)

WHAT TO BRING:
Take along standard gold mining gear including a dredge and sluice box. The camp will also sell or rent prospecting equipment.

INFORMATION:
The camp offers gold panning, dredging and sluicing. The area is also good for the rockhound looking for crystals, jade, jaspers, river rubies and garnets. A guide is available for fishing and to help you with prospecting for gold. Swimming is also available. Roaring Camp offers a roaring good barbecue on Saturday nights.

Cabins for non-families cost $550 per week for one or two persons, $165 for each additional person. Family rates start at $550 for the first two people over eighteen, while each additional person under the age of eighteen years is $120. The mining tour takes you to old mines, allows you to pan for gold, collect minerals, and visit the Wildlife and Mining Artifacts Museum.

ADDRESS:
The Oceanview Mine
The owners prefer to be contacted by phone or via the internet
(760) 489-1566
freespool1@cox.net
http://digforgems.com

DIRECTIONS:
From San Diego, take Interstate Highway 15 north to Highway 76 and drive west for five miles. From Los Angeles County, take Interstate Highway 5 south to Highway 76, and go east twenty-three miles. At the western edge of Pala. turn into the casino overflow parking lot. The tour will pick you up beside the two large propane tanks. Please arrive by 10:30 a.m., as the tour departs at 10:45 a.m. sharp.

Detailed directions and a map are available at the mine's website upon confirmation of scheduled tour.

SEASON:
Open Sundays

HOURS:
10:30 a.m. to 3 p.m. (Tours leave at 10:45 a.m.)

COST:
$60 per person adult–Fee
$50 per child–Fee
$200 per family of four (2 adults & 2 children)–Fee

WHAT TO BRING:
Bring gloves, sun hat, lunch, drinking water, comfortable shoes, a backpack or bucket to carry your finds.

INFORMATION:
    Visitors to the Oceanview Mine have an opportunity to find many different types of semi-precious stones. Pegmatite minerals that include pink tourmaline, green tourmaline, bi-colored tourmaline occur here. Garnets, mica, cleavelandite, kunzite, morganite, goshenite (clear beryl), purple lepidolite and aquamarine are also found here.
    Reservations are required, and the owners ask that visitors download the liability release form and send it with their reservations.
    Guests at the mine will be sifting through material using screens and water stations in search of treasure.
    There are specimen pieces and gemstones available for purchase at Oceanview.

ADDRESS:
Underground Gold Miners Museum
356 Main Street
Alleghany, CA 95910
(530) 287-3330
http://www.undergroundgold.com
info@undergroundgold.com

DIRECTIONS:
Call for directions and to make reservations before your visit.

SEASON:
May to October

HOURS:
Call for a reservation

COST:
Underground Tours:
$95 per person (minimum of two required)
Group Rates:
$60 per person—groups of 10 to 15 people
$40 per person—groups of 16and over
Call for non-profit/educational group rates
The Miner's Working Tour:
$300 per person (must be 18 or older)
The Executive Tour:
$600 per person

WHAT TO BRING:
Sweater or sweatshirt, work clothing and gloves if you plan a working tour.

INFORMATION:
   The underground tours take approximately four hours, and includes a one-mile walk into the mine at eight hundred feet to visit the historic mine area, geologic formations, and the hoist room where ore is lifted from the mine. The temperature is a constant 55°F in the mine, so dress appropriately.
   The miner's working tour is a full day (up to eight hours) tour with the miners geared towards the interest of the participant, and allows visitors to experience the underground operations of the mine. This tour includes a chance to learn about drifts, adits, stopes and winzes. A professional miner is your guide. Lunch is provided.
   The executive tour affords you a one-on-one tour of the surface and underground operation by the president of the corporation or mine manager. With luck, visitors will be among the first to see virgin gold ore.
   All tours require the ability to navigate steep terrain on foot.

ADDRESS:
Gems of Pala
P.O. Box 382
Pala, CA 92059
(760) 742-1356
mmmgems@hotmail.com
http://www.mmmgems.com

DIRECTIONS:
Located north of Escondido, seven and two-tenths miles east of Interstate Highway 15 on Highway 76 at Macgee Road. See their website for a map of their location.

SEASON:
March 15 through December 15
Call for winter hours

HOURS:
10:00 a.m. to 4:00 p.m., Thursday through Sunday
Call ahead for reservations

COST:
$50 per bucket–Fee for bucket of virgin material from the "Bridal Chamber"
$25 per bucket–Fee for bucket of material from the "pocket zone"
$10 per bucket–Fee for buck of general spillage material

WHAT TO BRING:
Sifting equipment and screens are provided. Bring a hat, sunscreen, drinking water, tweezers and a closed container to hold your gemstones.

INFORMATION:
   The Stewart Mine is world famous for its fine natural pink tourmaline. Specimens from this location are included in many museums and also cut into gemstones. Especially coveted are the blue-capped rubellite specimens.
   Gravel is gathered from three locations. Federal regulations prohibit visitors from entering the mines, but a virtual tour is available on their website.
   Visitors will begin with a five minute instructional video and then it is on to the tables where you use screens to classify the material and search for your own treasure.

ADDRESS:
Yuba River Ranger District
15924 State Highway 49
Camptonville, CA 95922
(530) 288-3231

DIRECTIONS:
Union Flat Casual Mining Area is located in Tahoe National Forest in the Yuba River Ranger District. Turn right off State Highway 49, approximately five miles east of Downieville, into the Union Flat Campground.

SEASON:
Open year-round–Panning
June 1 through October 15–Dredging

HOURS:
Daylight

COST:
Free

WHAT TO BRING:
Standard gold mining gear. Dredges up to four inches are permitted. Bring your own food, camping supplies and drinking water.

INFORMATION:
    Union Flat Casual Mining Area is located on federal land, overseen by the U.S. Forest Service. It has produced some nice gold flakes in the past. Camping is permitted in the campground area only, which has a fourteen-day limit. Panning is permitted all year round. Dredging requires a permit available from the California Department of Fish and Game at (530) 225-2300. Dredges up to four inches are permitted.
    Casual mining area rules from the forest service were established to protect the land and reduce conflicts with other users. Rules include: mine only the wet areas of stream; no bank mining or disturbing roots of any plants; hand tools only; do not build dams; leave the site as you found it; and no jet or nozzle mining.

ADDRESS:
Wild West Gold Mining Adventures
The owners prefer to be contacted by phone or via
the internet
(530) 675-2668
riverqueen1@softcom.net
http://www.goldminingadventure.com/

DIRECTIONS:
Call or e-mail for directions.

SEASON:
June through August, possibly September

HOURS:
One week mining adventure by reservation only

COST:
Please call for custom pricing
Reservations are limited

WHAT TO BRING:
Dredges, highbankers and other mining tools are provided. Bring your sleeping bag, pillow, personal belongings, and clothing. If you are planning to dredge, bring a wet suit, hood, booties, mask, gloves and a pry bar.

INFORMATION:
    Wild West Gold Mining Adventures will take guests to their claim, where they can camp in their facilities on the Northern Yuba River. They provide meals and instruction in basic dredging, highbanking, sluicing and panning. Individual and full-time instruction is available during the week guests are there. Food and accommodations are included in the price.
    Guests stay in large tents that include a screened-in eating tent. Tents contain a cot or mattress, and are right beside the river. The claim now has a Coleman water heating system to provide warm water for showering after a day of gold mining.
    When not searching for gold, guests may enjoy bird watching, fishing, swimming, tubing, photography, sunbathing, and taking nature hikes.
    Wild West Gold Mining Adventures guarantees you will go home with a minimum of one-half ounce of gold.

MUSEUMS

Site 24.
California State Mining & Mineral Museum
> P.O. Box 1192
> Mariposa, CA 95338
> (209) 742-7625
> http://www.parks.ca.gov/default.asp?page_id=588
> mineralmuseum@sti.net
> • This museum collection, begun in 1880, has over thirteen thousand minerals, rocks, gems and historic artifacts including the gold Fricot Nugget weighing two hundred one troy ounces. Also of interest is a recreated mining tunnel connected to the museum where visitors can see the working conditions of a century ago.

Site 25.
Natural History Museum of Los Angeles County
> 900 Exposition Boulevard
> Los Angeles, CA 90007
> (213) 763-DINO
> http://www.nhm.org/
> • The Gem and Mineral Hall includes: rocks, meteorites and minerals. The California collection displays local minerals, native gold and gem crystals.

Site 26.
Santa Barbara Museum of Natural History
> 2559 Puesta del Sol Road
> Santa Barbara, CA 93105
> (805) 682-4711
> http://www.sbnature.org/
> • The Geology and Paleontology Hall contains information on the formation and history of this region. Fossils include a giant "toothed" bird, a skull from a giant extinct toothed whale and the most complete pygmy mammoth skeleton ever found.

CAVES

Site 27.
Boyden Cavern
> 74101 E. Kings Canyon Road
> Kings Canyon National Park, CA 93633
> (209) 736-2708
> http://www.caverntours.com/BoydenRt.htm
> • Located deep in Kings Canyon Giant Sequoia National Monument, this cavern includes many unusual formations including a stalactite group called the Upside Down City and the Bat Grotto where bats sleep the summer days away. This cavern offers family walking tours, a nature gift shop and picnic facilities.

Site 28.
California Cavern
> 9565 Cave City Road
> Mountain Ranch, CA 95246
> (209) 736-2708
> http://www.caverntours.com/CalifRt.htm
> • This cavern offers tours or spelunking expeditions through the cave's unique crystalline formations and stalactites. Facilities include nature trails, picnic facilities, gemstone mining and a visitor center. Experience the cave toured by Mark Twain and John Muir.

Site 29.
Crystal Cave
Sequoia National Park
47050 Generals Highway, #10
Three Rivers, CA 93271-9651
(559) 565-3759
http://www.sequoiahistory.org/cave/cave.htm
• Rich and varied stalactites fill this cavern. Tickets are sold in advance at the Foothills or Lodgepole Visitor Center and not at the cave entrance.

Site 30.
Lake Shasta Caverns
20359 Shasta Caverns Road
Lakehead, CA 96051
(800) 795-2283
http://www.lakeshastacaverns.com
• Stalactite and stalagmite formations fill this cavern. Milky flowstone deposits and mini-waterfalls grace this limestone and marble cave. Be sure to look for the signature of James A. Richardson who marked his discovery, known for centuries by the indigenous tribes, on November 3, 1878.

Site 31.
Lava Beds National Monument
1 Indian Well, Headquarters
Tulelake, CA 96134
(530) 667-8100
http://www.nps.gov/labe/
• This area is volcanic in origin and thus somewhat devoid of vegetation. Lava tubes are a unique feature here with over two hundred caves within this area. Formed as hot lava pours from a volcano, the outer surface cools rapidly acting as an insulator for the inner core allowing it to flow. When the eruption stopped, the lava drained away leaving a tube or tunnel. Trails have been laid out with ladders to allow easy access to the tubes. Many caves lie off the Cave Loop Road near the visitor center.

Site 32.
Mercer Caverns
P.O. Box 509
Murphys, CA 95247-0509
(209) 728-2101
http://www.mercercaverns.com/
• Mercer Caverns has guest books dating back to the 1880s. This three million-year-old cave was first used by the Yokuts Tribe as a mortuary cave to bury their dead. Modern visitors are welcome to explore the living limestone formations preserved and protected here.

Site 33.
Mitchell Caverns Natural Preserve
Providence Mountains State Recreational Area
P.O. Box 1
Essex, CA 92332
(760) 928-2586
http://www.parks.ca.gov/default.asp?page_id=615
• Intricate limestone formations grace this cavern's tunnels and chambers. Highlights include stalagmites, stalactites, lily pads, helictites, curtains, popcorn and draperies. Tours depart from the visitor center.

Site 34.
Moaning Cavern

5350 Moaning Cave Road
Vallecito, CA 95251
(209) 736-2708
http://www.caverntours.com/MoCavRt.htm
• Gold prospectors found this cavern in 1851 and people have been enjoying the huge chambers ever since. Moaning Cavern got its name from the sound created by water flowing through the limestone creating a perpetual drumming moan. The guided tour descends two hundred thirty-five steps, and travels down one hundred sixty-five feet.

Site 35.
Subway Cave

Lassen National Forest
Hat Creek Ranger District
43225 E. Highway 299
P.O. Box 220
Fall River Mills, CA 96028
(530) 336-5521
http://www.shastacascade.org/forest/lassen/subway.htm
• This is a unique opportunity to walk through a one thousand three hundred-foot long lava tube that varies between six and seventeen feet high. Most lava tubes collapse over time, but the walls of this tube range from eight to twenty-four feet thick. It's cold in here—only 46ºF year-round—you'll need a sweater and a flashlight with good batteries for your trip.

Site 36.
Sunny Jim Cave

The Cave Store
1325 Cave Street
La Jolla, CA 92037
858-459-0746
http://www.cavestore.com/index.html
• This area name is Spanish for "the Jewel." Seven elongated fissures in the cliff wall, located north of the cove, are accessible from the beach at low tide. At other times, visitors travel down one hundred thirty-four steps hewn from the rock, leading to a rich chamber called Sunny Jim's Cathedral. At high tide the surf echoes against the chamber walls.

POINTS OF INTEREST

Site 37.
Bodie State Historic Park

P.O. Box 515
Bridgeport, CA 93517
(760) 647-6445
http://www.parks.ca.gov/?page_id=509
• Named for Waterman S. Body, who discovered the richest gold vein in the west in 1859. This area produced over $32 million in gold and $7 million in silver. The streak was short lived. Twenty years after the discovery, the decline began. Bodie is now a ghost town with a self-guided tour available at the park office. There is a museum on site.

Site 38.
Columbia State Historic Park
> 11255 Jackson Street
> Columbia, CA 95310
> (209) 588-9128
> http://www.parks.ca.gov/default.asp?page_id=552
> • This town has preserved the 1850s Gold Rush-era business district for visitors. Shop owners wear period costumes to conduct business. Visitors can take a stagecoach ride, pan for gold or tour an active gold mine.

Site 39.
Devils Postpile National Monument
> c/o Sequoia and Kings Canyon National Parks
> 47050 Generals Highway
> Three Rivers, CA 93271-9651
> (760) 934-2289
> http://www.nps.gov/archive/depo/depomain.htm
> • This national monument preserves two unusual geologic features, one hundred foot Rainbow Falls, and the huge columnar basalt formations known as Devils Postpile.

Site 40.
Empire Mine State Historic Park
> 10791 East Empire Street
> Grass Valley, CA 95945
> (530) 273-8522
> http://www.parks.ca.gov/page_id=499
> • The Empire Mine is one of the oldest, deepest and longest gold mines in California. Closed in 1956, this mine produced over five million ounces of gold. The park contains mine buildings, and provides guided tours and audio visual presentations.

Site 41.
Pinnacles National Monument
> Superintendent–5000 Highway 146
> Paicines, CA 95043-9770
> (831) 389-4485
> http://www.nps.gov/pinn/
> • This spectacular National Monument is the remains of an ancient volcano, eroded by rain, heat and tectonic-plate movement. The geology is so breath-taking and unique that the monoliths, spires and shear-walled canyons became a national monument in 1908. Hiking, climbing, exploring caves and picnicking are popular park activities.

FAIRS AND FESTIVALS

Site 42.
Pirate Faire
> Gold Coast Festivals, Inc.
> Lake Casitas, CA
> (805) 496-6036
> http://www.goldcoastfestivals.com/piratefaire/piratefestpg1.html
> • Grab your eye-patch and hook and join in this festival celebrating the Pirate Life. The faire has plenty of food, drink and activities to entertain and enchant the entire family.

"Pike's peak or bust."

The California Gold Rush touched off exploration for gold throughout the American West. Soon the Rocky Mountains were no longer the territory of Indians and Trappers. Prospectors arrived, and the search was on.

Gold was first discovered in 1858 by a Georgia miner in a dry creek in what is now suburban Denver. Word spread throughout the country. The rallying call to this new migration was "Pike's Peak or Bust." During the next year, over fifty thousand people arrived in Colorado.

More gold was discovered in Cherry Creek, Central City and then Blackhawk. By 1861, Colorado was large enough to become a territory. In 1887, a prospector named Tom Groves unearthed the largest gold nugget ever found in the state. He brought the seventeen-pound beauty to the assayer's office swaddled in a blanket and the find was dubbed "Tom's Baby."

In 1879, a greasy metal called molybdenum was discovered but no one knew what to do with it until the 1940s when it was used as an alloy to harden steel for armament.

When the placer gold disappeared, men moved underground and hardrock mining became the way to strike it rich. Silver and gold recovery required a transportation system to bring ore to the mill. A cog railroad was built to Cripple Creek. In 1893, an ambitious plan for removing gold ore from beneath the existing mines began. The Argo Tunnel Project aimed to build the longest tunnel ever constructed at the time, beginning in Idaho Springs and heading gradually up for over four miles. The purpose was to link with the mines above, provide ore transportation and ground water removal for a fee. It took seventeen years of hardrock mining, beginning with hand tools, to complete the work. The mines on the tunnel's route profited mightily from having ground water drained and ore removed quickly and efficiently. Mines not lucky enough to be on the route of the Argo dealt with their own rising water or abandoned their mines.

In 1894 Molly Brown, not yet unsinkable, and her husband were awarded a one-eighth share of the richest mine in the area, The Little Jonny, and their fortune was made. Molly used some of the money to gain the education she never got working in tobacco factories in Hannibal, Missouri or as a young wife in the mining camp of Leadville, Colorado. She learned to speak five languages. In 1912, she was reading in her berth aboard the *Titanic* when the collision with the iceberg threw her to the cabin floor. She survived the sinking, helping the other women stay warm by sharing some of the five pair of woolen stockings she had the foresight to put on and by insisting the women row. She was appalled that the man in charge of her boat refused to return for survivors after the ship sank. Back in New York she supposedly attributed her survival to typical Brown luck and may have said, "We're unsinkable." The nickname stuck. She was forever after The Unsinkable Molly Brown.

In 1914, Colorado made national news when a coal miners' strike turned ugly. During the Ludlow Massacre, a group of strike busters made of the Colorado Guard, coal guards and thugs doused the miners' tent camp with kerosene, torched the canvas and then sprayed the area with Gatling gunfire. Twenty people died including thirteen children.

The Argo Tunnel made its final ore run in 1943. A powder blast released a huge body of trapped ground water. A miner, William Bennetts, headed into the mine on an electric tram unaware of the wall of water crashing towards him. A little over a mile into the tunnel, the power shut down. He assumed a breakdown caused the outage and began walking out. He heard an unfamiliar rumble and he began to run. He reached the tunnel opening, struggling through waist deep water. Moments later the water, forced through the tunnel's narrow opening, exploded from the mountain under high pressure. The force of the water was great enough to throw the electric tram, weighing several tons, across the river and impale it into the mountain face on the opposite side of the valley. Four men died in the release of water, and the tunnel was closed for good. Silver and gold production continued to decline through the 1940s.

In the 1950's uranium was discovered and mining began. In 1975, diamonds were discovered and are now mined by the Kelsey Lake Mine. Today coal, diamonds, gold, silver and uranium are still mined. The housing and infrastructure boom in the 1990's has supported the mining of gravel, sand, marble, gypsum and clay. The state of Colorado has a rich mining past and will no doubt have a bright future.

Opportunities still exist for visitors to set their sluice in a river and find gold. Beginners will enjoy the digging sites where greenhorns learn how to pan for gold.

COLORADO SITE MAP

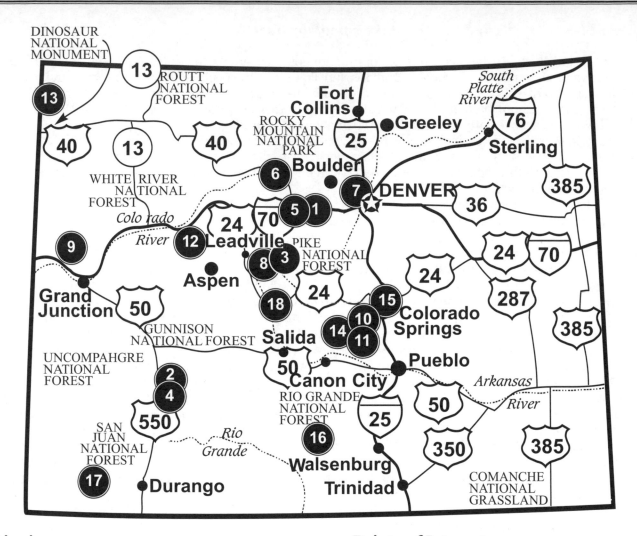

Diggings
1. Argo Gold Mine & Mill
2. Bachelor-Syracuse Mine Tour
3. Country Boy Mine
4. Old Hundred Gold Mine Tour
5. Phoenix Gold Mine
6. Vic's Gold Panning

Museums
7. Denver Museum of Science and Nature
8. The National Mining Hall of Fame & Museum
9. Museum of Western Colorado's Dinosaur Journey
10. Western Museum of Mining and Industry

Caves
11. Cave of the Winds
12. Fairy Caves

Points of Interest
13. Dinosaur National Monument
14. Florissant Fossil Beds National Monument
15. Garden of the Gods
16. Great Sand Dunes National Park
17. Mesa Verde National Park

Fairs and Festivals
18. Gold Rush Days

Map Not To Scale

ADDRESS:
The Argo Gold Mine & Mill
2350 Riverside Drive
Idaho Springs, CO 80452
(303) 567-2421
http://www.historicargotours.com

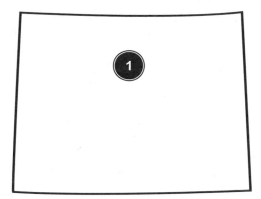

DIRECTIONS:
Take Interstate Highway 70 to Exit 241A, Idaho Springs, Colorado. Exit the highway and follow Miner Street to the Argo Gold Mine and Mill.

SEASON:
mid-April through mid-October

HOURS:
9:00 a.m. to 6:00 p.m.

COST:
$15–Adults
$7.50–Children ages 7–12
Free–Children ages 7 and under
$10–Miners bag of dirt with guaranteed placer gold
$6–Miners bag of dirt with guaranteed gemstones

WHAT TO BRING:
No special equipment or clothing is needed to visit this historic site.

INFORMATION:
The Argo Mine & Mill is listed as a National Historic Site. The tunnel was constructed to drain huge quantities of water from the gold mines between Idaho Springs and Central City, a distance of seventeen miles through solid rock. The tunnel provided drainage, ventilation and transport of ore from the mountains. The processing plant milled the ore, extracting over $100 million of gold at the 1892 prices of $8 to $35 per ounce.

The unique history of this site makes it worth the trip. Begin your visit with a guide who will tell you some of the Argo's fascinating history and show you the many minerals found in Colorado. Then you will be driven by bus up the huge tailing piles to the site of an abandoned gold mine. After you have toured the mine, you can walk past the Argo Tunnel and through the processing plant. Learn how gold was processed in the late 1800s as you walk through this self-guided tour. After you have toured the plant, you can get a gold panning lesson and then buy bags of dirt to pan for gold or screen for gemstones.

ADDRESS:
1222 CR 14
Ouray, CO 81427
(970) 325-0220 or (800) 227-8545
http://www.ouraycolorado.com/bachelor

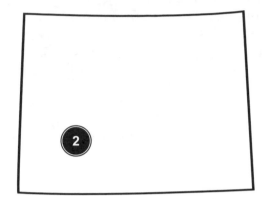

DIRECTIONS:
The Bachelor-Syracuse Mine is located in Ouray, Colorado. Take County Road 14 to Dexter Creek Road. Follow the signs to the mine.

SEASON:
May 20 through September 15, closed July 4

HOURS:
10:00 a.m. to 5:00 p.m.–May
9:00 a.m. to 6:00 p.m.–June to August

COST:
$15.95–Adults tour fee
$7.95–Children ages 11 and under tour fee
$4.00–Fee for gold panning with tour ticket
$6.00–Fee for gold panning with no tour ticket

WHAT TO BRING:
The mine will supply you with the equipment you need to pan for gold and give you a small bottle to hold your finds. This mine has great barbecue so there is no need to pack food.

INFORMATION:
Ouray is a town with a rich mining history. It is very scenic and worth the drive through the Rocky Mountains. The Bachelor Mine is a clean, well-maintained silver and gold mine. Silver was discovered here in 1884 by three bachelors, thus the name. The mine has produced fifteen million ounces of silver, and two hundred fifty thousand ounces of gold as well as lead, zinc and copper.

The tour is conducted by trained guides who can answer all your mining questions and relate their local history. A mine train (trammer) is boarded to advance into the mine. You will visit the work areas and see how explosives are used. Tours leave every hour on the hour. The temperature in the mine is 50°F, so bring a coat. A gold-bearing stream runs from the mine's entrance. An instructor will teach you how to pan for gold.

ADDRESS:

Country Boy Mine
Breckenridge Sleigh Rides
P.O. Box 2332
0542 French Gulch Road
Breckenridge, CO 80424
(970) 453-4405
info@countryboymine.com
http://www.countryboymine.com

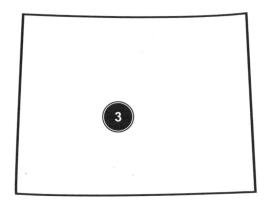

DIRECTIONS:

From Interstate Highway 70 take exit 203. At the third traffic light turn left onto Country Route 450, and drive two miles on French Gulch Road to Country Boy Mine.

SEASON:

March 1 through October 15

HOURS:

10:00 a.m. to 5:00 p.m. most days, closed Mondays in March and April

COST:

$17.95 adults–Fee for tour and gold panning
$12.95 children 12 and under–Fee for tour and gold panning

WHAT TO BRING:

Gloves, sun hat, lunch, drinking water, comfortable shoes, and a small container to carry your gold dust. Bring a sweater or jacket for the mine tour, as the mine shaft is cool year-round.

INFORMATION:

The Country Boy Mine was established in 1887, and was one of the largest gold mines in Breckenridge. This attraction offers an underground mine tour that runs every hour on the hour, and takes forty-five minutes. You'll enjoy hay rides in the summer, sleigh rides in the winter, and gold panning year-round, thanks to an indoor panning facility. During summertime, prospectors use Eureka Creek to search for gold.

The mine's newest attraction is a fifty-five foot ore chute water slide.

ADDRESS:
Old Hundred Gold Mine Tour
P.O. Box 430
Silverton, CO 81433
(800) 872-3009 or (970) 387-5444
info@minetour.com
http://www.minetour.com/

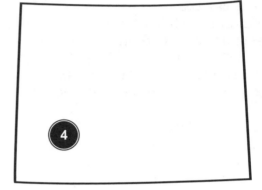

DIRECTIONS:
Take U.S. Highway 550 (San Juan Skyway) to Silverton. Drive past the courthouse and museum and take a right hand turn onto County Road 2. Drive two more miles. Once you pass the Mayflower Mill entrance, the road becomes gravel. After another two miles you come to the ghost town of Howardsville. Cross the creek and turn right on County Road 4 and drive one mile to the mine on County Road 4-A. You will see the blue and white "Mine Tour" signs located every half-mile outside of Silverton.

SEASON:
May through October

HOURS:
10:00 a.m. to 4:00 p.m.

COST:
$16.95–Adults
$7.95–Children ages 5–12
$14.95–Seniors 60 and older

WHAT TO BRING:
The temperature underground is 48°F, so bring a sweater or jacket. You will be fitted with hard hats and coats. Panning equipment is provided.

INFORMATION:
    The mine itself is located at ten thousand feet. The fun starts with a ride on the mine trammer, an electric train, to take you one thousand six hundred feet underground. At the main level, you will take a walk of one-third of a mile through a real gold mine. This tour features actual mining demonstrations of authentic equipment including antique tools of the trade, some of which include a single-jack drill, drifter drill, jack-leg drill and tugger hoist. The tour takes about forty-five minutes.
    Your tour ticket of the Old Hundred Mine entitles you to pan for gold for free. The sluice box is "salted" with real gold so you are sure to see some color.
    The Old Hundred Mine has restrooms, gift shop, snacks and a picnic area available to visitors. If you are in Silverton, stop by this historic landmark and find some gold.

PHOENIX GOLD MINE

SITE 5

GOLD MINE TOUR & GOLD PANNING

COLORADO

ADDRESS:
Phoenix Mine
2060 Miner Street
Idaho Springs, CO 80452
(303) 567-0422
http://www.phoenixgoldmine.com

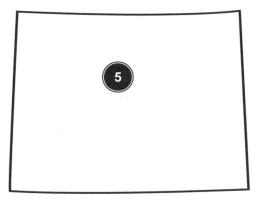

DIRECTIONS:
Traveling east on Interstate Highway 70, take Exit 234 and cross under the highway. Turn right and follow Stanley Road to Trail Creek Road. Travel up the road to the mine. If you are traveling west on Interstate Highway 70, disembark and Exit 239 and travel west on Stanley Road to Trail Creek Road. The mine is approximately thirty minutes from Denver.

SEASON:
May through October
November through April, weather permitting

HOURS:
10:00 a.m. to 5:00 p.m.

COST:
$10–Adults
$8–Seniors age 65 and over
$5–Children ages 5–11
$5–Panning fee
Free–Children 4 and under

WHAT TO BRING:
Wear old clothes and a light jacket. The mountains are cool and, the mine is cooler. Small gold pans are provided to use in the stream, but they do not provide shovels or trowels. Check first to see if you can use these items.

INFORMATION:
Experienced guides will orient you to the history of the Colorado Gold Rush. Then it's time to go underground and see how the old-timers worked the rock using steel tools and black powder. Your guide will explain the techniques and evolution of the gold mining process as you tour the mine. With wooden timber supports and steel racks for the ore cars, the mine looks as it did one hundred fifty years ago. In at least two places, gold veins and nuggets of gold are visible in the quartz vein. Before leaving the tunnel, the guide explains the refining process for extracting gold from ore. Finally, guests are given a gold pan and a quick lesson before heading to the creek and picnic area. Pan as long as you like, and keep what you find.

ADDRESS:
Vic's Gold Panning
Colorado Prospector
P.O. Box 478
Rollinsville, CO 80474
prospector@coloradoprospector.com
http://www.coloradoprospector.com/Vic's_Gold_Panning/vics.html

DIRECTIONS:
Located on Highway 119, below Blackhawk.
Contact Jesse Peterson by e-mail for directions.

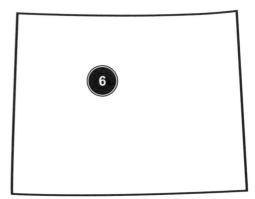

SEASON:
Open year-round

HOURS:
8:00 a.m. to 6:00 p.m. daily, weather permitting

COST:
$10–Fee for gold panning
$15–Fee for sluice box three foot or less
$20–Fee for sluice box 4 foot or greater
$40–Fee for high banker
$40–Fee for dredging

WHAT TO BRING:
You may bring your own equipment, or the mine will provide you with a gold pan at no additional charge. Bring any prospecting gear you need, in addition to drinking water, a hat and sunscreen.

INFORMATION:
Vic's Gold Panning has a twenty-one acre area on Clear Creek, near Blackhawk, Colorado. Gold panning, sluicing, high banking and dredging are all permitted at this claim. Open since 1957, this site is open to the public, and is a fine place to learn gold prospecting basics. This site is affiliated with the Colorado Prospectors Association.

Reservations are required so that there will be someone to welcome you and get you oriented.

MUSEUMS

Site 7.

Denver Museum of Nature & Science

2001 Colorado Boulevard
Denver, CO 80205
(303) 322-7009
http://www.dmns.org/
• The Coors Mineral Hall includes a mine tunnel and reconstructed pocket of deep red rhodochrosite crystals from the world famous "Sweet Home" Mine. The most celebrated specimen is the Alma King, a four and one-quarter-inch deep pink crystal. Other must see exhibits include a collection of Colorado gold nuggets, including "Tom's Baby," a nugget found in 1887 and weighing thirteen pounds!

Site 8.

The National Mining Hall of Fame & Museum

120 West Ninth Street
P.O. Box 981
Leadville, CO 80461-0981
(719) 486-1229
http://www.mininghalloffame.org/
• This museum celebrates the history of mining in America. A replica of an underground hardrock mine, complete with mine-gauge track, ore cars, chutes, hammers, hand steels and mechanical drills, leads visitors to the Gold Rush Room. This room displays gold specimens and artifacts from each of the seventeen states that hosted gold rushes. Specimens of gold, silver, other ores and minerals are on display along with a twenty-three-ounce specimen of native gold from Leadville.

Site 9.

Museum of Western Colorado's Dinosaur Journey

Dinosaur Journey
550 Jurassic Court
Fruita, CO 81521
(970) 858-7282
http://www.dinosaurjourney.org/
• The Museum of Western Colorado's Dinosaur Journey features exhibits and information about dinosaur excavations, realistic robotic dinosaurs and a working paleontology laboratory.

Site 10.

Western Museum of Mining and Industry

225 North Gate Boulevard
Colorado Springs, CO 80921
(719) 488-0880
http://www.wmmi.org/html/index.htm
• This museum offers a historical look at the process of mining, including a working stamp mill, mining equipment and lessons on gold panning. Tours take approximately one and one half hours.

CAVES

Site 11.
Cave of the Winds
    P.O. Box 826
    Manitou Springs, CO 80829
    (719) 685-5444
    http://www.caveofthewinds.com
    • Two boys heard wind blowing across the cave's natural entrance and discovered this site. During the height of the Great Depression, railroad official George Jeffries provided funds to develop this cave with the stipulation that his name be inscribed on a wall, and mentioned on each tour. And so it is. The Cave of the Winds takes visitors past an astonishing array of flowstone and rock formations. The tour begins and ends in a large gift shop.

Site 12.
Fairy Caves
    Glenwood Caverns Adventure Park
    51000 Two Rivers Plaza Road
    Glenwood Springs, CO 81601
    (970) 945-4CAV or (800) 530-1635
    http://www.glenwoodcaverns.com/
    • Fairy Caves was open to the public in 1886 and billed as the eighth wonder of the world. The cave was closed around 1910, and reopened when two of the largest chambers in Colorado were discovered.

POINTS OF INTEREST

Site 13.
Dinosaur National Monument
    4545 Highway 40
    Dinosaur, CO 81610-9724
    (970) 374-3000
    http://www.nps.gov/dino/
    • Dinosaur bones were found here in 1909. The site was designated a National Monument in 1915 when excavation continued, but the fossils were left where they were found. The park stretches into Utah, but the visitors center is in Colorado and was built on top of a fossil-bearing wall of sandstone. The surrounding canyons contain ancient petroglyphs.

Site 14.
Florissant Fossil Beds National Monument
    P.O. Box 185
    Florissant, CO 80816
    (719) 748-3253
    http://www.nps.gov/flfo/
    • An ancient volcano trapped many creatures here and preserved them forever. These fossil beds are world-renowned and have provided unique specimens of insects, plants and animals. A trip to the visitor's center or along an interpretive trail is the best place to see these fossils.

Site 15.
Garden of the Gods
    Visitor Center
    1805 North 30th Street (at Gateway Road)
    Colorado Springs, CO 80904
    (719) 634-6666
    http://www.gardenofgods.com/home/index.cfm?&Flash=1

• Garden of the Gods is a unique city park, which became a National Landmark because of its geological uniqueness. The red rock formations are spectacular and easily accessible because of a network of sidewalks that circle major formations. The visitor center includes exhibits and a film presentation along with free maps.

Site 16.
Great Sand Dunes National Park

11999 Highway 150
Mosca, CO 81146
(719) 378-6319
http://www.nps.gov/grsa

• These dunes are the tallest in North America, rising seven hundred fifty feet and covering an area of approximately forty miles. A product of erosion of the San Juan and Sangre de Cristo Mountains, they collect in this place on the prevailing winds. Over the years the sand accumulated grain by grain and the dunes continue to grow. Like a living sculpture, the dunes change with the prevailing wind. A campground is open year-round, and backpacking is permitted.

Site 17.
Mesa Verde National Park

P.O. Box 8
Mesa Verde National Park, CO 81330
(970) 529-4465
http://www.nps.gov/meve/

• Mesa Verde is Spanish for "green table" which refers to the color of the cliff tops. This park preserves over seven hundred years of human history. The stone villages on cliff tops and wedged into the cliffs are remarkable and elaborate. The cliff dwelling period lasted about one hundred years, after which the area was abandoned. Today visitors can tour the ruins and wonder at a people known as the "ancient ones".

FAIRS AND FESTIVALS

Site 18.
Gold Rush Days

Buena Vista Area Chamber of Commerce
343 Highway 24 South
P.O. Box 2021
Buena Vista, CO 81211
(719) 395-6612
http://www.fourteenernet.com/goldrush/

• Each August, Buena Vista celebrates its Gold Rush heritage with the Gold Rush Days. Check out the burro races, rubber ducky race down the Cottonwood Creek or watch an old fashioned melodrama by the Pick and Shovel Player. Also, watch out for gunfights in the street. Lots of fun things take place besides gold panning. Many food booths and vendors are there as well, so come and try your luck at panning.

HAWAII

Tears of Pele, Goddess of Fire.

The Hawaiian Islands are the peak of the biggest mountain range in the world. Mountains are usually measured from sea level, by which standard Everest is king at 29,028 feet. But when the measurement is taken from the mountain's base, Hawaii's Mauna Kea is the champion, rising 33,476 feet from its base on the ocean floor. Hawaii is also the place where visitors will find the youngest rocks on the planet, some only minutes old.

Magma is constantly forced from its home thirty miles beneath the surface through active volcanoes. Eruptions are either rapidly-moving with intense brief periods of high volume output, or slow-moving with prolonged low volume outputs of magma. Both can be very destructive, consuming homes and forcing evacuations. This process also adds new land. The Hawaiian Islands are young and still growing.

Magma is a mixture of silica, black crystalline, obsidian, olivine and feldspar. The color of the lava varies depending on its composition, with black being most common, green showing a high concentration of olivine (peridot), and red, most rare, results from oxidation. There is a myth about lava, which says it is bad luck to take lava home with you. This myth did not come from Hawaiian culture, and the Park Service denies originating the story. Could it be the airline and tourist industries conspired to avoid having to cart tons of rock collected by visitors? Maybe the locals grew tired of watching their island shrink one piece of lava at a time. Or perhaps the Fire Goddess, Pele, disapproves of rock collectors and brings bad luck. In any case, rockhounding in Hawaii may be more dangerous than in other states.

The volcanic flow brings to the surface a gemstone born of fire—peridot. Small crystals are often found in lava rocks, sometimes in such magnitude to give them a green luster. On the island of Oahu, some beaches are composed entirely of olivine grains. Hawaiian legend tells that these green gemstones are tears from the volcano goddess—Pele. Perhaps lava saturated with peridot is unlucky because it holds her sorrows.

Another island gemstone is coral. Occurring in pink, gold and black, these living gems are harvested from deep waters and fashioned into jewelry. Hawaiian black coral is a rare and relatively new addition to the market, only having been discovered in 1958 and becoming Hawaii's official gemstone in 1987.

Mining in the Hawaiian Islands is confined to extracting sand and gravel for use in building and industry. New technologies are being developed that may make mining mineral resources offshore profitable. Deposits of sand, coral and shell are currently extracted in shallow water. Deep mineral resources are known to exist including: magnesium, sulfur and placer deposits of diamonds, tin and gold. Environmental issues and the exceedingly high cost of deep-sea extraction currently make such efforts unprofitable. But who knows what future technological breakthroughs will bring.

HAWAII SITE MAP

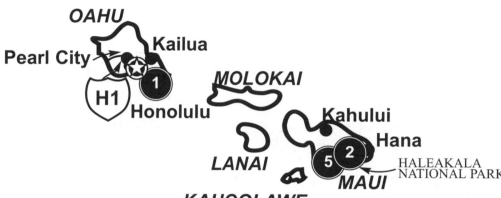

KAUAI

NIIHAU

OAHU

Pearl City   Kailua

1

H1   Honolulu

MOLOKAI

Kahului

Hana

LANAI

5 **2**

HALEAKALA
NATIONAL PARK

MAUI

KAHOOLAWE

HAWAII

19

190   Hilo

3 **11**

4

HAWAII
VOLCANOES
NATIONAL
PARK

Museums
  1. Honolulu Community College
Caves
  2. Hana Lave Tube (Ka'eleku Caverns)
  3. Thurston Lava Tube/Hawaii Volcanoes National Park
Points of Interest
  4. Hawaii Volcanoes National Park
  5. Haleakala National Park

N

W ← → E

S

Map Not To Scale

MUSEUMS

Site 1.
Honolulu Community College
874 Dillingham Boulevard / Honolulu, HI 96817
(808) 845-9211
http://www.hcc.hawaii.edu/dinos/dinos.1.html
• Located on the campus grounds is a permanent exhibit of replica fossils cast from the American Natural History Museum Collection in New York.

CAVES

Site 2.
Hana Lava Tube (Ka'eleku Caverns)
P.O. Box 40 / Hana, HI 96713
(808) 248-7308
http://www.mauicave.com
• Guides take visitors deep into subterranean passages of one of the world's largest lava tubes. Lava tubes are fragile and guests are asked not to touch the cavern system.

Site 3.
Thurston Lava Tube/Hawaii Volcanoes National Park
P.O. Box 52 / Hawaii National Park, HI 96718-0052
(808) 985-6000
http://www.botany.hawaii.edu/faculty/bridges/bigisland/thurston/thurston.html
• This lava tube is available for self-guided tours. Tubes are generally cool and moist and may have tree roots protruding from the roof of the cave. The cave is accessible through a collapsed portion of the roof and a smaller roof exit a bit farther along.

POINTS OF INTEREST

Site 4.
Hawaii Volcanoes National Park
P.O. Box 52 / Hawaii National Park, HI 96718-0052
(808) 985-6000
http://www.nps.gov/havo
• This is the only park in the United States that posts updates on lava flows. Since Hawaii's volcanoes are less explosive than other places, visitors can get an up close look at the formation of a land mass. The Thurston Lava Tube is a major attraction on Crater Rim Drive. Visitors will see cinder cones, chasms and barren lava frozen into fantastic shapes. The park is also a refuge for native plants and animals. Activities include: backpacking, camping, interpretive talks, nature walks, star gazing, slide shows and exhibits on volcanoes.

Site 5.
Haleakala National Park
P.O. Box 369 / Makawao, HI 96768-0369
(808) 572-4400
http://www.nps.gov/hale/
• The Hawaiian Islands are located on the Pacific Plate where land masses move away from each other and magma wells upward to fill the gap. Here visitors can see the earth's surface in motion. Haleakala National Park, on the island of Maui, preserves the Haleakala Crater and the fragile ecosystem of Kipahulu Valley. Visitors will find a natural environment and tropical wilderness.

The Gem State

How can you not love a place called the Gemstone State? Idaho has gemstones including opal, the very rare star garnet, agates and sapphires. But that is not all you should know about Idaho. The state history is fascinating, the landscape breathtaking and the mining opportunities endless.

Let's focus on history. The first Europeans to wander this way were explorers and trappers. Native Americans lived here long before, and there is evidence they did mining before European prospectors ever considered Idaho as a destination. The Oregon Trail crossed Idaho, and so did countless wagons bound for the fertile Pacific coast. Gold was found in 1849 and prospectors rushed into the mountains. By 1860, Idaho had its first town, Franklin. The same year major strikes were found near what is now Idaho City and Silver City. Chinese workers flooded into Idaho's mines. Men dug everywhere. One prospector and hotel owner in the area, now called Silver Valley, missed staking a profitable claim so he ripped up the floor of one of his bedrooms and dug straight down for thirty feet to bedrock and then began mining. The Bedroom Mine Bar is still open for business in Murray, Idaho.

Through the 1860s and 1870s, there were several Indian wars as Europeans claimed territory from the previous inhabitants. In 1885, a miner named Noah Kellogg arrived in the town of Murray broke. To make some money, he convinced two businessmen to stake him. His "grubstake" consisted of money to buy food, and the loan of a burro to carry his gear. He headed up the Coeur d'Alene River and south over the mountains. He made camp and the next morning he discovered his burro had wondered off. He found the irritating creature high up on the hillside. Beneath the burro's feet was the glitter of galena, otherwise known as lead. What Noah found, or rather what the little burro found was Bunker Hill—the largest silver strike in the nation, surpassing even Nevada's Comstock Lode. Noah always gave his borrowed burro full credit for the discovery, but they named the town after Noah Kellogg.

News of Kellogg's discovery soon reached James Wardner, an entrepreneur of the first caliber. Wardner got the news at his grocery store in Warren and headed out on a fast horse carrying nothing but two bottles of whiskey. He reached the camp of Kellogg, and O'Rourke and got the lucky miners drunk. While they slept one off, he proceeded to borrow their axe and spent the next few hours blazing trees, thus staking his claim. Kellogg and O'Rourke knew they'd been had and made Wardner a partner.

In 1879, a gold prospector named Tom Irwin discovered a gold-bearing quartz vein. He mined there successfully for three years, during which time he managed to lay down his track, mine car and tools in the tunnel and blast open an entrance. The fact that he put his tools and equipment inside the shaft, rather than selling them indicates he meant to return. He never did and the location of the mine disappeared for a hundred years. In 1991, the owner of the property noticed ground water seeping from the hillside. Hoping to find a spring, he unearthed the portal to the mine. During the hundred lost years, smithsonite crystals formed on the walls. Gold and wire silver are still visible in places. In 1996, the property was sold to a retired miner, who has turned the gold mine into a tourist attraction. Visitors to Kellogg, Idaho can see the Crystal Gold Mine and take a tour.

The geography of Idaho often made mineral riches difficult to reach. Burke, Idaho is a case in point. This mining town is located in the valley of two very steep mountains. Burke's mineral wealth attracted two railroads before they ever had a road. Hundreds of miners lived in a canyon so narrow there was little room for streets, and buildings resembled cliff dwellings. In 1888, the Tiger Hotel in Burke was built across the canyon with the railroad running beneath it. Another railroad arrived in 1890 and it ran through the hotel lobby. Finally a road joined the rails, and this also ran through the hotel. The establishment had one hundred fifty rooms, and was listed in *Ripley's Believe it or Not*. In 1923, a fire swept through the town, destroying many buildings, including the hotel.

Not all of Idaho's mining history is fortunate. On May 2, 1972 in Wallace, Idaho, the Sunshine Mine suffered one of the worst mining accidents in the state. Ninety-one miners died in a mine fire. A statue of a miner holding a rock drill was erected on Interstate Highway 90 to honor the dead.

Idaho still provides visitors many opportunities to find gold, opals, garnets and star garnets. The Spencer Opal Mine is famous. Garnets and star garnets are found at the Emerald Creek Garnet Area. As for gold—there are many sites for beginners and experts. Check the digging list for locations.

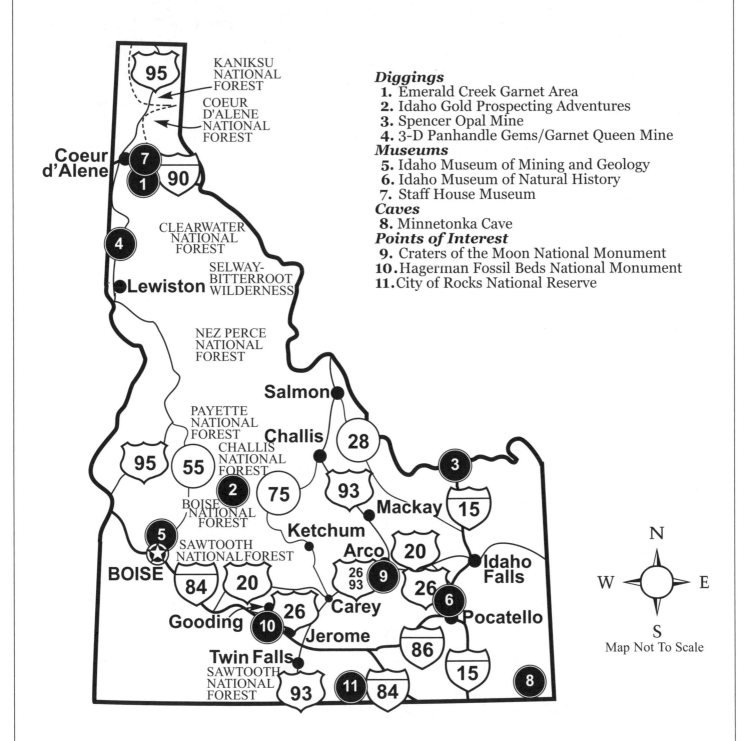

Diggings
1. Emerald Creek Garnet Area
2. Idaho Gold Prospecting Adventures
3. Spencer Opal Mine
4. 3-D Panhandle Gems/Garnet Queen Mine

Museums
5. Idaho Museum of Mining and Geology
6. Idaho Museum of Natural History
7. Staff House Museum

Caves
8. Minnetonka Cave

Points of Interest
9. Craters of the Moon National Monument
10. Hagerman Fossil Beds National Monument
11. City of Rocks National Reserve

Map Not To Scale

ADDRESS:
St. Joe Ranger District
222 South 7th Street, Suite 1
St. Maries, ID 83861
(208) 245-2531
http://www.fs.fed.us/ipnf/rec/activities/garnets

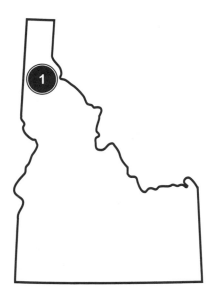

DIRECTIONS:
From St. Maries, follow State Highway 3 south twenty-four miles. Take Road 447 southwest for eight miles to the Emerald Creek Garnet Area parking area. The admission permit, information and digging area are a one half-mile hike up 281 Gulch.

SEASON:
Memorial Day through Labor Day

HOURS:
9:00 a.m. to 5:00 p.m.—closed Wednesday and Thursday

COST:
$10 per day—Adults
$5 per day—Children ages 6-14

WHAT TO BRING:
You should bring lined rubber gloves, a small hammer and brush, container with lid for garnets and a change of clothes—this is wet, muddy work. You are provided with buckets, shovels and special screen boxes.

INFORMATION:
The twelve-sided (dodecahedron) star garnets are found in only two places in the world. Crystals can range in size from a grain of sand to a golf ball or larger. Stars found here are both four-ray and six-ray. Some material is of gem quality. You may carry away up to five pounds of garnets. If you want more than five pounds of material you must buy another permit (limit of thirty pounds per person per year).

The Forest Service has constructed an area where the public can purchase a permit, remove material from stockpiled, garnet-bearing gravels and take them to one of two sluice boxes to wash the material in search of the garnets. This location has an administration building with restrooms, visitor's information and assistance, permit sales and a garnet display. Four miles east of Emerald Creek Garnet Area is Emerald Creek Campground. The camping fee is $6 per night. Food, gas and other supplies are six miles away in Clarkia. No drinking water is available at the garnet site so bring plenty of your own beverages.

ADDRESS:
Idaho Gold Prospecting Adventures
c/o Ed Easley
4401 West Hubbard
Kuna, ID 83634
(208) 884-3142

DIRECTIONS:
Gold Prospecting Adventures is located in Idaho's Boise National Forest on private gold claims. Call for specific directions.

SEASON:
July through October 15

HOURS:
Full-, half-, two- and three-day trips available (half-day for locals only)

COST:
$145 per day—Adults
$70 per day—Children ages 9 to 13
Free—Children ages 8 and under

WHAT TO BRING:
All prospecting equipment is provided. Adventures, one-, two- or three-day, include meals, camping and gold mining equipment. Pack your personal gear, bug repellent, sunscreen, a hat and bring a camera.

INFORMATION:
Idaho Gold Prospecting Adventures offer a real outdoor experience in the grandeur of the Boise National Forest. The forest is home to elk, deer, trophy fish and other critters. The water is crystal clear. You may even see a hot spring or two.

An experienced prospector guide will teach you what you need to know. You can pan for gold, sluice, metal detect, power sluice and learn to operate a dredge. Tenderfeet are welcome. The prospectors guarantee visitors will find some gold, and they never add gold to their claims.

This is a wilderness experience with no phones, beepers, shopping malls or gift shops. You'll camp outdoors and meals are prepared over a campfire. If you enjoy roughing it in a truly magnificent mountain area, this outing is made for you.

ADDRESS:
Spencer Opal Mine
27 Opal Avenue
Spencer, ID 83446
(208) 374-5476
info@SpencerOpalMine.com
http://www.spenceropalmines.com

DIRECTIONS:
Spencer is just south of the Idaho/Montana border on Interstate Highway 15. The mine is located off Interstate Highway 15 and State Highway 22 outside of Spencer. Mine headquarters are located in the town of Spencer, on the north end of Main Street at the gas station and trailer park.

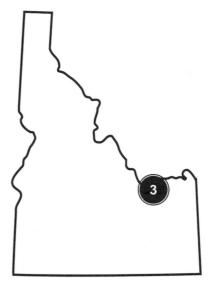

SEASON:
May through October

HOURS:
9:00 a.m. to 5:00 p.m.–closed Wednesdays

COST:
Opal Mine–Call for dates and availability
$40 per day per person–Fee for mining, includes up to five pounds of opals

Mini-Mine–Located at the headquarters
$5 per person–Fee for mining at the mini-mine

WHAT TO BRING:
Bring a spray bottle (most important), points and chisels, a three- to four-pound rock hammer, eight-pound sledgehammer and a carrying bucket. Safety glasses are REQUIRED.

INFORMATION:
The headquarters is open six days a week from 9:00 a.m. to 5:00 p.m. (closed Wednesdays). There is more than one mine office in town, so be sure to get the right one. They carry a full line of opal-cutting supplies, rough opal and finished jewelry. They have a stockpile of mine run material that you can search through. The charge is $5 per pound.

You need to obtain a permit at the mine office to dig through the pile. Water is available for washing the material, but not for drinking. You must bring your own. You will be digging in opal-bearing rock ranging in size from gravel to small boulders.

The opal mine is not open for fee mining on a daily basis. Call for open dates.

ADDRESS:
Louise Darby
P.O. Box 9082
Moscow, ID 83843
(208) 882-9496

DIRECTIONS:
3-D's Panhandle Gems & "Garnet Queen Mine" is on 1026 Juliene Way. From Moscow, go east on State Highway 8 and turn right at Milepost 7. Turn left at the second place on the left.

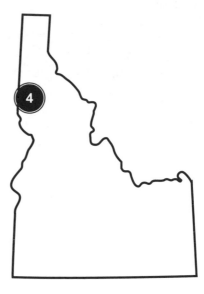

SEASON:
Memorial Day weekend through Labor Day weekend

HOURS:
By appointment only

COST:
$65 per person–Fee

WHAT TO BRING:
All equipment as well as instructions are supplied. You may choose to bring a container with a lid. You will need to bring your own lunch and beverages. Old clothes and lace boots or sneakers are recommended.

INFORMATION:
Due to the popularity of these garnet mining trips, reservations must be made at least thirty days in advance. Your cost includes the U.S. Forest Service fee, user fee and Idaho sales tax. To get to the mining area there is a three-fourths of a mile walk on an inclined road.

Louise Darby will teach you where to look and a bit about how the garnets are formed. You will learn how to tell a star garnet from a facet-grade garnet. Garnets found can be the size of sand particles up to over two inches in diameter. Trips take place within the Idaho Panhandle National Forest.

Louise Darby is a licensed guide and outfitter. She will take you on a mining trip that you will never forget.

MUSEUMS

Site 5.
Idaho Museum of Mining and Geology
2455 North Penitentiary Road
Boise, ID 83712
(208) 368-9876
http://www.idahomuseum.org
• Idaho's colorful history of mining and geology is highlighted with historical photographs, artifacts from early Idaho mining days and an extensive collection of gem and mineral specimens.

Site 6.
Idaho Museum of Natural History
Idaho State University Campus
ISU Building 12, Room 205C
5th Avenue and Dillon Street
Pocatello, ID 83209
(208) 236-3317
http://www.imnh.isu.edu/
imnh@isu.edu
• The Earth Science Division maintains collections of vertebrate and invertebrate fossils, geology and mineralogy.

Site 7.
Staff House Museum
Shoshone County Mining & Smelting Museum, Inc.
820 McKinley Avenue
Kellogg, ID 83837
(208) 786-4141
http://www.staffhousemuseum.com
• This museum focuses on local mining history and includes rock and mineral displays, local historic exhibits, mining equipment and a three dimensional model of the Bunker Hill Mining and Smelting Company.

CAVES

Site 8.
Minnetonka Cave
Montpelier Ranger District
322 North 4th Street
Montpelier, ID 83254
(435) 245-4422
http://www.fs.fed.us/r4/caribou-targhee/about/minnetonka_cave.shtml
• Four hundred forty-eight steps descend into the Minnetonka Cave and take visitors past limestone formations with such names as Three Sisters, Kermit's Castle and the Grasshopper.

Points of Interest

Site 9.
Craters of the Moon National Monument

Park Headquarters
P.O. Box 29
Arco, ID 83213
(208) 527-3257
http://www.nps.gov/archive/crmo/home.htm
• This otherworldly area was made a National Monument in 1924. The surface of this eighty some mile area is strewn with lava from a volcano that erupted fifteen thousand years ago and up until two thousand years ago. A seven-mile drive takes you through the strange landscape and to such places as a half-mile lava tube cave. The park offers many challenges to hikers since the black lava can reach temperatures of 175°F in the summer.

Site 10.
Hagerman Fossil Beds National Monument

221 North State Street
P.O. Box 570
Hagerman, ID 83332
(208) 837-4793
http://www.nps.gov/archive/hafo/home.htm
• It is hard to believe that the quantity and quality of Pliocene fossils unearthed in this area come from a narrow bluff only six miles long. About two to three million years ago, sediments primarily consisting of sand, silt and clay settled to form the geology of most of the six hundred foot thick fossil bed. The area was created from a fluvial and floodplain environment that formed around the edge of ancient Lake Idaho. Also notable is that this monument is one of only three units within the U.S. National Park system which contains original parts of the Oregon National Historic Trail. The Oregon Trail traverses the southern portion of the fossil beds.

Site 11.
City of Rocks National Reserve

P.O. Box 169
Almo, ID 83312
(208) 824-5519
http://www.nps.gov/ciro
• These granite rock formations are some of the oldest in the United States, 2.5 billion years old, and have weathered into fantastic shapes. Visitors claim to see animals, faces and buildings in the rocks. These rocks lie within the Albion Mountain Range and offers numerous recreational activities such as hiking, wildlife viewing, picnicking, rock climbing, backpacking, Nordic skiing, photography and horseback riding. City of Rocks is a very popular destination among rock climbers.

"Home, Home on the Range."

This state is as far from the ocean as a person can get. But this was not always the case. Kansas was once beneath a vast inland sea. Fossil remains attest to this, and the rock of Kansas has revealed fantastic creatures long gone from this world. One particularly unusual animal is the extinct animal called the mosasaur. This swimming reptile was neither dinosaur nor fish, but most closely related to the monitor lizard and modern day snakes. With flippers, rather than feet, this creature resembled a crocodile and included forty species that ranged in length between ten and fifty feet. Its massive jaws filled with rows of teeth made mosasaurs ideally suited for snapping up prey and swallowing them whole. The mosasaurs shared the waters with giant fish and a huge variety of sharks, judging by the fossilized teeth and bones left behind. The Smoky Hill Chalk area of Kansas is famous for these and many other fossils. Visitors can see mosasaur fossils and others at the Johnson Geology Museum.

Over 80 million years ago the same continental shift that created the Rocky Mountains raised the plains above sea level, and the inland sea receded leaving behind tons and tons of chalky algae, shell and other sediment. Time and pressure changed this sediment to limestone. River sediment covered the limestone and changed to sandstone. Erosion took most of the limestone here, but it remains in places like Castle Rock, Rock City, Monument Rocks and Mushroom Rocks. The latter is a strange collection of rocks resembling mushrooms, with the tougher sandstone cap resisting erosion better than the underlying limestone stem. The result is huge stone mushrooms, some fifteen feet in height.

Anyone who has been to Kansas knows that the central portion of the state is nearly devoid of trees. Early settlers, accustomed to using wood for fuel, construction and fence posts now found no raw materials. Their solution to the fence post problem was to make the posts of limestone. In the area known as Post-Rock County around the Smoky Hills, a farmer could buy quarried limestone posts for $.25 each. That fee included delivering the three to four hundred-pound stone columns to the farmer's fence line. There is a small museum in Lacrosse, Kansas dedicated to post rock.

Before the settlers busted sod here, Spanish explorers led by Francisco Vasquez de Coronado traveled to interior Kansas in 1541. They searched for the famed Seven Golden Cities of Cibola, but did not find them and left.

In 1802 Kansas became a United States territory with the Louisiana Purchase. For the next eighty years, settlers and Native Americans battled for the territory with the settlers finally triumphing. Sixty-nine years later in a peaceful prairie, Dr. Brewster M. Higley, M. D. wrote the song "Home on the Range." The land filled with cattle and sodbusters, but no miners dallied in Kansas any longer than it took to travel through it to the goldfields of California.

Just before the turn of the twentieth century, a type of gold was discovered in Kansas—black gold. Oil and natural gas reserve discoveries brought wildcatters, and oil companies began drilling. By 1913 Kansas City was an oil boomtown producing over twenty-four thousand barrels a year. By the end of World War 1, the population of Wichita doubled as oil reserves were discovered nearby. During the Great Depression more oil was discovered in western Kansas, sustaining many in the state in hard times. The oil boom continued into the 1950s. Visitors can learn more about Kansas' oil history at the Butler County History Center & Kansas Oil Museum.

Kansas still produces salt, oil, Portland clay and crushed stone, but they get their fence posts from states that have lumber.

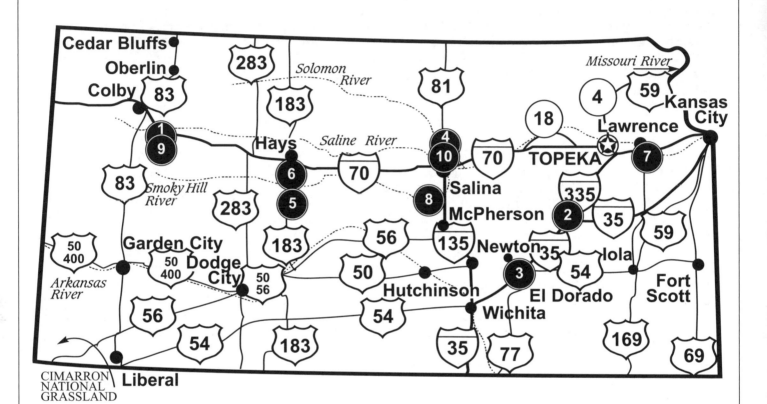

Museums
1. Fick Fossil and History Museum
2. Johnston Geology Museum
3. Butler County History Center & Kansas Oil Museum
4. Ottawa County Historical Museum
5. Post Rock Museum
6. Sternberg Museum of Natural History
7. University of Kansas Natural History Museum & Biodiversity Research Center

Points of Interest
8. Mushroom State Park
9. Monument Rocks National Natural Landmark
10. Rock City

Map Not To Scale

Museums

Site 1.
Fick Fossil and History Museum
700 West Third Street
Oakley, KS 67748
(785) 672-4839
http://www.discoveroakley.com/Document.aspx?id=1353/
• This museum's exhibits include rocks, fossils and minerals. Admission is free, but donations are greatly appreciated.

Site 2.
Johnston Geology Museum
a.k.a Emporia State University Geology Museum
ESU Cram Science Hall
14th and Merchant Streets
Emporia, KS 66801
(620) 341-5330
http://www.emporia.edu/earthsci/museum/museum.htm
• This university museum has fossils on display including Cretaceous fish and plant fossils, invertebrate fossils, a Pteranodon wing, a giant ground sloth, a mastodon tusk and mosasaur fossil. The geology displays include items from the Hamilton Quarry and petrified tree stumps, among others. Most of the geological specimens are from Kansas. Admission is free.

Site 3.
Butler County History Center & Kansas Oil Museum
383 East Central Avenue
El Dorado, KS 67042
(316) 321-9333
http://www.kansasoilmuseum.org/index.cfm
• This museum is dedicated to the discovery and development of the oil industry in Kansas.

Site 4.
Ottawa County Historical Museum
110 South Concord Street
Minneapolis, KS 67467
(785) 392-3533
http://www.ottawacounty.org/index.asp?DocumentID=293
• Exhibits include the most famous dinosaur of Kansas, the Silvisaurus Condrayi, rocks and other fossils.

Site 5.
Post Rock Museum
Rush County Historical Society
202 West First
LaCrosse, KS 67548
(785) 222-2719
http://www.rushcounty.org/postrockmuseum/
• The plains of central Kansas had few trees. Early settlers used the available resources and made fence posts from the local limestone. In the 1880s farmers and ranchers could purchase a six-foot tall post weighing three hundred pounds and have them delivered to their fence line for $.25 each. The Post Rock Museum, built from—you guessed it—post rock, examines the geology of post rock limestone, the quarrying process and the uses of this versatile stone.

Site 6.
Sternberg Museum of Natural History
3000 Sternberg Drive
Hays, KS 67601
(877) 332-1165
http://www.fhsu.edu/sternberg/
• This museum is named for paleontologist George F. Sternberg. The museum has many fossils from around the world. The museum includes a four-story exhibit of animated, life-sized dinosaurs in their recreated environment.

Site 7.
University of Kansas Natural History Museum & Biodiversity Research Center
Dyche Hall
1345 Jayhawk Boulevard
Lawrence, KS 66045
(785) 864-4540
http://nhm.ku.edu/
• Exhibits include fossilized dinosaurs, fish, birds, mammals, reptiles and invertebrates of Kansas and the Great Plains.

POINTS OF INTEREST

Site 8.
Mushroom State Park
Kanopolis State Park
200 Horsethief Road
Marquette, KS 67464
(785) 546-2565
http://www.kdwp.state.ks.us/news/state_parks/locations/mushroom_rock
• This park, a satellite of Kanopolis State Park, is the smallest state park in Kansas. Nonetheless it's worth a look because of the unusual rock formations, which resemble giant mushrooms rising from the plains. Their prominence made them natural meeting places for Native Americans and trappers such as Kit Carson. Available for day use only.

Site 9.
Monument Rocks National Natural Landmark
Southwest Gove County
West of Castle Rock area in Gove County, Kansas
http://www.washburn.edu/cas/art/cyoho/archive/KStravel/bigrocks/pyramids.html
• This rock formation, also known as the chalk pyramids is located on private land. The owner allows visitors to walk around the formations, but there are no facilities on premises. The area is remote, located twenty miles south of Oakley, Kansas. There are two formations towering seventy feet above the plains.

Site 10.
Rock City
1051 Ivy Road
Minneapolis, KS 67467
(785) 392-2577
http://www.washburn.edu/cas/art/cyoho/archive/KStravel/rockcity/
• Over two hundred giant rocks cover the landscape here. Formed millions of years ago, these concretions of Dakota Sandstone were deposited when Kansas was beneath an inland sea.

MONTANA

A cigar box full of blue pebbles.

Montana has always been a place of wild beauty. The first Europeans saw this territory when the Lewis & Clark Expedition crossed Montana. Later came the trappers and then the pioneers. In 1862, gold was found on Grasshopper Creek near Bannack and another gold rush commenced. The area was divided into two hundred-foot claims. Businessmen from Hell Gate and Frenchtown mainly took these claims as they arrived first to the site. Drifting prospectors arrived after the best claims were taken, as was usually the case. The placer played out by 1874, but the hard rock mining continued until 1885. In the early days, the mining locations were so isolated and supply lines so poor, that real problems arose in supplying adequate food and shelter to the hordes of arriving men. "Packers" as the men carrying supplies were called made a fortune selling merchandise at inflated prices. Towns and cities began to appear, and shops and businesses flourished as money from the mines poured in. As with any mining area, the real money was made by saloons, mercantile stores and by anyone who offered supplies or creature comforts to hungry, dirty and temporarily rich men.

While the miners struggled for gold, the federal government struggled against the Sioux Nations and in 1876, Custer fell at the Little Bighorn in Montana. The following year the Sioux tribes lay in tatters, while Chief Joseph and the Nez Percé Indians retreated across Montana toward Canada.

As gold vanished, significant copper deposits were discovered and mining began near Butte. This became this world's greatest copper mine producing thirteen and one-fourth billion pounds of copper to date.

In 1888, the mining of silver, lead and zinc commenced on Flat Creek, north of Superior and the next year Montana joined the Union as the forty-first state. The most unusual mining discovery came seven years later in an unlikely sounding spot—Pig-eye Basin.

A gold prospector named Jake Hoover made a trip to a likely gold-bearing area. Instead of flakes of heavy gold, he noticed something unusual lining his pan. Heavy blue pebbles lay among the black sands. He collected a number of these oddities in a cigar box and sent them to Tiffany & Co. They turned out to be corundum with aluminum oxide and traces of iron and titanium. In other words, they were cornflower blue sapphires. A gem expert, Dr. George Kunz, declared them the finest gem quality sapphires ever found in the United States.

The Sapphires of Yogo Gulch are legendary for their superior clarity and brilliance. Four main deposits have been identified in Montana. Yogo Gulch is famous for blue and purple sapphires; Dry Cottonwood Creek produces yellow, gold, green, pink and blue sapphires; the Missouri River contributes green, blue, yellow, orange and pink sapphires; and Rock Creek has a full range of colorful sapphires, including some bicolor stones. The last three sites have on a few occasions produced the rarest of all corundum, a red ruby.

There are sites open to the public for sapphire mining at the L Diamond E Ranch and Spokane Bar Sapphire Mine. The list of amazing finds does not end here. Montana has opportunities for rockhounds to find opals, garnets, petrified wood, quartz crystals, gold, agates and, of course, dinosaur fossils.

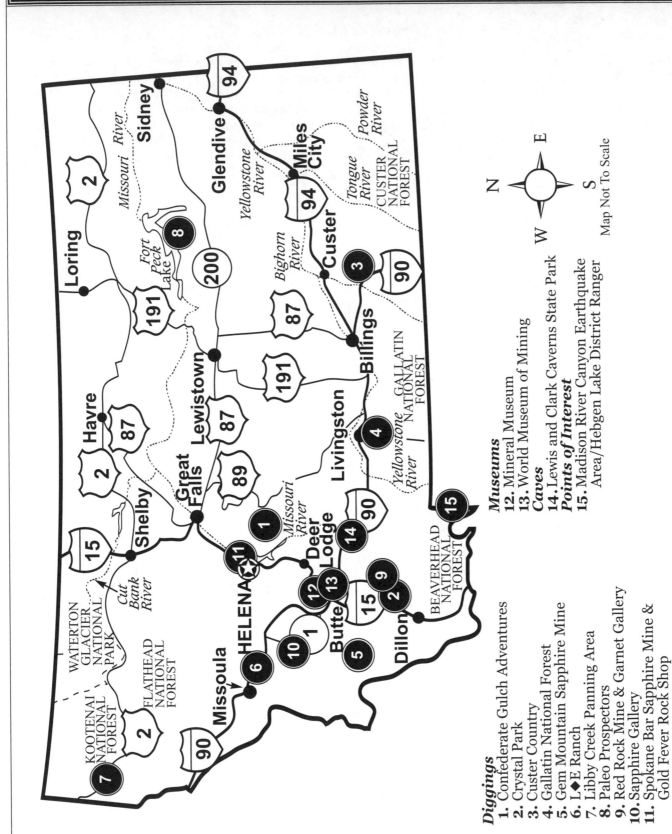

Diggings
1. Confederate Gulch Adventures
2. Crystal Park
3. Custer Country
4. Gallatin National Forest
5. Gem Mountain Sapphire Mine
6. ◆L E Ranch
7. Libby Creek Panning Area
8. Paleo Prospectors
9. Red Rock Mine & Garnet Gallery
10. Sapphire Gallery
11. Spokane Bar Sapphire Mine &
   Gold Fever Rock Shop

Museums
12. Mineral Museum
13. World Museum of Mining
Caves
14. Lewis and Clark Caverns State Park
Points of Interest
15. Madison River Canyon Earthquake
   Area/Hebgen Lake District Ranger

ADDRESS:
Confederate Gulch Adventures
P.O. Box 592
Townsend, MT 59644
(406) 459-3404
contactus@confederategulchadventures.com
http://www.confederategulchadventures.com

DIRECTIONS:
From Townsend, go east on Highway 12 approximately twelve miles. Turn north onto Highway 284 and drive fifteen miles. Turn east up Confederate Gulch Road. The mine is approximately eight miles up the road.

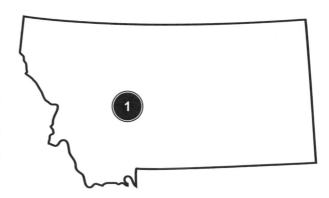

SEASON:
May 15 through November 30

HOURS:
7:00 a.m. to 5:00 p.m.

COST:
$15 per day–Fee for panning
$90 per week–Fee for panning
$20 per day–Fee for panning and sluicing
$120 per week–Fee for panning and sluicing
BY APPOINTMENT ONLY:
$25 per day–Fee for high banking ($15 for each additional person)
$150 per week–Fee for high banking($60 for each additional person)

WHAT TO BRING:
Some supplies are available such as pans, shovels, buckets, classifying screens and some hand sluices. Appointments must be made in advance to arrange for high-banking equipment, and is allowed in designated areas only.

INFORMATION:
   Confederate Gulch Adventures is located in the western mountains in a rich placer gold area. Guests can pan, sluice and high-bank at this site. Lessons in panning and sluicing <u>may</u> be available with advance notice.
   On-site camping is available for $10 per night by reservation only. There are no hook-ups, water or electricity.
   Visitors may also wish to inquire about the trommel runs, a communal operation where each participant receives a portion of the yield of gold.
   Other activities include hiking, fishing, boating and picnicking. The nearby towns of Townsend and Helena offer museums, shopping and more.

ADDRESS:
Dillon Ranger District Office
Beaverhead National Forest
Dillon, MT 59725
(406) 683-3900
http://goldwest.visitmt.com/listings/11967.htm

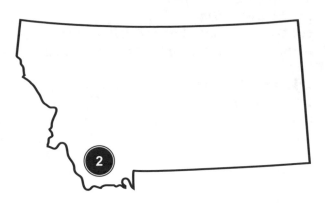

DIRECTIONS:
From Butte, take Interstate Highway 90 west to Interstate Highway 15 south. Drive fifteen miles south to the town of Divide. Turn west onto State Highway 43 toward Wise River and travel twelve miles. Past the town of Wise River, turn south on a two-lane, paved road called the Wise River-Polaris National Scenic Byway. Go south twenty-seven miles into the Pioneer Mountains. The park is on the south side of the road.

SEASON:
May 15 through October 15

HOURS:
Sunrise to sunset

COST:
Free–Donations accepted

WHAT TO BRING:
Standard mining tools, plus a 1/4-inch mesh screen, and a container to hold your crystals.

INFORMATION:
Dig your own quartz crystals and amethyst on this forty-acre site within the national forest. Use hand tools and a 1/4-inch screen to sift the sandy soil and search for treasure. There is a short walk from the parking area to the mine site, so bring a pack to carry your tools. A volunteer host is available to answer questions during the summer.

The quartz crystals have six sides and resemble prisms. They are clear and cloudy, white, gray or purple. Crystals range from thumb size to several inches in length. Only hand tools are permitted for digging. No claims may be staked. No tunneling or working on vertical walls higher than four feet is allowed. The camp is closed overnight. Be prepared for cool weather, because it rains and snows at these higher elevations even in the summer.

ADDRESS:
Custer Country
P.O. Box 904
Forsyth, MT 59327
(800) 346-1876

DIRECTIONS:
Montana agates can be found along the Yellowstone River parallel to Interstate Highway 94 and State Highway 16 from Custer to Sidney.

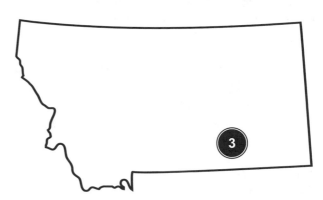

SEASON:
Spring and Summer

HOURS:
Daylight

COST:
Free

WHAT TO BRING:
You will need a small shovel, other hand-held tools and a bucket to carry your finds. Bring your own food and drink. We also recommend you bring a change of clothes.

INFORMATION:
Montana agate is one of the official gemstones of the state. You may also find petrified wood, colored jaspers and fossils. The Montana agates are called plume or moss agates for the interesting formations within the stone which resemble plumes and moss growth. Good quality specimens are beautiful and valuable.

Agates are found in the terrace gravel high above the river. These deposits are difficult to access, as they are mainly on private land. Additional specimens are located along the river in gravel deposits. These stones are much more approachable. Agates found in the area are translucent, meaning that some light does pass through them. They often appear cloudy when found in nature. Colors vary and can be white, tan or bluish.

Acquire permission from the owner if you want to collect on private land. Contact local rock shops for guide service or trips for searching out these gems.

ADDRESS:
P.O. Box 130
Bozeman, MT 59771
(406) 848-7375 or (406) 587-6701
http://www.fs.fed.us/r1/gallatin/?page=passespermits#petrifiedwood

DIRECTIONS:
From Emigrant, take U.S. Highway 89 south for fifteen miles. Then take Tom Miner Basin Road west for seven miles. Go to the campground near the head of a beautiful mountain valley in Gallatin National Forest.

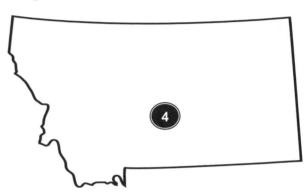

SEASON:
Spring and Fall

HOURS:
Daylight

COST:
Free with permit

WHAT TO BRING:
No equipment is needed or permitted.

INFORMATION:
    The petrified forest is between thirty-five and fifty-five-million-years-old. This forest is worth a visit because of it's natural beauty. Collecting opportunities are extremely limited. The forest service maintain that you must stop at the one of these three district offices, Bozeman, Livingston and Gardner, first to obtain a permit to enter. There is no fee for entering the forest. You are allowed to collect only one sample with a maximum size of twenty cubic inches. The piece must be loose on the ground. Digging is not permitted.

    This forest was established to preserve the fossils and petrified wood. Trails have been constructed for visitors to see first hand petrified specimens. The trail is one-half mile long. Hiking is permitted throughout the forest.

ADDRESS:
Gem Mountain Sapphire Mine
3835 Skalkaho Road
P.O. Box 148
Philipsburg, MT 59858
(406) 859-4367 or (866) 459-4367
info@gemmtn.com
http://www.gemmtn.com

DIRECTIONS:
The mine is located between Butte and Anaconda on Route 38, the Skalkaho Road. Six miles south of Philipsburg, turn from Highway 1 and drive sixteen miles west. Look for the signs, then cross a small bridge over the West Fork of Rock Creek to the mine's parking lot. Their website is linked to MapQuest to help you get exact directions.

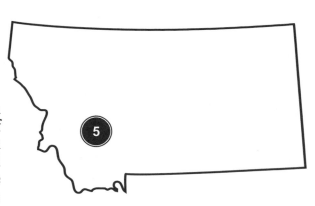

SEASON:
May 19 to October 9, seven days a week

HOURS:
9:00 a.m. to 5:00 p.m.

COST:
$12—Fee for a single bucket of material
$72—Fee for the "Lucky Seven" (buy six buckets and get one bucket free)
$120—Fee for the "Dirty Dozen Deal" (buy ten buckets and get two free)

WHAT TO BRING:
All supplies and equipment are provided, just bring your personal gear.

INFORMATION:
 Gem Mountain is situated between Yellowstone National Park and Glacier National Park in southwest Montana. The mine offers three digging options. Guests can purchase single buckets of gravel or try the 'lucky seven' bucket deal, or the 'dirty dozen deal'.
 Guests will use the washing stations to clean the gravel in their search for sapphires.
 In addition to gravel washing, this site also has a gift shop and jewelry store. Can't make the trip? This mine ships sapphires all over the world.

ADDRESS:
24210 Bonita R/S Road
Clinton, MT 59825
(406) 825-6295 or (888) 725-8747
info@ldiamonde.com
http://www.ldiamonde.com/

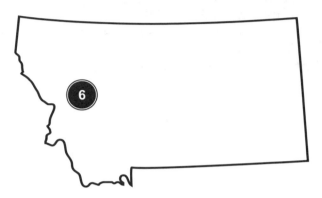

DIRECTIONS:
The L◆E (L Diamond E) Ranch is located east of Missoula, just off Interstate Highway 90, at Exit 126. Take Rock Creek Road northeast to the ranch.

SEASON:
Summer pack trips leave late June through mid-September

HOURS:
Call for information

COST:
$250 per person–Fee for summer pack trips (four-day minimum)

WHAT TO BRING:
All supplies for sapphire mining will be provided by the L◆E Ranch. For more information on what to pack and information on the trips available please call the L◆E Ranch.

INFORMATION:
    The L◆E Ranch offers pack trips to suit many needs. Among the fishing, hunting, photography and horseback riding pack trips are the sapphire mining pack trips.
    You may work the claim for sapphires, hike, or ride the trails. The mining consists of digging and sifting through the dirt, then sorting the concentrate. The trip to the mine is breathtakingly beautiful.
    The trip consists of a thirty-two-mile ride from the ranch to the trailhead, then an eleven-mile ride on horseback to the sapphire camp. At camp you are housed in a nine foot by nine foot, summer tent with foam mattresses. An outdoor shower facility and home-cooked meals are provided. The outdoor camp is set up for the entire summer and is quite comfortable.

ADDRESS:
Kootenai National Forest
1101 US Highway 2 West
Libby, MT 59923
(406) 293-6211
http://www.fs.fed.us/r1/kootenai/recreation/activitiesx/panning.shtml

DIRECTIONS:
Libby is sixty-four miles northwest of Kalispell. From Libby, take U.S. Highway 2 south to Libby Creek. At Libby Creek, turn right onto Bear Creek Road/Forest Service Road 231. Travel ten miles on the paved forest road and eight additional miles on the same road as it turns to gravel.

SEASON:
May 15 through October 15

HOURS:
Daylight

COST:
Free

WHAT TO BRING:
You need to bring gold mining equipment. No dredges, highbankers or other motorized equipment is permitted.

INFORMATION:
    At Libby Creek Panning Area you can try your luck gold panning on a stream in a national forest. The creek is thirty feet from the road. You can pan all you want, but no motorized equipment, sluices or rocker boxes are allowed. This location is for those who have some experience in panning. You will not find instructors or staff to assist you, just you and the stream.
    You may camp for free in the national forest for up to fourteen days. A fee campground with toilets is available one mile south at Howard Lake.
    Historic items from earlier mining days are still in evidence up the hillside. Additionally, several historic cabins that were built in 1932 still remain standing and can be viewed nearby a bridge that crosses Libby Creek. Please view, but do not disturb, these structures.

ADDRESS:
Paleo Prospectors
Steve Niclas, Ph.D
6625 Highway 53 East, Suite 410-98
Dawsonville, GA 30534
(678) 316-4983
http://www.paleoprospectors.org
steve12@alltel.net

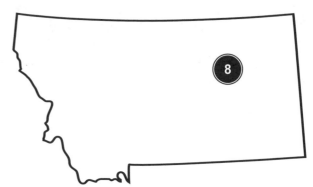

DIRECTIONS:
To be provided when booking your excursion.

SEASON:
June, July and August

HOURS:
This is a week-long trip. Your day begins with a wake-up call at 6:30 a.m., followed by breakfast. You will leave for the field at 8:15 a.m. Lunch is provided in the field and the group returns to the hotel each night before dinner.

COST:
$2,320—Fee which includes: insurance, meals, room for seven nights, landowner fees, guide fees, transportation to and from the field, hand tools, instructions and fossil collecting

WHAT TO BRING:
Rain coat, wind breaker, camera, file, canteen, hat, sun block, gloves, good boots, shorts, long pants, knee pads, light coat and a large backpack.

INFORMATION:
These excursions take place in the Hell Creek Formation of South Dakota, North Dakota and Montana, spanning one hundred thirty thousand acres and eight ranches. The collecting formations are between sixty-five and sixty-eight million years old. Vertebrate fossils recovered on past excursions include: Triceratops, crocodile, edmontosaurus, turtles, T. Rex and small theropods. Some trips are planned for areas in Nebraska for mammals including: saber toothed cats, small mammals and birds. You are able to keep almost everything you find up to $3,000. The only items excluded are individual bones valued at over $1,000 or articulated bones. If you unearth one of these rare finds, you will be paid a three percent finders fee.
Excursions are one week in length, and are limited to fifteen participants.

ADDRESS:
2040 Highway 287
Alder, MT 59710
(406) 842-5760

DIRECTIONS:
The Red Rock Mine is located one and one-half miles east of Alder on State Highway 287, between Alder and Virginia City.

SEASON:
May 1 through October 31

HOURS:
9:00 a.m. to 5:00 p.m. Monday-Saturday
12:00 p.m. to 5:00 p.m. Sunday

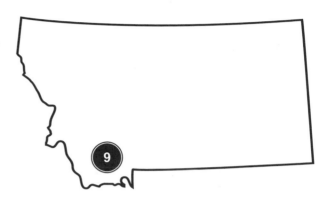

COST:
$15 per day–Fee for digging
$10 per bucket–Fee for collecting

WHAT TO BRING:
You will need a spray bottle with water, a film container to hold your stones and long tweezers to pluck up your stones. Bring work gloves, a shovel and a pick, if you plan to dig your own dirt. The mine will rent some equipment.

INFORMATION:
The proprietors at the Red Rock Mine are clearing an area of concentrated, pond bank gravel. This gravel was a waste product of gold dredges used during the gold rush days. Miners at the Red Rock Mine are finding red and pink rhodolite and gray and purple corundum (sapphires). Gem-quality garnets in colors ranging from light pink to deep blood red are also found here.

The mine also sells Montana gold and sapphire gravel from other mines along with gems, jewelry, rocks and minerals. Gravel can also be mail ordered in bags ranging in price from $20 to $80.

You and your family can camp at the KOA Campground, which is only one mile west of the Red Rock Mine.

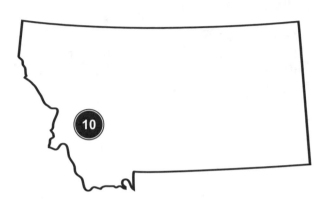

ADDRESS:
Sapphire Gallery
P.O. Box 2002
115 East Broadway
Philipsburg, MT 59858
(800) 525-0169 or (406) 859-3236
sapphire@sapphire-gallery.com
http://www.sapphire-gallery.com/

DIRECTIONS:
From the east take Interstate Highway 90 to Exit 153 to Route 1 to Philipsburg. From the west take Interstate Highway 90 to Exit 208 take Route 1 to Philipsburg.

SEASON:
Open year-round–Sunday through Friday, closed Saturday

HOURS:
10:00 a.m. to 5:00 p.m.–September through May
10:00 a.m. to 6:00 p.m.–June through August

COST:
$25–Fee per bag of stones

WHAT TO BRING:
No equipment or special clothing are necessary.

INFORMATION:
   The storefront dates back to the 1890s when the establishment was a harness and grocery shop. The Sapphire Gallery specializes in quality gold sapphire and ruby jewelry. What is truly unique about this shop, other than the jewelry design, is the fact that you can dig your own sapphire from dirt provided by the Sapphire Gallery. Once revealed, your stone can be heat-treated to enhance color, faceted and set into a one-of-a-kind piece of jewelry.

ADDRESS:
Spokane Bar Sapphire Mine & Gold Fever Rock Shop
5360 Castles Road
Helena, MT 59602
(406) 227-8989 or (877) DIG-GEMS
sales@sapphiremine.com
http://www.sapphiremine.com

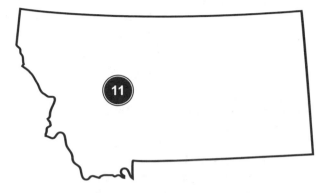

DIRECTIONS:
From Helena, take York Road east eight miles to
Hart Drive. Bear right at Milepost 8 onto Hart
Drive to the Spokane Bar Sapphire Mine. Follow
the signs. If you pass Deal Lane you have passed
Hart Drive.

SEASON:
Open year-round

HOURS:
9:00 a.m. to 5:00 p.m.–Seven days a week
Winter hours vary–Call for appointment

COST:
Call (877) DIG-GEMS for fees or visit their website

WHAT TO BRING:
Equipment is available. If you are digging your own dirt bring a shovel, 1/4-inch screen (available
there), whisk broom, pry bar, screwdriver and gloves. To sort your sapphires you need a pair of
tweezers, a spray bottle and a container with a lid.

INFORMATION:
The Spokane Bar Sapphire Mine has beautifully colored stones varying from white to green
to light blue. Sapphires of a half-carat up to ten carats are fairly common. The largest sapphire
found here was one hundred fifty-five carats. Minerals frequently collected here include moss
agate, petrified wood, fossils, mammoth teeth, jasper, hematite and lizard rock. Also found, but
extremely rare, are diamonds, topaz, citrine and rubies.

You may dig your own dirt here in an open pit, or buy it by the bucket. The staff will help
you learn how to screen, sift and concentrate your dirt and find the sapphires. There is a rock
shop at the mine. Gold prospectors dig here for flake and nugget gold. This entire area was once
a gold prospecting area. The sapphires were passed over in the search for gold.

MUSEUMS

Site 12.
The Mineral Museum
Montana Tech University
Butte MT 59701
(406) 496-4414
http://www.mbmg.mtech.edu/museum.htm
• Over one thousand three hundred mineral specimens from around the world are displayed here with a large exhibit of Montana's rich mineral resources. Displays include the Highland Centennial Gold Nugget, weighing 27.475 troy ounces, recovered in September 1989 from a placer mine south of Butte and a 400 pound smoky quartz crystal, called "Big Daddy." Don't miss the blue sapphires from Yogo Gulch and Montana's other state stone, the agate.

Site 13.
World Museum of Mining
155 Museum Way
Butte, MT 59701
(406) 723-7211
http://www.miningmuseum.org/
• The World Museum Of Mining, a national historical site, has recreated an 1890s mining camp called "Hell Roarin' Gulch" at the base of the towering Orphan Girl Mine. Hell Roarin' Gulch includes a bank, funeral parlor, jail, post office, city hall, union hall, school, church and Chinese laundry to name a few. Many of the tools and equipment used in underground mining are displayed, including a sixty-five-ton experimental electric truck, a one hundred-year-old Chilean mill, and an armored pay car. The Orphan Girl Express, a three-car train pulled by a 1911 underground trammer engine, takes patrons around the perimeter of the museum grounds.

CAVES

Site 14.
Lewis and Clark Caverns State Park
P.O. Box 489
Whitehall, MT 59759
(406) 287-3541
http://fwp.mt.gov/lands/site_281895.aspx
• Explorers, trappers, miners and immigrants all passed beneath this cave unaware. The cave might be better named for the hunter who noticed the cavern opening in the winter of 1892, or for the Native Americans who left arrowheads inside the cavern's entrance. Today visitors still marvel at the impressive limestone formations hidden in this cavern.

POINTS OF INTEREST

Site 13.
Madison River Canyon Earthquake Area/Hebgen Lake District Ranger
P.O. Box 520
West Yellowstone, MT 59758
(406) 823-6961
http://montanagroups.com/p22.htm
• On Monday, August 17, 1959, a severe earthquake measuring 7.5 on the Richter scale rocked the area around Yellowstone. The quake caused tidal waves to crash the Hebgen dam as a seven thousand foot high mountain collapsed. The mountain blocked the canyon and the water surged back up the canyon. In eight seconds eighty million tons of rock fell to the valley below. The final death toll for the earthquake was miraculously only twenty-eight. This area is now preserved for visitors.

NEBRASKA

The discovery of so many intact fossils posed a mystery.

In the age of dinosaurs, Nebraska was covered by a shallow inland sea. Gigantic prehistoric fish and sharks swam through warm waters. Over time the ocean receded leaving in its place tropical lowlands filled with dinosaurs. The time of the dinosaurs' extinction coincided with the Rocky Mountains emergence. Nebraska rose with the mountains and sediment from the inland sea dried on the surface. River sediment collected above the ocean sediment. These layers, pressed by time became the familiar whitish limestone capped with darker sandstone. Toadstool State Park shows these layers with fascinating results. The softer limestone erodes at a faster rate than the top layer of sandstone, leaving rocks shaped like giant toadstools. Scotts Bluff National Monument, Indian Cave State Park and Chimney Rock National Historical Site all show Nebraska's limestone eroding with astonishing beauty.

During this period, the climate changed, temperatures dropped, and rainfall diminished. The tropical lowlands gave way to arid plains. On Nebraska's plains, herds of three-toed horses, camels, woolly mammoths and rhinoceroses mingled with giant tortoises as they tried to avoid predators like the saber-tooth cat and beardog. And both the saber-tooth cat and the herd animals avoided the "terrible pig," which rose over seven feet tall at the shoulder. Drought caused many animals to die and leave their remains in what is now Nebraska. Many of these fossils have been unearthed at Agate Fossil Bed National Monument.

These species all disappeared, replaced by buffalo, antelope and man. The great eroding limestone became meeting places, resting places and places of wonder. The Native Americans had names for these formations, and so did the white settlers who rolled across the prairie in covered wagons, following the Oregon Trail and leaving ruts in the earth that can still be seen at Ash Hollow State Park. Pioneers looked for Chimney Rock and recorded its sighting in their journals. Eventually settlers did not just past through on the way west. They came to stay, producing vast quantities of grain, corn sorghum, corn and wheat. Cattle and hog replaced buffalo, as the Great Plains became America's breadbasket. The gravel and sand left by the inland sea and river sediment were mined and used in concrete production, landscaping, glass manufacturing and sand casting in foundry operations.

In 1971, after a heavy rain, a complete rhino skull was found in a cornfield in Antelope County. Fossils like these had been found before in the 1920s and 1950s. But this specimen was exceptionally well-preserved and intact. Digging revealed more fossils, hundreds more. Rhinos, three-toed horses and camels were unearthed. Beneath them lay the skeletons of birds, musk deer and turtles, all dated ten million years ago. Infant animals were found beside their pregnant mothers and strangely most of the fossils were intact. This is highly unusual. Most animals die or are killed and scavengers scatter the bones. This did not happen here. The question arose—what kind of disaster could kill all these healthy animals? Some kind of cataclysmic event first killed the smaller animals, and then the larger ones. The answer is in the volcanic ash surrounding the find. It seemed somewhere to the west an enormous volcano or series of volcanoes erupted sending huge quantities of glassy ash into the air. Over a foot of sediment fell on Nebraska and it drifted up to eight feet in places. These animals inhaled the glassy dust and died as their lungs were choked of oxygen. The smaller animals died first, while the larger ones struggled on. Last to die were the rhinos who fell on top of the rest and were buried in ash. The digging continues today at Ashfall Fossil Beds State Historical Park with hopes of finding a rare large predator like a saber-tooth cat.

NEBRASKA SITE MAP

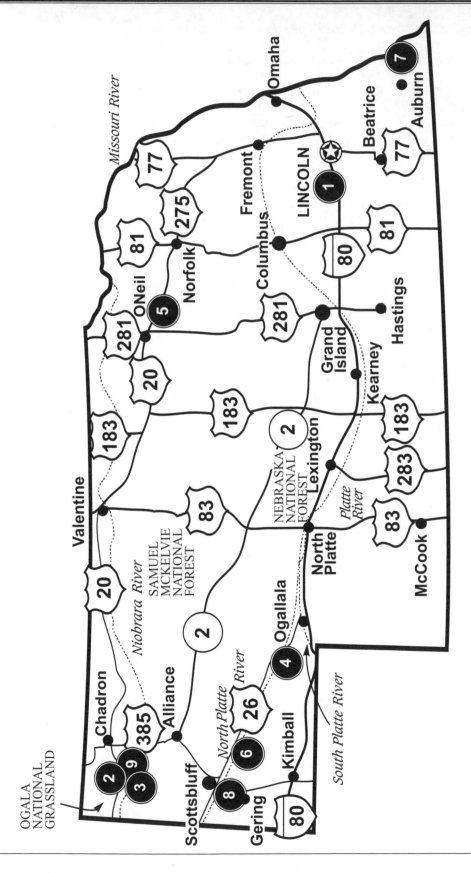

N E
W S

Map Not To Scale

Museums
1. University of Nebraska State Museum
2. Trailside Museum of Natural History at
   Fort Robinson State Park
Points of Interest
3. Agate Fossil Beds National Monument
4. Ash Hollow State Historical Park
5. Ashfall Fossil Beds State Historical Park
6. Chimney Rock National Historic Site
7. Indian Cave State Park
8. Scotts Bluff National Monument
9. Toadstool Geologic Park

112

MUSEUMS

Site 1.
University of Nebraska State Museum
307 Morrill Hall
University of Nebraska-Lincoln
Lincoln, NE 68588
(402) 472-2642
http://www-museum.unl.edu/
• Dinosaur fossils exhibited include: allosaurus, coelophysis, stegosaurs, triceratops and tyrannosaurus. The museum closely follows and highlights significant fossil discoveries in Nebraska.

Site 2.
Trailside Museum of Natural History at Fort Robinson State Park
University of Nebraska State
Fort Robinson State Park
Box 462
Crawford, NE 69339
(308) 665-2929
http://www-museum.unl.edu/trailside/
• This museum highlights the life and death of woolly mammoths in this area. Other fossils include fossils from western Nebraska, the rhino and giant tortoise.

POINTS OF INTEREST

Site 3.
Agate Fossil Beds National Monument
301 River Road
Harrison, NE 69346-2734
(308) 668-2211
http://www.nps.gov/agfo/
• Site of the excavation of many important skeletons including the now extinct two-horned rhinoceroses and "terrible pig," which rose over seven feet tall at the shoulder.

Site 4.
Ash Hollow State Historical Park
P.O. Box 70
Lewellen, NE 69147
(308) 778-5651
http://www.ngpc.state.ne.us/parks/guides/parksearch/showpark.asp?Area_No=8
• This park has been a resting place for man for over six thousand years as evidenced by artifacts found in a small rock shelter near the visitor center. Modern visitors can learn about the large mammals (rhinoceros, mammoth and mastodon) that roamed the plains before the last Ice Age. Pioneers left their mark as well. The ruts from westward wagons remains deeply etched in the ground here.

Site 5.
Ashfall Fossil Beds State Historical Park
86930 517th Avenue
Royal, NE 68773
(402) 893-2000
http://www.ngpc.state.ne.us/parks/guides/parksearch/showpark.asp?Area_No=279

• Visitors will witness the fossil evidence of a great disaster ten million years old. Rhinos, two-toed horses, camels and giant tortoises were among the many animals devastated by the falling ash cloud from great volcanoes. Learn about this fascinating location at the visitor center, which includes interpretive displays and a working fossil laboratory. Nearby at the Rhino Barn, guests see the fossil skeletons as they were discovered and where they continue to be unearthed.

Site 6.
Chimney Rock National Historic Site
P.O. Box F
Bayard, NE 69334-0680
(308) 586-2581
http://www.nebraskahistory.org/sites/rock/
• Chimney Rock became a historic site because of its significance as a landmark on the Oregon and California Trails. An estimated half-million emigrants passed Chimney Rock.

Site 7.
Indian Cave State Park
65296 720 Road
Shubert, NE 68437-9801
(402) 883-2575
http://www.ngpc.state.ne.us/parks/guides/parksearch/showpark.asp?Area_No=91
• This park contains a huge sandstone cavity. The petroglyphs etched on the walls of the cave are the only known examples found in Nebraska. Who made them and when they were made remains a mystery. The pictures form shapes and scenes of wildlife. In 1830 a tract of land was set aside here for homeless children of traders and trappers who married Indian women and then moved on. The park is a popular spot for campers, hikers, anglers, horseback riders and picnickers. Restrooms are available.

Site 8.
Scotts Bluff National Monument
P.O. Box 27
Gering, NE 69341-0027
(308) 436-4340
http://www.nps.gov/scbl/index.htm
• Scotts Bluff was named for a fur trapper, Hiram Scott, who was allegedly wounded and deserted by his companions but somehow managed to reach this rock formation before expiring. The Native American name is the more practical "Me-a-pa-te" which means Hill that is hard to go around. This landmark on the Oregon, Mormon and California Trails is home to a museum recording the bluff's geologic and human history.

Site 9.
Toadstool Geologic Park
Nebraska National Forest- Pine Ridge Ranger District
1240 West 16th Street
Pine Ridge Ranger District
Chadron, NE 69337
(308) 432-4475
http://www.fs.fed.us/r2/nebraska/units/prrd/toadstooltemp.html
• Toadstool Park presents an odd landscape that makes a visitor feel like Alice beneath a gigantic toadstool. Wind erosion created these top-heavy formations of clay and sandstone, some of which are twenty feet high and fifteen feet across at the tops. Picnic tables, water pumps and fire grates are available. The Admission fee is $3 and the camping fee is $5.

"Some people are malicious enough to think that if the devil were set at liberty and told to confine himself to Nevada Territory, he would get homesick and go back to hell again."
– Mark Twain –

As with many places in the west, the first miners here were Native Americans and their ancestors who dug obsidian, opalite, chalcedony, quartz and jasper to make hunting and scraping tools beginning around 300 AD. Modern prospectors were likely led to these ancient places in the 1880s. Early prospectors reported finding wedges, chisels and hammers of stone along with lapidary stones for polishing turquoise in what is now Nevada.

In 1856, prospectors returning to Utah from the California gold fields discovered lead deposits, which provided bullets for areas as far away as Salt Lake City. But it was in 1858 that discoveries in Nevada were to make history with the discovery of the Comstock Lode.

Gold was still the precious metal of choice. Miners found gold in Six-Mile Canyon in the 1850s. Prospectors were discouraged and hampered by a thick, viscous bluish mud. It clung to picks and shovels and made gold extraction nearly impossible. Someone finally recognized the blue-gray mud. assayer's confirmed the sample was high quality silver ore. This discovery was so huge it drew the attention of President Abraham Lincoln, who needed these resources along with the gold and silver from Colorado and California to help win the Civil War. Virginia City, named after a miner called "Old Virginny" rose practically overnight. Denver and San Francisco also profited from the boom and fortunes were made by the likes of George Hearst, Leland Stanford and John Mackay.

Prospectors flooded the area and became miners in the biggest silver strike in United States history. Among them was a slender man from Connecticut who quickly gave up his pick for a pen. Mark Twain became a writer for Nevada's first newspaper, the *Territorial Enterprise*. He wrote that he could feel the explosions in the mines from his seat in his office.

The mines went deeper and became hotter and more dangerous. Mines ran twenty-four hours a day and shafts reached depths of two thousand feet. The heat rose with each foot. Steam obscured a man's vision and wooden pick handles were too hot to hold without gloves. Many were killed, maimed or seriously injured. Those who survived suffered from pneumonia, miner's lung (emphysema) and rheumatism. Forests were stripped to supply timber for the mines. Silver did not come cheap.

Virginia City produced so much silver it set in motion the wheel for the bust to come. The abundance of silver caused prices to drop. Silver was no longer king. Rumors of discoveries bigger than the Comstock came from South Dakota and Montana. Miners moved quickly on the new rail system to the next boomtown.

Today Nevada mines for copper, silver, lead, tungsten, iron ore and zinc. But Nevada's mineral industry still centers on silver and gold, currently supplying ten percent of the world's gold.

Today rockhounds have a chance to search for opals at Rainbow Ridge and the Royal Peacock Opal Mine. Even Mark Twain would agree that Nevada has grown much more hospitable.

NEVADA SITE MAP

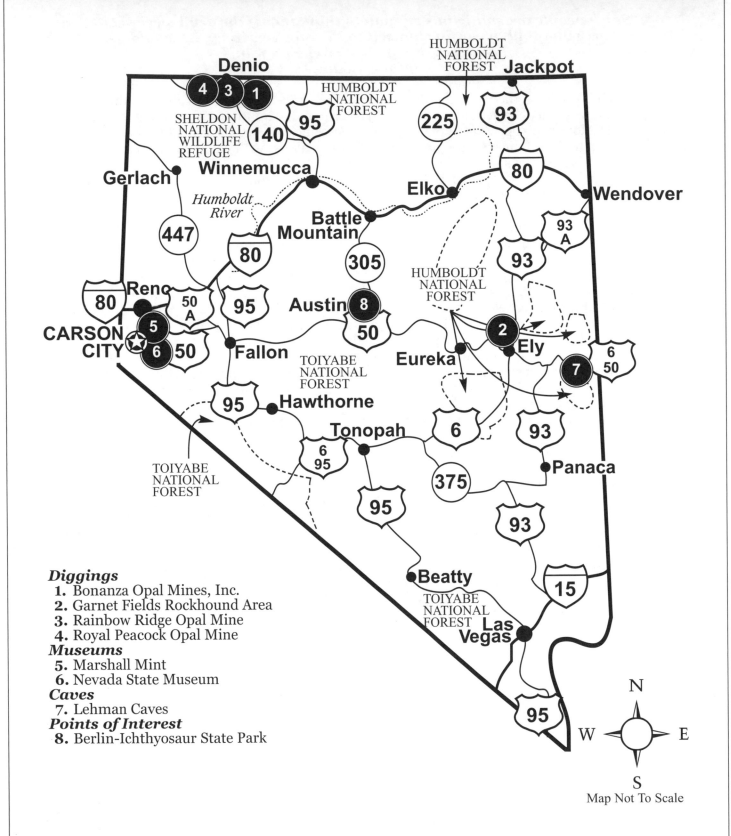

Diggings
1. Bonanza Opal Mines, Inc.
2. Garnet Fields Rockhound Area
3. Rainbow Ridge Opal Mine
4. Royal Peacock Opal Mine

Museums
5. Marshall Mint
6. Nevada State Museum

Caves
7. Lehman Caves

Points of Interest
8. Berlin-Ichthyosaur State Park

Map Not To Scale

ADDRESS:
Bonanza Opal Mines, Inc.
P.O. Box 121
Denio, NV 89404
(775) 941-0121
Nadine1700@aol.com
http://www.bonanzaopals.com

DIRECTIONS: From Lakeview, Oregon, head east on Highway 140 for eighty-five miles. After the rest area on the right, drive one-half mile and turn onto the dirt road on the right. From the campground to the Bonanza turnoff is four and one-half miles. Follow the signs.

SEASON:
Memorial Day Weekend to September 30

HOURS:
8:00 a.m. to 4:00 p.m.

COST:
$45–Fee per day
Free–Children under 12

WHAT TO BRING:
A hat, sunscreen, camera and other personal belongings, water and snacks.

INFORMATION:
　　Bonanza Opal Mine boasts that their opal is unsurpassed in beauty and rarity. The digging site is close to other opal mines listed in this book including: Opal Queen, Rainbow Ridge and Royal Peacock. Digging is limited to tailings. Bank digging is reserved for shareholders.
　　Free camping is available to miners and includes showers and a 'soaking pond'.
　　For those who do not wish to dig, opal can also be purchased by appointment at the mine's millsite in Virgin Valley or by mail.

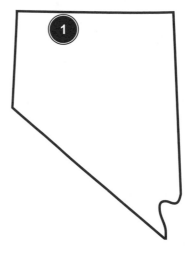

MAILING ADDRESS:
Bureau of Land Management, Ely Field Office
H.C. 33, Box 33500
Ely, NV 89301

STREET ADDRESS:
702 North Industrial Way
Ely, NV 89301
(775) 289-1800
http://www.fs.fed.us/htnf/garnet.htm

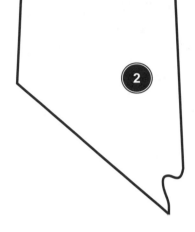

DIRECTIONS:
Garnet Fields Rockhound Area is located on U.S. Highway 50 near Ely. From Ely, at the traffic light at the junction of U.S. Highway 93 and U.S. Highway 50, take U.S. Highway 50 west six and four-tenths miles. The access road to the area is one-fourth of a mile north of the turnoff to Ruth, Nevada. Take the access road three and one-tenth miles to Garnet Hill. The access road is winding and somewhat steep, but is suitable for all types of vehicles. Garnet Hill is a one thousand two hundred eighty-acre site on public land.

SEASON:
Open year-round—Weather permitting

HOURS:
Daylight

COST:
Free

WHAT TO BRING:
You'll need standard mining equipment as well as a knife, screwdriver and pry bar.

INFORMATION:
This area is famous for its dark red garnets found in volcanic rock. These garnets are of the almandine variety and are dark red. Most are flawed, but some gem-quality stones are found. Garnets can be found by searching the surface and drainage areas for dark colored stones that have weathered from their host rock or by breaking open garnet-bearing rock with a pick or hammer to reveal the gems. The garnets usually occur as a single crystal inside air pockets, vugs within the volcanic rock. Look for rock with veins of quartz. Garnets found inside a vug must be carefully extracted with a knife or similar tool. Be careful, as the garnets are hard, but brittle and may shatter.

Limited space for tent camping and small RVs is available. Also visible from this site is the large, open-pit copper mine and multicolored, waste rock dumps at the nearby Robinson Mining District.

ADDRESS:
P.O. Box 97
Denio, NV 89404
(775) 941-0280 November through May
(541) 941-0270 after May 10 through October
glen@nevadaopal.com
http://www.nevadaopal.com

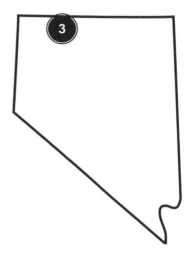

DIRECTIONS:
From Denio Junction, travel west on State Highway 140 for twenty-two and one-half miles to a dirt road on the left (the turnoff is 90 miles from Lakeview, Oregon). Travel on the dirt road two and one-half miles to the CCC Camp. Signs from the CCC Camp will lead you to the final five miles to the mine. The last seven and one-half miles are dirt and gravel roads.

SEASON:
Memorial Day through September 15

HOURS:
8:00 a.m. to 4:00 p.m.–closed Wednesdays

COST:
$50 per day–Fee for adults to dig on tailings piles
Half-price–Fee for children ages 10 to 15

WHAT TO BRING:
Standard mining tools including tweezers and a spray bottle.

INFORMATION:
The opal found here is some of the most beautiful in the world. Most of the common opal found at the Rainbow Ridge Opal Mine is black, white or wood opal. All of the opal found here occurs in wood-opal combinations or wood casts. The mine allows digging on tailings piles only. New material is bulldozed several times a week and dumped on the tailings piles.

The petrified wood and opal occurring here was once part of a pine forest. Rare opalized pine cones have been found. Long ago the Roebling Black Opal was found here. It is eighteen ounces and is now owned by the Smithsonian Institution.

Finding opal involves knowing what to look for and a bit of good luck. The mine suggests you stop by the rock shop on the premises to see what the specimens you are searching for look like. Some minerals are for sale. There is no overnight camping at the mine, but it is available at the CCC Camp five miles away.

ADDRESS:
P.O. Box 165
Denio, NV 89404
(775) 941-0374
maestes@frontier.net
http://www.royalpeacock.com/mineinfo.htm

DIRECTIONS:
From Denio take State Highway 140 west for twenty-five miles. Turn left at the BLM sign onto a dirt road and follow the signs to the Royal Peacock Opal Mine. The CCC Campground is two and one-half miles down this road. The mines are seven miles farther along the dirt road.

SEASON:
May 15 through October 15–Weather permitting

HOURS:
8:00 a.m. to 4:00 p.m.

COST:
$145–Fee for bank digging
$40–Fee for tailings digging
$20–per night–Fee for RV camping
$6–Fee for all other camping
$40 per night–Fee for furnished trailer rentals, reservations required

WHAT TO BRING:
You will need equipment for opal mining listed in the front of the book on page 18.

INFORMATION:
    You can keep all that you find at the Royal Peacock Opal Mine. Black opals are found here, as well as some fire and wood opals. This area was once a forest. The trees fell, and over time, were buried in silica and became opals of extraordinary beauty. Mining of opals has taken place in this valley since the 1900s. Since then, millions of dollars of opals have been mined in this region. Over two hundred private claims are mined here. In 1992, a man found an opalized log weighing one hundred thirty pounds.

    Several of this region's opals are on display at the Smithsonian Institution in Washington, DC. You can dig in the banks, or in the tailings pile. No rock hammers are permitted. There is a full service opal shop on-site with equipment, specimens and cut stones. Full RV hookups, furnished trailers and tent camping sites are available. The camp has a shower and laundry facility. Call in advance for camping reservations.

MUSEUMS

Site 5.
Marshall Mint
96 North C Street
Virginia City, NV 89440
(800) 321-6374
http://www.marshallmint.com/?page=about
• Located in an 1876 assay office in the heart of the richest silver strike in America, the Comstock Lode, this museum now displays gems and minerals, silver and gold nuggets and demonstrates the process of stamping metal.

Site 6.
Nevada State Museum
600 North Carson Street
Carson City, NV 89701-4004
(775) 687-4810
• http://dmla.clan.lib.nv.us/docs/museums/cc/carson.htm
This state museum occupies the old Carson City Mint building. Exhibits include a recreated silver mine shaft including a three hundred-foot tunnel, items of Nevada's history including silver and a coin press used in the 1870s to strike U.S. coins.

CAVES

Site 7.
Lehman Caves
Great Basin National Park
100 Great Basin National Park
Baker, NV 89311-9702
(775) 234-7331, ext. 242
http://www.nps.gov/grba/lehmancaves.htm
• This cave has abundant quantities and varieties of calcite formations. The United States Forest Service has managed and protected the cave since 1922, allowing visitors to enjoy these unique formations. Visitors must purchase advance tickets at the visitor center at Great Basin National Park to gain admission to this wonder.

POINTS OF INTEREST

Site 8.
Berlin-Ichthyosaur State Park
H.C. 61 Box 61200
Austin, NV 89310
(775) 964-2440
http://www.parks.nv.gov/bi.htm
• This park was established in 1957 to preserve two very different things. First the park preserves and displays North America's largest concentration of ichthyosaur fossils. These were marine reptiles that somewhat resembled a dolphin and grew up to fifty feet in length. About forty ichthyosaurs were excavated from this site in the 1950s. Today visitors can tour the fossil house to see these swimming reptiles, and the excavation site. The second attraction is a turn-of-the-twentieth-century mining town. Berlin boomed in 1863 when gold was mined into the early 1900s. Many buildings have been preserved here. Visitors can walk through the old town, read descriptive signs and peer into Nevada's past. Guided tours are available at times during the year and include tours of the Diana Gold Mine.

Turquoise has been mined here for thousands of years.

New Mexico is full of history. Billy the Kid met his end here, shot by Sheriff Pat Garret at Fort Sumner on a hot July night in 1881. This is also the place where the world's first atomic bomb was detonated, at Los Alamos in 1945.

This state conjures images of a lone miner searching the desert with his overloaded burro. In fact the best-known mining area is much older than any forty-niner. The Cerrillos Mines, containing lead, copper, silver, zinc, iron and traces of gold, is best-known for turquoise and galena. Ancient peoples of this area mined veins of precious blue stone as early as 900 AD and used lead as a glaze on pottery. With axes, mauls, hammers and anvils, they mined and shaped the mystical turquoise into beads, pendants and to trade with other tribes.

Navajo and Pueblo Indians wore turquoise as ornaments. Native tribes ground turquoise and red coral to make intricate sand paintings created to bring the rain. Apache shamans used this stone as a powerful healing tool. Some tribes placed turquoise on the graves of their dead. Navajo kept turquoise carvings of sheep and horses to guard against bad luck. The proliferation of this vivid blue stone did not go unnoticed by the Spaniards who knew turquoise is an indicator for copper.

In 1581, Spanish expeditions discovered the copper, silver and galena deposits. They used mercury to extract the metals from ore and began the process of smelting. By 1630, many of the Spanish residents in this area were silversmiths, although there was no written record of the discovery of the area's wealth. This may have been a way to avoid paying taxes to the Spanish Crown and continue to control these undisclosed riches. Native Americans learned the craft of fashioning silver from these Spanish interlopers.

By the 1850s, American miners had possession of this land. The American Turquoise Company developed claims in 1914, but discovery of turquoise in other places in the west decreased the company's monopoly of the gemstone. The decline in price brought a drop in production. Today the mines are mostly used for gravel mining.

Another gemstone known in New Mexico is peridot. This green gemstone is known to form in volcanic rock. Peridot occurs in pockets within the basalt, and occasionally in large gemmy masses without flaw or fissure. New Mexico's Kilbourne Hole is an ancient volcanic crater where rockhounds gather in the desert to search out masses of peridot.

Turquoise is generally collected on reservations or private mines that are closed to the public. But the Nitt Mine is open to the public for the collection of lovely specimens of Azurite in vivid blue and green.

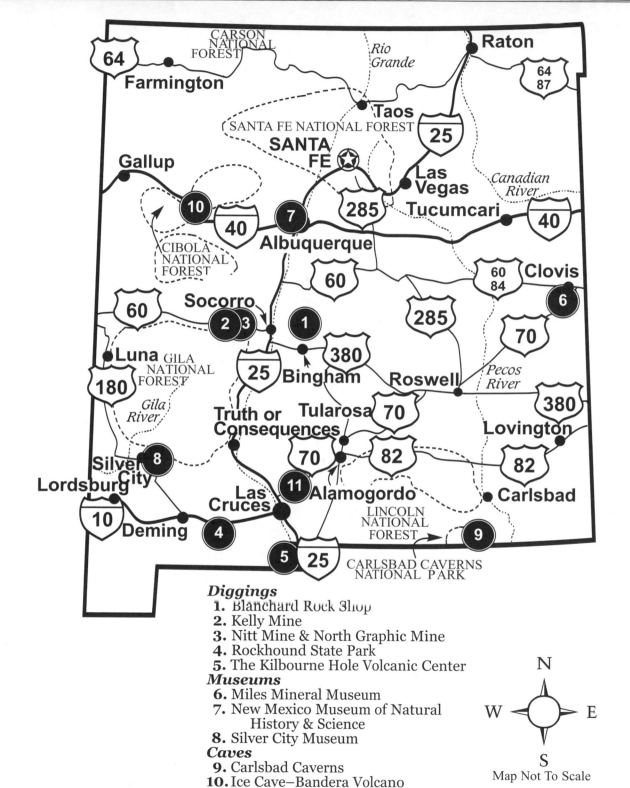

Diggings
1. Blanchard Rock Shop
2. Kelly Mine
3. Nitt Mine & North Graphic Mine
4. Rockhound State Park
5. The Kilbourne Hole Volcanic Center

Museums
6. Miles Mineral Museum
7. New Mexico Museum of Natural History & Science
8. Silver City Museum

Caves
9. Carlsbad Caverns
10. Ice Cave–Bandera Volcano

Points of Interest
11. White Sands National Monument

Map Not To Scale

ADDRESS:
Blanchard Rock Shop
2972 Highway 380
Bingham, NM 87832
(505) 423-3235
blanchardrock@plateautel.net
www.blanchardrockshop.com

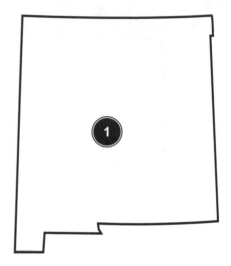

DIRECTIONS:
The Blanchard Rock shop is located in Bingham, on U.S. Highway 380 about thirty miles east of San Antonio. Bingham is one hour and forty-five minutes south of Albuquerque. It is halfway between Socorro and Carrizozo. Bingham has only seven residents. Directions and maps to the claims are provided from the shop.

SEASON:
Open year-round, but call ahead

HOURS:
9:00 a.m. to 6 p.m.

COST:
$10—Adult fee for first ten pounds of material collected
Material after initial ten pounds will be charged according to the quality of specimens collected

WHAT TO BRING:
Safety glasses. Bring food and plenty to drink.

INFORMATION:
The owners of the rock shop will provide you with a map and direct you to the best places to collect specimens. Only surface searching is permitted. There is an abundance of minerals here. Specimens found include: fluorite, barite, galena, calcite, selenite, and quartz. Rarer minerals include linarite and brochantite.

ADDRESS:
Kelly Mine
c/o Chamber of Commerce
P.O. Box 281
Magdalena, NM 87825
(866) 854-3217
(505) 854-2401 Tony's Rock Shop
http://www.ghosttowns.com/states/nm/kelly.html

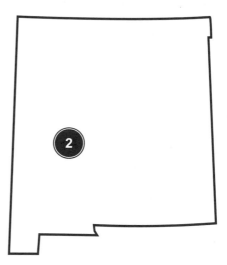

DIRECTIONS:
In Magdalena take Kelly Road south for two and one-half miles and look for the mine on the left. Magdalena is west of Socorro and Interstate Highway 25.

SEASON:
May through October

HOURS:
10:00 a.m. to 4:00 p.m.

COST:
$10 per person per day—Fee

WHAT TO BRING:
Collecting bucket, pick, hammer, sifting screen, shovel and eye protection. Bring a hat, sunscreen, water and anything you want to eat.

INFORMATION:
This area has been mined since 1866 when galena (lead) outcroppings were discovered. Later zinc was revealed and also mined. In the 1900s, silver and lead were mined and the greenish waste rock discarded in huge piles. Later it was discovered that this was a zinc carbonate called smithsonite. When the owners became aware of the value of the tailings piles were striped. Eventually the tailings were exhausted and in the 1930s the mine and town fell on hard times and the population that once reached three thousand dropped away to almost nothing. Tailing dumps, mine buildings and headframes still stand.

Today's visitors need to purchase a visitors pass at Tony's Rock Shop, which is located on the left side as you drive toward the Kelly Mine. The phone number at Tony's Rock Shop is (505) 854-2401.

The Old Kelly Mine is known for the vivid blue smithsonite, though other minerals are also found including azurite, barite, pyrite, bornite, iron ore and occasionally smithsonite. Two other mining sites are available to interested miners: the Nitt and the North Graphic. The Nitt site has large pyrite specimens and the North Graphic has more azurite, sphalerite and smithsonite.

ADDRESS:
Bill's Gem & Mineral Shop
P.O. Box 141
Magdalena, NM 87825
(505) 854-2236

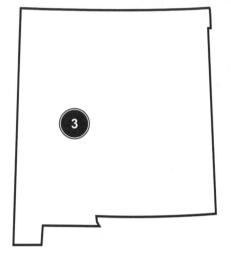

DIRECTIONS:
From Albuquerque take Interstate Highway 25 south to Exit 150 (Exit 147 from Truth or Consequences). Take U.S. Highway 60 west twenty-eight miles to Magdalena. Bill's Gem and Mineral Shop is on U.S. Highway 60 on Magdalena's main street which is the corner of First and Pine. The shop is in a large house next to the Ponderosa Restaurant and the Women of the Mountain Inn.

SEASON:
Open year-round
(mine may be closed due to poor weather conditions)

HOURS:
8:00 a.m. to 5:00 p.m.–Monday to Saturday
8:00 a.m. to 3 p.m.–Sunday

COST:
$5 per person per day–Adult fee with twenty-pound limit
$4 per person per day–Senior fee
Free–Children under 12

WHAT TO BRING:
Standard mining tools may be helpful, but are not necessary to find specimens. Bring sun protection, food and drink.

INFORMATION:
Nice pyrite specimens can be found on the tailings piles of these two mines. You will be digging in the tailings piles for all sorts of minerals. There is copper, azurite, bornite, iron ores and some blue smithsonite. The Nitt Mine is best for pyrite, and the Graphic Mine is often better for smithsonite, azurite and sphalerite in small quantities. You will need to be patient with your searching and digging.

Call ahead to make sure that you can gain access to the mine(s). You will need a key to get by the two gates to access the mine. You may camp at the site, but there are no facilities. Bring a Coleman stove. Drought conditions make open fires a hazard.

ADDRESS:
P.O. Box 1064
Deming, NM 88030
(505) 546-6182
http://www.emnrd.state.nm.us/PRD/Rockhound.htm

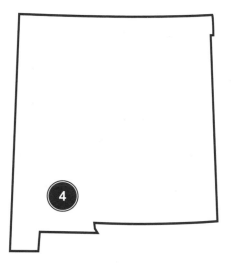

DIRECTIONS:
Rockhound State Park is located outside of Deming. Take State Highway 549 east six miles from where it intersects State Highway 11 in the middle of town. Then proceed south five and nine-tenths miles on State Highway 143, following the well-marked signs to the park.

SEASON:
Open all year round

HOURS:
7:30 a.m. until sundown

COST:
$5–Admission fee per vehicle–day use
$8–Fee per night camping at a primitive site
$10–Fee per night camping at a developed site
$4–Fee for electrical hookup
$4–Fee for sewage hookup

WHAT TO BRING:
General mining supplies, camping supplies, food and beverages.

INFORMATION:
Located on the west side of the Little Florida Mountains, the two hundred fifty-acre Rockhound State Park allows visitors to dig for agates, jaspers, geodes and other semiprecious minerals. Jaspers found here are yellow, pink, orange, brown and variegated. Thundereggs and geode nodules are filled with agate or common opal, or a combination of both. They may be hollow, lined with crystals or solid. Perlite and quartz crystals are also found along with numerous other minerals. Visitors are welcome to take fifteen of material from the park.

The landscape is rough, with loose rocks and inconspicuous drop-offs, so watch your step. There are numerous trails, throughout the park. As with all things, the easy access trails offer the least opportunities and specimens. You'll have to work a bit and travel the extra mile to find extraordinary rocks and minerals.

The camping area is used as a base camp for exploration and collection activities and offers restrooms, dump stations and showers.

ADDRESS:
New Mexico Bureau of Mines & Mineral Resources/New Mexico Tech Las Cruces District Office
1800 Marquess Street
Las Cruces, NM 88005-3370
(505) 835-5420 or (505) 525-4300
http://www.nm.blm.gov/recreation/las_cruces/kilbourne_hole.htm

DIRECTIONS:
This is a desert area, so be prepared. It is sixty miles from El Paso, Texas, to Kilbourne Hole, New Mexico. The specific directions are available for a small fee from the New Mexico Bureau of Mines & Mineral Resources by calling the number above. Directions are lengthy and since this is a desert area, you should have the complete directions in hand before setting out.

SEASON:
Open year-round

HOURS:
Daylight

COST:
Free

WHAT TO BRING:
Standard tools are needed. Take along a shovel, rock hammer, collecting buckets and a pick.

INFORMATION:
    This destination is for rockhounds with experience in the desert. Summer temperatures exceed 100ºF, and winter temperatures are below freezing. Spring and fall may be hot or wet and bring intense thunderstorms. Rattlesnakes are active in late spring. Kilbourne Hole is on public land managed by the Bureau of Land Management. When planning a trip, let a friend know where you plan to be and when you will leave and return. Make sure check in when you get back home.

    The Kilbourne Hole is a volcanic crater. Peridot appearance coincides with volcanic explosions that occurred twenty-five thousand years ago. The crystals are small and may appear in the sand, however their origin is in "xenolith bombs" which are elliptical rocks two to forty centimeters in length. The exterior of these "bombs" vary; the interior is full of green to greenish-yellow crystals. Peridot found here is of gem quality.

MUSEUMS

Site 6.
Miles Mineral Museum
Roosevelt Hall/Eastern New Mexico University
Portales, NM 88130
(505) 562-2651
http://www.enmu.edu/academics/excellence/museums/miles-mineral/index.shtml
• This university museum displays minerals, rocks, meteorites and fossils found in New Mexico.

Site 7.
New Mexico Museum of Natural History & Science
1801 Mountain Road NW / Albuquerque, NM 87104
(505) 841-2800
http://www.nmnaturalhistory.org/
• This museum focuses heavily on dinosaurs with many recreational activities and fossil displays.

Site 8.
Silver City Museum
312 West Broadway/Silver City, NM 88061
(505) 538-5921
http://www.silvercitymuseum.org/
• This house museum contains a large collection of photographs dating back to the 1870s. Objects related to the town's mining past date back to before the turn-of-the-twentieth century and include mineral specimens and small mining equipment.

CAVES

Site 9.
Carlsbad Caverns
3225 National Parks Highway / Carlsbad, NM 88220
(505) 785-2232
http://www.nps.gov/cave/index.htm
• Carlsbad Caverns contains a fossilized coral reef and has numerous caves, including the nation's deepest limestone cave, Lechuguilla Cave, reaching depths of one thousand five hundred sixty-seven feet.

Site 10.
Ice Cave/Bandera Volcano
c/o Ice Caves Trading Co.
12000 Ice Caves Road / Grants, NM 87020
(888) ICE-CAVE
http://www.icecaves.com/
• Advertised as "The Land of Fire and Ice", visitors are lead along an ancient lava trail to the Ice Cave containing layers of glistening blue-green ice. The trading post displays ancient artifacts and sells contemporary Native American artwork.

POINTS OF INTEREST

Site 11.
White Sands National Monument
P.O. Box 1086 / Holloman AFB, NM 88330-1086
(505) 679-2599
http://www.nps.gov/whsa
• Mountains of gypsum eroded to form a huge sandy white plain of fine gypsum crystals. The park road runs eight miles into this unusual landscape.

T-Rex and the largest lignite coal deposit in the world.

North Dakota was originally populated by Native American tribes including, Crow, Cheyenne and Lakota Sioux. The first European to arrive here was a French Explorer named La Verendrye who claimed the area for France. By 1781, there was a fur trading post near the Souris River but attacks by the Native American tribes quickly drove them out. In 1804, Lewis and Clark spent a winter in what is now North Dakota. For the next eighty years Europeans traveled nervously and quickly through the territory. Some hunted and trapped with a constant eye out for hostile Indians. The year 1884 marked the end of the Sioux, Crow and Cheyenne domination of the territory because gold was discovered in South Dakota and Europeans flooded in from the east and west. Many bloody battles ensued with the Native Americans ultimately defeated and pushed out of the territory promised to them by U.S. treaty.

Most of the claims and mining occurred south in the sacred Black Hills of South Dakota. Little gold was found in North Dakota. What was found was thought to have originated in Canada, and was carried south by glaciers during the Ice Age.

In 1889, the Sioux surrendered and one hundred thousand settlers arrived in the Dakota Territory. Northern residents wanted Bismarck for their capital and southern residents chose Pierre. Congress divided the territory into the states of North Dakota and South Dakota.

The area in Ransom County was tested in 1936 and reports showed gold. Prospecting for gold had a brief resurgence in the 1930s, fueled by desperate poverty and unemployment during the Great Depression. Small mining plants used various gold prospecting methods including jigging, sluicing, cyanide and floatation to squeeze any gold from the gravel. Most gold recovered was only the size of a grain of wheat, with nuggets occurring very rarely. Prospecting efforts here were largely unsuccessful. The federal government did some testing of samples and confirmed that indigenous gold existed, but in amounts too small to make commercial mining profitable. Hobbyists do most of the gold prospecting now. The government did find something else of value—coal. This is the real mineral wealth of North Dakota.

One of the stranger places to visit in North Dakota is on U.S. Forest Service Land. It is a park called Burning Coal Vein, and is a thick coal vein that has been on fire for at least a hundred years. Lack of oxygen makes this a very slow burn, but occasionally the coal turns to ash and the ground above collapses, giving the landscape a unique topography.

The first ton of coal came from the Knife River Coal Company in 1917. This state may have the largest deposit of lignite coal in the world, estimated at thirty-five billion tons. Currently the Freedom Mine is the largest in the state.

Gravel, sand, clay and lime make up the majority of the remaining mine industry in North Dakota. The clay mined here has been used to manufacture bricks since 1904.

North Dakota is also a hot spot for paleontologists. Dinosaurs, such as a duck-billed Edmontosaurus and a complete Triceratops, have been found in an area known as Hell Creek Formation. One of only twelve known T-Rex skeletons ever found came from the area near Rhames in the Badlands. If you'd like to learn more about North Dakota's dinosaur history, visit the Dakota Dinosaur Museum.

NORTH DAKOTA SITE MAP

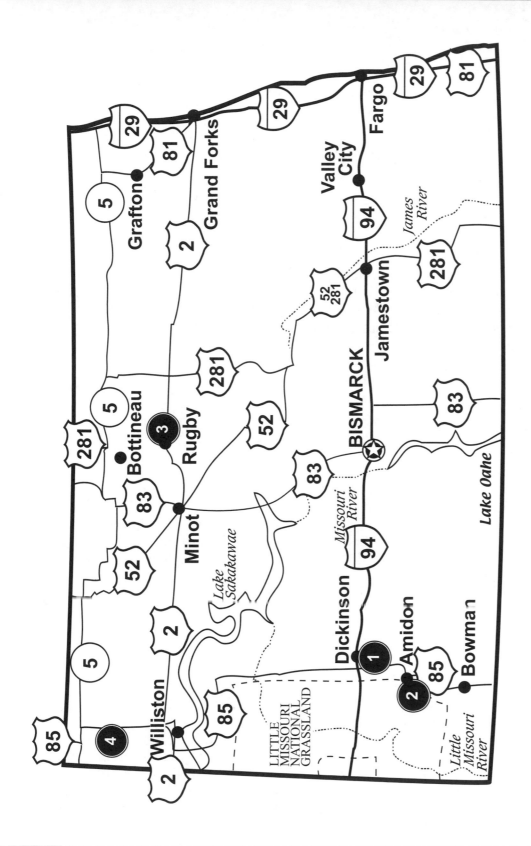

N
W — E
S
Map Not To Scale

Museums
1. Dakota Dinosaur Museum
Points of Interest
2. Burning Coal Vein
3. Geographical Center of North America
4. Writing Rock State Historic Site

MUSEUMS

Site 1.
Dakota Dinosaur Museum
200 Museum Drive
Dickinson, ND 58601
(701) 225-DINO
http://www.dakotadino.com/
• This museum exhibits a complete Triceratops skeleton, as well as several thousand rock, mineral and fossil specimens. Exhibits include a Velociraptor sculpture, eggs carved from minerals and petrified wood.

POINTS OF INTEREST

Site 2.
Burning Coal Vein
Little Missouri National Grasslands/U.S. Forest Service
Route 6, Box 131B
Dickinson, ND 58601
http://www.npwrc.usgs.gov/resource/habitat/natareas/burncoal.htm
• Located fifteen miles northwest of Amidon, North Dakota, this badlands landscape hides a burning coal vein beneath the ground. White settlers noticed the fires from this coal layer over a hundred years ago. The unusual landscape is a result of the coal turning to ash and collapsing, bringing the surface layer down with it. The burning is slow, due to a lack of oxygen and creeps only about ten feet each year. Cracks in the earth admit oxygen and emit hot fumes, which affected the way the junipers grow.

Site 3.
Geographical Center of North America
Chamber of Commerce & Convention Visitor Bureau
224 U.S. Highway 2 SW
Rugby, ND 58368
(701) 776-5846
http://rugbynorthdakota.com/Tourism/GCenter.aspx
• Defined as the place where the surface area of North America would balance if it were a plane of uniform thickness. But don't try balancing it alone. If you happen through Rugby you will find a Geographical Center of North America, a pioneer village, and one of the best views of the Northern Lights anywhere.

Site 4.
Writing Rock State Historic Site
Historic Sites Division
State Historical Society of North Dakota
North Dakota Heritage Center
Bismarck, ND 58505
(701) 224-2666
http://www.tradecorridor.com/grenora/gren-a.htm
• Two large boulders are now enclosed to protect the prehistoric Indian petroglyphs covering their surface. The site was discovered in 1864. These amazing examples of picture language show communication used before written language. The surface of these granite stones is carved with an unknown picture language including thunderbirds and human forms. Much about these petroglyphs remains unknown. The park also contains images that depict the mythological figure of the thunderbird.

"Oil made Oklahoma."

Oil was discovered in Oklahoma accidentally by a driller seeking water. The first oil well in Oklahoma was sunk in 1859. Before the turn-of-the-twentieth century, oilmen or wildcatters invaded the Indian Territory searching for "black gold." Oklahoma's oil fields are part of a huge mid-continental oil region including Oklahoma, central Texas and eastern Kansas. New oil discoveries brought new boomtowns and wealth that gushed with the oil. Most towns disappeared as fast as they appeared, dribbling away with failing wells.

Oil isn't all you will find here. This state has unusual rocks and minerals; some are found nowhere else in the country. The barite rose is the official state rock. Unique to Oklahoma, it occurs in the red sandstone in the central portion of the state. Barite-cemented red sand forms clusters that are shaped like a blooming rose. These clusters are found in very few other places in the world. Cherokee legend tells that these roses formed from the tears of the Cherokee people during their long forced march from Georgia and Tennessee to Oklahoma known as the Trail of Tears.

April through October, Oklahoma rockhounds are found on the Great Salt Plains, near the city of Jet, (located sixty-four miles west of Ponca City along U.S. Highway 64) digging for selenite crystals. Native Americans and early settlers collected the thin layer of salt found here. Selenite is formed from gypsum, which takes on many unusual forms. Digging is not difficult, but finding a complete crystal and extracting it intact takes an equal measure of luck and skill. Visitors are welcome to dig for selenite at the Salt Plains National Wildlife Refuge.

The area north of the city Broken Arrow (located about fifteen miles southeast of Tulsa along the Muskogee Turnpike) is known for quartz crystals. A unique feature of some of the specimens here is an inclusion of liquid trapped in quartz. These "bubble crystals" are highly prized. Because of a boom in the metaphysical market, quartz crystals are now in demand.

Fossils of different varieties are found in Oklahoma. Petrified wood and dinosaur bones are unearthed throughout the state. Works Progress Administration (WPA) workers discovered dinosaur bones during the Great Depression as they built roads, dams and bridges. Giant footprints left in soft sand, now solid rock have also been discovered in Oklahoma. Large trilobites are found in the south-central portion of the state, and these specimens are shipped throughout the world.

From the late 1800s, up until about 1910, zinc and lead were mined. Oklahoma lead the nation in zinc production during those years. The tailing piles in the northeastern portion of the state now yield beautiful sphalerite, galena and calcite crystals.

The town of Lampasas became famous for celestine more than one hundred years ago. This crystal is a lovely blue and so is named for the sky. Rockhounds searching the streambeds and bluffs of Lampasas County may have luck finding crystals ranging from a half-inch in length to a foot across.

Oklahoma does have some industrial mining, though no precious metals are mined here. The less glamorous and more utilitarian mining products extracted from Oklahoma include coal, clays, gypsum, lead, iodine and crushed stone. This state ranks a distant twenty-second in national production of coal.

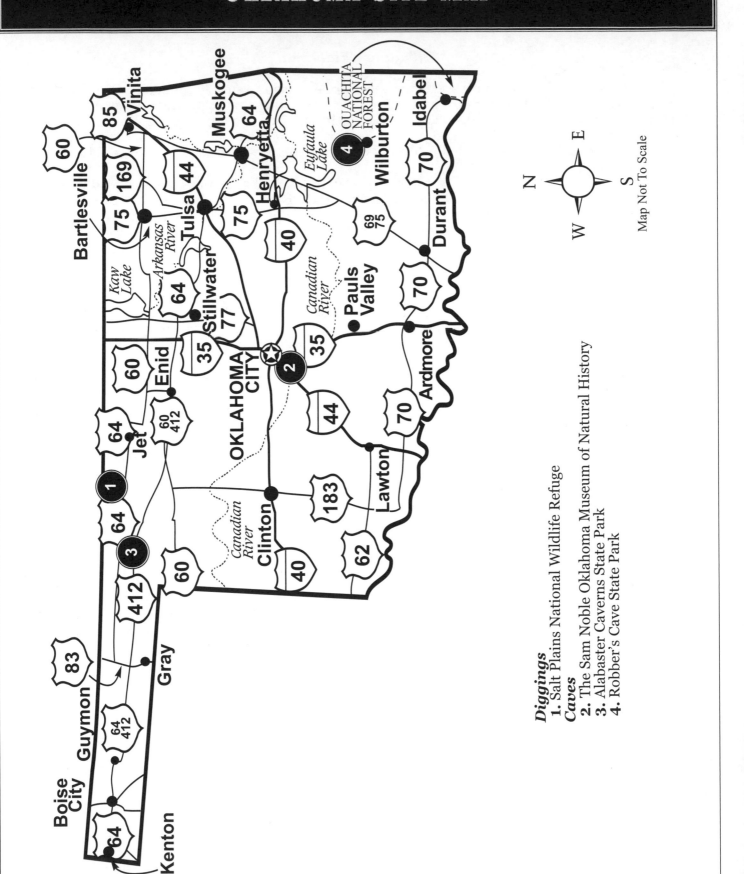

Diggings
1. Salt Plains National Wildlife Refuge
Caves
2. The Sam Noble Oklahoma Museum of Natural History
3. Alabaster Caverns State Park
4. Robber's Cave State Park

Map Not To Scale

ADDRESS:
Salt Plains National Wildlife Refuge
Route 1, Box 76
Jet, OK 73749
(580) 626-4794
fw2_rw_saltplains@fws.gov
http://www.fws.gov/southwest/refuge/saltplains/

DIRECTIONS:
From Cherokee, take U.S. Highway 64 south three miles. Then travel six miles east on a paved country road following the signs to Selenite Crystal Collecting Area.

SEASON:
April 1 through October 15

HOURS:
Daylight

COST:
Free

WHAT TO BRING:
Take small garden tools, a shovel, a container to hold your crystals, plus your own food and water. A change of clothes, socks and shoes is recommended, as you are likely to get wet. Sunscreen is also recommended.

INFORMATION:
Selenite crystals are crystallized gypsum, brownish in color and somewhat translucent. The crystals are found just below the thin layer of salt covering the muddy soil.

Dig carefully into the mud, using the water that seeps into the hole. Splash the water onto the sides of the hole to expose the crystals in the hole wall. The crystals found here range from single selenite crystals a few inches long to clusters weighing several pounds. Single, twin and clusters of crystals are also found. Ten pounds of crystals per day are permitted to be removed for personal use.

Be sure to wear old clothes, as the salt and mud will stain. A cushion or pad to kneel upon is recommended. Crystals newly exposed from the mud are fragile and you should place them in a carton or box to dry.

No camping is permitted. However, camping is available on the east side of the lake in the Great Salt Plains Dam and State Park. The nearby town of Cherokee has several restaurants and lodging.

Museums

Site 2.
The Sam Noble Oklahoma Museum of Natural History
2401 Chautauqua Avenue
Norman, OK 73072
(405) 325-4712
http://www.snomnh.ou.edu/
• Take a trip through Oklahoma's prehistory with this museum's extensive fossil collection.

Caves

Site 3.
Alabaster Caverns State Park
Highway 50 & 50A
Box 32
Freedom, OK 73842
(580) 621-3381
http://www.touroklahoma.com/detail.asp?id=1+5U+920
• This cave actually is formed of alabaster, which is a form of gypsum and as such is the largest publicly operated natural gypsum cave in the world. Selenite formations, colored alabaster and five species of bats highlight this cave tour experience. The park includes a gift shop and educational center.

Site 4.
Robber's Cave State Park
Highway 2
Wilburton, OK 74578
(918) 465-2565
http://www.touroklahoma.com/detail.asp?id=1+5U+3607
• This cave hid some very famous robbers and notorious characters including Frank and Jesse James and Belle Starr. Deserters from both sides of the Civil War made this cave their home and the cave's proximity to Texas roads made it a great place to stash ill-gotten gains. Visitors can hike past the entrance of this infamous cave, camp, picnic or ride a horse on the bridle trails. A grocery store is open on the park grounds.

OREGON

Gold brought them, fertile lands kept them.

The Native Americans who inhabited Oregon for over ten thousand years had it right. This area is better used for hunting, fishing, ranching and agriculture. The tribes of this area changed the land drastically by burning forests to provide grasslands, which lured herds of game. Coastal peoples relied upon salmon and other seafood. They were among the first to see Europeans who arrived as early as the 1700s trading trinkets for provisions.

The first European to arrive overland came in 1806. The Lewis & Clark Expedition reached the mouth of the Columbia River and wintered here. Upon their return to Washington, DC, they revealed their discovery of the fertile land beyond the Rocky Mountains. Trappers were the first to face the perils of the wild land, but they were followed by wagons in 1842, reaching the rich Willamette Valley where timber was abundant and wheat, cattle, fruit and vegetables grew plentifully. Native tribes were not pleased with the interlopers arrival and battles ensued.

In 1848, gold was discovered in the Klamath River in northern California and southern Oregon. Prospectors headed to Oregon to stake claims. In 1852, placer gold found in Jackson County and Josephine County triggered a rush of sufficient size to establish gold mining as an industry in the state. As everywhere else, the placer deposits were quickly exhausted and mining went underground. Gold-bearing quartz found in Jackson was worked well into the 1860s, and eventually played out by 1870. The boom in Oregon was responsible for attracting many people to the territory, significantly enlarging the population. The first railroad arrived because of the gold mining operations.

Many prospectors moved on with the news of gold in other territories. But many stayed to farm, raise cattle and begin the states first industries. Other minerals and metals were discovered and mined including nickel, mercury and uranium. Gold is still found on the Klamath River, judging from the number of weekend prospectors found in the area.

Travelers to Oregon will find many opportunities to search for gold with many mining sites listed in this book. But that is not the extent of the interesting outings available here.

Agates and jaspers of all variety can be found on many of Oregon's beaches. The stones you collect will remind you of your visit to the cold Pacific waters. Another interesting digging site is the Dust Devil Mining Company where you can dig for Oregon sunstone. This official state gemstone is actually feldspar, but it is the most magnificent feldspar you will ever see. These red, green and orange beauties can be faceted. Native Americans collected the stones for barter with other tribes.

Another collecting opportunity not to be missed is gathering thundereggs. Thundereggs were first collected by Native Americans, whose legend said these rocks, which are approximately the size of a naval orange, were actually the eggs of the great thunderbird. Apparently angry gods launched them at each other high in the mountains. This explained the violent thunder and lightening storms and the appearance of this strange round rock lying about. These "eggs" are nodules filled with different agatized material occurring with a great range of color and pattern variety. Most rare and valuable of all are opalized thundereggs.

OREGON SITE MAP

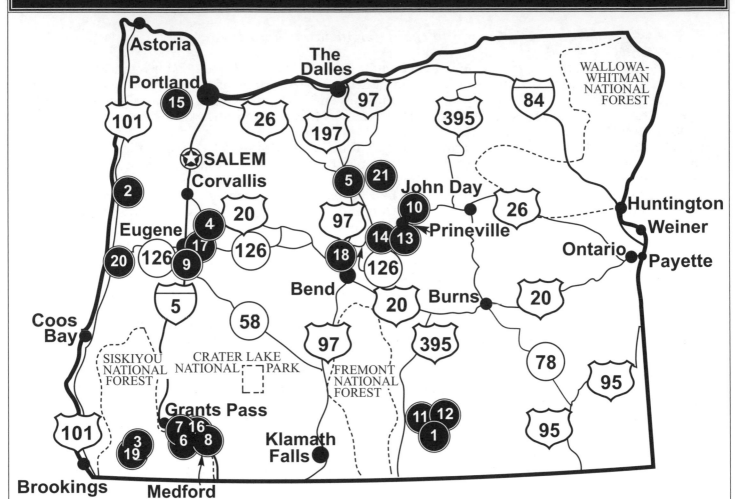

Astoria

Portland
(15)

The
Dalles
97

WALLOWA-
WHITMAN
NATIONAL
FOREST

101

26

197

84

395

SALEM

Corvallis

5   21

John Day

Huntington

2

20

4

97

10

13   Prineville

26

Weiner

Eugene

17

14

18

126

Ontario

Payette

20

126

9

Bend

20   Burns

20

5

58

97

395

78

95

Coos
Bay

SISKIYOU
NATIONAL
FOREST

CRATER LAKE
NATIONAL   PARK

FREMONT
NATIONAL
FOREST

95

101

Grants Pass

7 16

11 12

3
19

6   8

Klamath
Falls

1

Brookings   Medford

Diggings
1. Dust Devil Mining Company
2. Oregon's Ocean Beaches
3. Oregon Gold Trips, LLC
4. Quartzville Recreational Corridor/Dogwood Recreation Site
5. Richardsons Rock Ranch
6. Rogue River National Forest/Little Applegate Recreation Area
7. Rogue River National Forest/Golden Nugget Recreation Area
8. Rogue River National Forest/Tunnel Ridge Recreation Area
9. Sharps Creek Recreation Area
10. Lucky Strike Mine
11. Spectrum Sunstone Mines
12. Spectrum Sunstone Mines Gem Tours
13. Whistler Springs
14. White Fir Springs

Museums
15. Rice Northwest Museum of Rocks & Minerals
16. Crater Rock Museum
17. University of Oregon Museum of Natural and Cultural History

Caves
18. Lava River Cave
19. Oregon Caves National Monument
20. Sea Lion Cave
21. John Day Fossil Beds National Monument

N

W   E

S

Map Not To Scale

ADDRESS:

May to October
P.O. Box 55
Plush, OR 97637
(503) 559-2495
DDMC@oregoncoast.com
http://www.dustdevilmining.com

November to April
P.O. Box 279
Cloverdale, OR 97112
(503) 965-7707

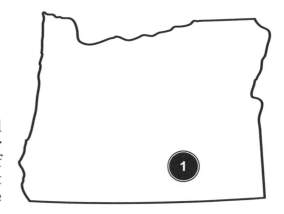

DIRECTIONS:
From Plush travel north on Hogback Road (Country Road 3–10) for about ten miles (pavement ends about four miles). Turn right on County Road 3–11 and drive for half a mile. Turn left on the BLM Road 6155 and drive for eight miles left into Dust Devil Mining Company or right for one mile on BLM Road 6115 into the public collection area.

SEASON:
Memorial Day weekend through October 15 (later if weather permits)

HOURS:
Daylight

COST:
Fee digging prices are based on the wholesale rates that they charge dealers. When fee-digging you will pay about 25% to 33% of the dealer's wholesale rate for usable stones. You are not obligated to purchase any stones that you do not want to take. Clear and mostly clear schiller is free.

WHAT TO BRING:
You should bring a picnic lunch and a camera.

INFORMATION:
The mine has four miles of area open to the public for digging and primitive camping is permitted (pit toilets and no showers). Camping is also available on public land. The nearest campsite is thirty-four miles away. The nearest town is twenty-six miles from the mine. The road to the mine is rough and is graded only twice a year. Bring along a good spare tire. The mining is done in the sun, but there is a covered area with table and chairs available.

Sunstone is a type of feldspar that comes in various colors and has a metallic luster which gives it its name. Most common at this mine is the pink schiller and light red through peach-colored stones. The rarest of all is the blue-green and bicolored stones. This mine is known for its exceptionally large stones and its red/green bicolors, watermelons and color change stones.

Dust Devil Mining Company allows two types of mining. You can dig through their tailing pile for a half- or full-day and keep what you find, or you can search the new ore that has been removed from their mine. The new ore can be screened for a fee and is the same material the mine processes. Stones from one hundred to three hundred carats have come from this pit. Prices are based on wholesale prices. The mine sells stones, cabochons and finished jewelry on the premises.

ADDRESS:
U.S. Highway 101 (north of Newport)
No phone

DIRECTIONS:
The best spot for collecting agates is on Agate Beach on the Oregon Coast, just north of Newport on U.S. Highway 101.

SEASON:
Open all year round

HOURS:
Daylight

COST:
Free

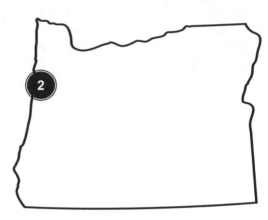

WHAT TO BRING:
You need a container or pail to carry your agates. The Pacific Ocean is COLD, so you may want to wear rubber boots.

INFORMATION:
    This beach lies at the mouth of Big Creek, which carries the agates down from northeast of Newport, Oregon. Agate Beach Wayside is a pull-off for your day use of these beaches. This blacktop parking area has clean restrooms and a tunnel under Ocean Drive (U.S. Highway 101) to the beach.
    Agates have a smooth, glassy feel. They are found in many earth colors and the rock surface may have an orange-peel texture. Agates may appear translucent; jaspers are opaque. Agates and jaspers are easier to spot when they are wet. On the beach you will see some small streams which outlet to the ocean. Streambeds and wet sandy beaches are good places to search. Local rock shops sell the beach agates and jasper in both their natural form and the polished variety. Local artists have also made some beautiful jewelry from the stones.

ADDRESS:
Oregon Gold Trips, LLC
P.O. Box 285
Grants Pass, OR 97528
(877) 672-8877 (call for brochure)
http://www.oregongoldtrip.com

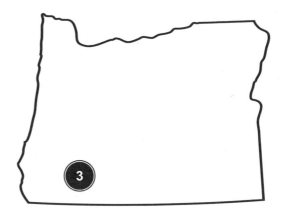

DIRECTIONS:
Oregon Gold Trips' land is in southwestern Oregon, approximately one hour from Grants Pass. From Interstate Highway 5, you will take a one-hour drive on rough road and some steep gravel roads. Be sure to check the weather. Off-road vehicles are advised. Limited transportation from Interstate Highway 5 is available on request.

SEASON:
May through October

HOURS:
three- and four-day trips are available

COST:
$450—Fee for a three-day trip
$550—Fee for a four-day trip
$100 deposit required
Trip fee includes equipment rentals, food and cabin lodging. Discounts available. $100 discount if you elect to tent camp with your equipment. There is an additional $100 discount if you provide your own gold mining equipment (three-inch gold dredge). For example, if you tent camp and bring a dredge, your $550 four-day trip would cost $350.

WHAT TO BRING:
Ask what to bring when you book your trip.

INFORMATION:
The mining site is located on four hundred forty acres of gold-bearing territory. The three- and four-day trips are scheduled frequently. Your stay is in a miners cabin built after World War II for mining activities, with all the comforts of home. The cabins are nestled deep in the heart of the mining district in wooded areas and by mountain streams. A walk around the land will reveal discarded relics of the rich local mining history. Flumes, watergates and long toms are all in evidence. The area you mine is virgin territory untouched by the earlier mining operations. You can work a common dig operation, or on your own. Trips are limited to five to eight people to give you the personal attention you need.

ADDRESS:
Bureau of Land Management Office Salem
1717 Fabray Road SE
Salem, OR 97306
(503) 375-5646

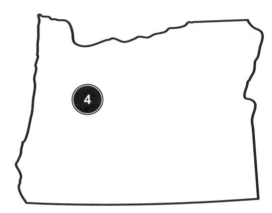

DIRECTIONS:
Sweet Home is slightly northeast of Eugene. From Sweet Home travel northeast on Quartzville Access Road past Green Peter Reservoir. The Dogwood Recreation Site is twenty-two miles from Sweet Home.

SEASON:
Open year-round
July 1 through September 1 only (dredging)

HOURS:
Daylight

COST:
Free

WHAT TO BRING:
Bring standard mining and gold mining equipment. Sluice boxes and dredges up to four inches are permitted. Bring your own food, camping supplies and drinking water. This is a national forest and camping is primitive.

INFORMATION:
Quartzville Corridor has been producing gold since the 1800s. In the 1860s, Quartzville was a tent city of gold miners. Gold panning and dredging are permitted. Dredging requires a permit which can be obtained by calling the Department of Environmental Quality at (503) 378-8240. Keep all mining activity inside the ten-mile Quartzville Recreational Corridor. This location should produce some gold and is a beautiful area of the country.

Camping is permitted in Dogwood Recreation Site, and seven miles north at Yellowbottom Recreation Site. The camping is primitive and on a first come, first served basis. No reservations are accepted. Camping is limited to fourteen days. Quartzville's campgrounds are also nearby and charge a small fee.

ADDRESS:
Gateway Route
Box 440
Madras, OR 97741
(541) 475-2680
richardsonranch@bendnet.com
http://www.richardsonrockranch.com/

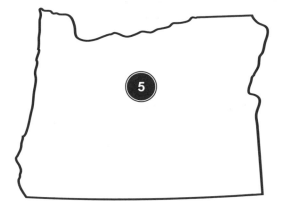

DIRECTIONS:
From Madras take U.S. Highway 97 north 11 miles.
Turn right at Milepost 81 on U.S. Highway 97 and
travel three miles to the ranch office.

SEASON:
Open daily–Weather permitting
call (800) 433-2680 to check digging availability

HOURS:
7:00 a.m. to 5:00 p.m. (office hours)

COST:
$.75 per pound–Fee for material you dig yourself

WHAT TO BRING:
The ranch provides free use of rock picks. You will need gloves, rock hammers, buckets, chisels
and wedges to do any hard rock mining.

INFORMATION:
   Richardsons Rock Ranch is famous for its thundereggs. They range in size from one fourth
of an inch in diameter to five feet in diameter. Thundereggs are geodes which are round rock
bubbles formed by gases. The outside of the rock is ordinary. The inside is filled with agate or
jasper, and in some cases crystals. Other rocks found here include moss agate, jasper, jasp-
agate, Oregon sunset and rainbow agates.
   The thundereggs received their name from Native American legend. They were said to be the
eggs of the thunderbird gods and used by other gods as weapons.
   The area is very scenic, so bring your camera. Camping without hookups and showers is free,
bring your own supplies the store does not sell wood or other camping items.

ADDRESS:
Rogue River National Forest
Applegate Ranger Station
6941 Upper Applegate Road
Jacksonville, OR 97530
(541) 899-3800

DIRECTIONS:
Applegate Recreation Area and Rogue River National Forest are located fourteen and one-half miles south of Jacksonville. Take State Highway 238, west of Medford, through Jacksonville to Ruch. Turn right onto Applegate Road/National Forest Primary Road 10 for two miles. Cross the Little Applegate River and turn left onto Little Applegate Road.

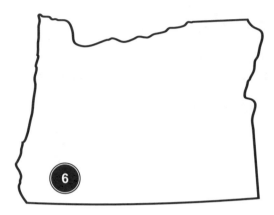

SEASON:
Open year-round

HOURS:
Daylight

COST:
$1 per day–Fee for panning
$5 per day–Fee for dredging

WHAT TO BRING:
Bring standard mining and gold mining equipment. Sluice boxes and dredges up to three inches are permitted. Bring your own food, camping supplies and drinking water. This is a national forest and camping is primitive.

INFORMATION:
　　Rock collecting is a popular activity in this national forest. Soapstone is found throughout the district, but much of it is under claim. Soapstone is white to green, and feels greasy to the touch. It is soft and easily carved, used in cosmetics, talc, sculpture and as an electrical insulator. Quartz and green serpentinized peridotite are also collected throughout the area, but are not concentrated in one location. Copper and red cinnabar are found here, but are rare.
　　Jacksonville was a gold boom town. In the 1850s, when the gold ran out, it became a copper and cinnabar mining town. Jacksonville is on the National Registry of Historic Places with many buildings dating back to the 1800s. Mining permits for the Oregon territory of the national forest are available at the ranger station.

ADDRESS:
Rogue River National Forest
Bureau of Land Management
Medford District Office
3040 Biddle Road
Medford, OR 97504
(541) 618-2200

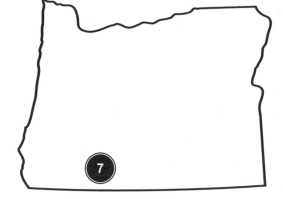

DIRECTIONS:
From Medford, take Interstate Highway 5 northwest to Gold Hill. Take State Highway 234 north approximately two miles and look for signs for the Gold Nugget Recreation Area.

SEASON:
Open year-round
June 15 through September 15 (dredging)

HOURS:
8:00 a.m. to 6:00 p.m.

COST:
$1 per day–Fee

WHAT TO BRING:
Bring standard mining and gold mining equipment. Sluice boxes and dredges up to three inches are permitted. Bring your own food, camping supplies and drinking water. This is a national forest, and camping is primitive.

INFORMATION:
Located east of Grants Pass on the Rogue River, the Gold Nugget Recreation Area is maintained by the Bureau of Land Management. This area is supported by your tax dollars and is available for your use.

If you plan to dredge you must obtain a permit by calling (503) 229-5431. The sites are open year round for panning and from June 15 to September 15 for dredging. Dredges can be operated from 9:00 a.m. to 6:00 p.m. Digging into or undermining the stream and riverbanks is not permitted.

Camping is permitted free for up to fourteen days in the primitive sites. Both sites charge a dollar a day to pan for gold. These areas have produced gold and have good potential.

ADDRESS:
Rogue River National Forest
Bureau of Land Management
Medford District Office
3040 Biddle Road
Medford, OR 97504
(541) 770-2200

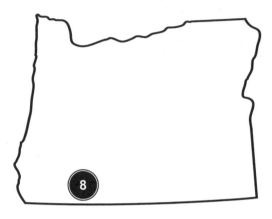

DIRECTIONS:
Tunnel Ridge Recreation Area is located on State Highway 238, west of Medford. Go through Jacksonville to Ruch. Turn right onto Applegate Road for two miles. Cross the Little Applegate River and turn left onto Little Applegate Road.

SEASON:
Open year-round
June 15 through September 15 (dredging)

HOURS:
8:00 a.m. to 6:00 p.m.

COST:
$1 per day–Fee

WHAT TO BRING:
Bring standard mining and gold mining equipment. Sluice boxes and dredges up to three inches are permitted. Bring your own food, camping supplies and drinking water. This is a national forest and camping is primitive.

INFORMATION:
This area has two spots in close proximity to search for gold, Tunnel Ridge and, upstream, Little Applegate. If you plan to dredge you must obtain a permit by calling the number listed above. The sites are open year-round for panning, and from June 15 to September 15 for dredging. Dredges can be operated from 9:00 a.m. to 6:00 p.m. Digging into or undermining the stream and riverbanks is not permitted.

Camping is permitted free for up to fourteen days in the primitive sites. Both sites charge a dollar a day to pan for gold. These areas have produced gold and have good potential.

ADDRESS:
Eugene District Bureau of Land Management
2890 Chad Drive
Eugene, OR 97440
(541) 683-6600
or090mb@or.blm.gov

DIRECTIONS:
From Cottage Grove head east on Row River Road. Travel fifteen miles. Row River Road becomes Shoreline Drive. Travel approximately twelve miles to Sharps Creek Road. Turn right onto Sharps Creek Road at the sign for the Sharps Creek Recreation Area. Drive three miles to the site.

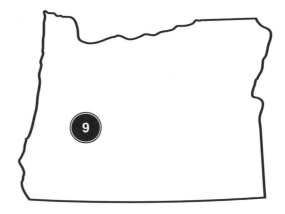

SEASON:
Open June through November (prospecting)
Open May 15 through November 15 (camping–ten sites available)

HOURS:
Daylight

COST:
Free–Prospecting
$5 per site–Fee for camping

WHAT TO BRING:
Bring standard mining and gold mining equipment. Sluice boxes and dredges up to four inches are permitted. Bring your own food, supplies and drinking water.

INFORMATION:
Sharps Creek Recreation Area allows gold panning and dredging after the fish spawning season, which is March 1 to May 31. Dredging requires a permit which can be obtained by calling the Department of Environmental Quality at (503) 378-8240.

The district office asks you to be conscious of other recreational users. If people are swimming in this popular area, please set up your dredge or sluicing equipment downstream of swimmers. Many areas along the stream are private claims so be sure to stay within the recreational area boundaries. The district office will provide you with a map for a small fee, which will help you stay off private claims.

The campground is open between May 15 and November 15. Camping is limited to fourteen days. Sites are primitive.

ADDRESS:
Lucky Strike Mine
P.O. Box 128
Mitchell, OR 97750
(541) 462-3073
info@luckystrikemine.com
http://www.luckystrikemine.com

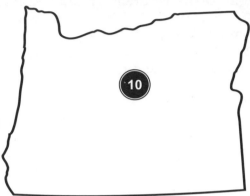

DIRECTIONS: The mine is located thirty-five miles northeast of Prineville.

SEASON:
Mid-May through mid-November–weather permitting

HOURS:
8:00 a.m. to 5:00 p.m., closed Tuesday and Wednesday

COST:
$1.00 per pound–Fee
Free–Fee for camping, water and outhouse

WHAT TO BRING:
Digging equipment, gloves, buckets and camping gear. The mine does not provide equipment.

INFORMATION:
These volcanic agates come in a range of color and contain mosses, banding, fortifications and plumes. The mine is well known as they have been open to the public for over fifty years. Located in the Ochoco Mountains, the mines are at an elevation of over one mile.

The digging area is bulldozed periodically to expose fresh material. Thundereggs are plentiful, and are dug from the ground using pick and shovel. Children will have great luck finding their own treasures. If you don't want to dig there is a mountain of thundereggs for sale at the mail office.

There is a rock shop on premises selling cut and uncut geodes, thundereggs, picture jaspers in rough or finished form. Some jewelry is available.

Camping is primitive. Spring water is available.

ADDRESS:
Spectrum Sunstone Mines
The owners prefer to be contacted by phone or via the internet.
(775) 772-7724 or (775) 830-5797
info@highdesertgemsandminerals.com
http://www.highdesertgemsandminerals.com

DIRECTIONS: The Spectrum Sunstone Mine is located twenty-four miles east of Plush. There is a detailed map available at the mine's website.

SEASON:
May 15 through through November 1

HOURS:
9:00 a.m. to 6:30 p.m.

COST:
Free–one day
$50 per day–Fee per person after first day

WHAT TO BRING:
Drinking water, a hat and sunscreen are a must. The mine provides some sifting areas and tables. Bring your own classifying screens, buckets, shovel, gloves, 1/4" screen, collecting bottles and containers for gems and larger specimens and a spray bottle for cleaning discoveries.

INFORMATION:
Both red and green sunstones of exceptional quality are found at the Spectrum Sunstone Mine. This twenty-acre, privately owned mine once belonged to Tiffany's of New York, and is Oregon's first commercial sunstone mine.

The Spectrum Sunstone Mine allows visitors to dig from their unprocessed ore all-day for free. Rockhounds regularly find reds, greens and dichroic sunstone. Clubs and families are welcome.

Primitive camping is available on the property, as well as water

ADDRESS:
Spectrum Sunstone Mines Gem Tours
The owners prefer to be contacted by phone or internet.
(775) 772-7724
info@highdesertgemsandminerals.com
http://www.highdesertgemsandminerals.com

DIRECTIONS: Call for reservations and directions.

SEASON:
May 15 through November 1

HOURS:
By appointment only

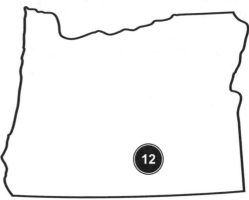

COST:
$1,850 per person—Fee (minimum of four people required for trip)

WHAT TO BRING:
Bring basic camping gear, including a tent. You will also want to pack 1/4" screen, bucket, shovel, gloves, hat and sunscreen.

INFORMATION:
This gem tour includes a visit to five mines: golden opal, fire opal, blue chalcedony, sunstone, and smokey quartz and amethyst mines.

The owners boast that rockhounds will go home with 'a suitcase full of rocks' and you keep all you find!

Transportation and meals are included.

ADDRESS:
Prineville-Crook County Chamber of Commerce
390 Fairview NE
Prineville, OR 97754
(541) 447-6304
pchamber@prineville.org

DIRECTIONS:
From Prineville, travel east on U.S. Highway 26 to
Milepost 49 and 50. Turn left after the sign reading
Bandit Springs and travel six miles on Forest
Service Road 27. At Forest Service Road 500 turn
right and drive a short distance to Whistler Springs.

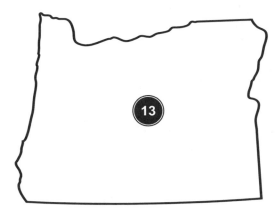

SEASON:
Open year-round—Weather permitting

HOURS:
Daylight

COST:
Free

WHAT TO BRING:
You need standard mining tools. This is an open area, not a private mine, so you need to bring
all your own tools.

INFORMATION:
Thundereggs in the Whistler Springs area have been found in blue, carnelian, plume and
moss colors of agatized jasper. Many eggs' cross sections appear to resemble seascapes, animal
pictures and other formations within the rock. This area is heavily worked and rocks may be
more difficult to find.

A thunderegg may be a nodular, solid sphere of rock or a hollow rock (geode). Geodes may
hide beautiful crystals within. These eggs have a brown or russet-colored outer shell that may be
knobby or ribbed. The inner shell may have a thin or intermediate lining of iron or manganese,
occasionally quartz or opal. The center is usually quartz with or without inclusions, pattern
growth or crystals. Opal interiors are rare but do occur. Plume patterns also occur and are
valuable finds. Rock sizes range from less than an inch to five feet in diameter. Most specimens
are the size of baseballs.

Stop by the Prineville-Crook County Chamber of Commerce for a free map of the area. Maps
are also available at the Forest Service Office.

ADDRESS:
Prineville-Crook County Chamber of Commerce
390 North Fairview
Prineville, OR 97754
(541) 447-6304

DIRECTIONS:
From Prineville take U.S. Highway 26 to Milepost 41. Turn left on Forest Service Road 3350 and continue five miles to the Chamber of Commerce claim sign.

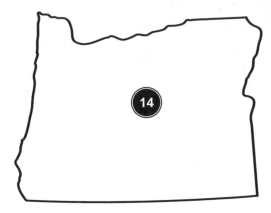

SEASON:
Open year-round–Weather permitting

HOURS:
Daylight

COST:
Free

WHAT TO BRING:
You will need rock hammers, picks, shovels, bucket, safety goggles and gloves.

INFORMATION:
White Fir thundereggs are made up of an agatized jasper composition with a rhyolite matrix. They occur in many colors and combinations of brown, tan, yellow, red and mauve. The thundereggs range in size from quarter-inch in diameter to five feet in diameter. Thundereggs are geodes which are round rock bubbles formed by gases. The outside of the rock is ordinary; the inside is filled with agate or jasper.

The Chamber of Commerce maintains several claims in the area. Be sure to stay on the chamber's claim, which is marked. Leave the gates as you found them. If the gates are open, leave them open; if closed, close them again after you leave. Please don't litter. This is an open area, not a private mine, so you need to bring all your own tools.

MUSEUMS

Site 15.
Rice Northwest Museum of Rocks & Minerals
> 26385 NW Groveland Drive
> Hillsboro, OR 97124
> (503) 647-2418
> http://www.ricenwmuseum.org//
> • This museum has an extensive collection of rock, mineral, gems and fossils from around the world including crystallized minerals, metal ores and gemstones.

Site 16.
Crater Rock Museum
> 2002 Scenic Avenue
> Central Point, OR 97502
> (541) 664-6081
> http://www.craterrock.com/
> • Crater Rock Museum contains excellent specimens of minerals, thundereggs (local geodes), fluorescent rocks, fossils and geodes. Other exhibits include cut and polished gemstones, a collection of early American Indian artifacts, effigies and small fired clay figures. One exhibit depicts the process of making stone tools. There are exhibits on meteorites and fossils, including four dinosaur eggs.

Site 17.
University of Oregon Museum of Natural and Cultural History
> 1680 East 15th Avenue
> Eugene, OR 97403-1224
> (541) 346-3024
> http://natural-history.uoregon.edu/Pages/
> • Museum collections include items discovered by Dr. Thomas Condon, father of Oregon geology, during the late nineteenth and early twentieth centuries, extensive fossil collections, and one of Oregon's most significant collections of Native American cultural and archaeological artifacts.

CAVES

Site 18.
Lava River Cave
> Lava Lands Visitor Center
> 58201 South Highway 97
> Bend, OR 97701
> (541) 593-2421
> http://www.fs.fed.us/r6/centraloregon/newberrynvm/interest-lavariver.shtml
> • This lava tube cave is tall and nearly constant in diameter. The tour is self-guided and there are no paths or lights. The visitor center provides directions and rents lanterns. Other area caves include; Boyd Skeleton Cave, Arnold Lavatube System, Surveyors Cave, Wind Cave, Charcoal Cave, South Ice Cave and Lavacicle Cave.

Site 19.
Oregon Caves National Monument
19000 Caves Highway
Cave Junction, OR 97523
(541) 592-2100 ext. 262
http://www.nps.gov/orca/index.htm
• This national monument contains hiking trails through a coniferous forest, and guided tours through a living marble cave.

Site 20.
Sea Lion Cave
91560 Highway 101 N
Florence, OR 97439
(541) 547-3111
http://www.sealioncaves.com/
• Visitors to this unusual cave will travel from a cliff top by elevator down two hundred ten feet to a sea-level chamber that is twelve stories high, and filled with seals of three varieties.

POINTS OF INTEREST

Site 21.
John Day Fossil Beds National Monument
22651 Highway 19
Kimberly, OR 97848
(541) 987-2333
JODA_Interpretation@nps.gov
http://www.nps.gov/joda
• Ancient plants and animals are trapped in heavily eroded volcanic deposits leaving a complete record of time spanning sixty-five million years during the Cenozoic era (mammals and flowering plants).

Sue the T-rex, Custer, Crazy Horse and the lust for gold.

The La Verendrye brothers, French explorers, first entered South Dakota in 1742. They buried an inscribed lead plate near Pierre, which marked the land as belonging to France. It is doubtful they asked permission of the Sioux nations before leaving this mark, but they did survive the trip, which is remarkable. In 1804 Lewis and Clark passed through South Dakota on the way west, and again in 1806 on the return trip. Despite these travelers, life remained unaffected in the area now called Dakota. The Sioux Indians did little mining, devoting their time to hunting, preparing weapons and tools, tanning hides and making war. They did mine for pipestone in what is now the eastern border of South Dakota. The soft reddish stone is easily carved into ornaments or pipe heads. Both the Black Hills, and the pipestone quarries were considered sacred places by all tribes. The Sioux peoples vigorously defended their territories from all intruders.

Settlers continued to encroach in larger numbers. Conflict occurred and bloody skirmishes ensued. The Sioux and representatives of the federal government signed a treaty in 1868, and the sacred Black Hills were established as Indian land forever. The United States kept their word for a short six years.

A young officer on a scouting expedition changed everything in 1874. Gold was discovered in the Black Hills. Colonel George A. Custer reported his discovery to the world. Prospectors poured in from the east and the west. The Sioux immediately protested the treaty violations and war broke out. The United States cavalry was ordered to protect the incoming prospectors, rather than enforce the treaty.

During this period of lawlessness and battle, several boomtowns appeared where gold was found. One of the most famous is Deadwood. In 1876 Wild Bill Hickok settled in to play poker in Deadwood sitting uncharacteristically with his back to the door. He held the winning hand, a pair of aces and a pair of eights, but he was shot in the back of the head before the round ended. This combination of cards is now known as "the Dead Man's Hand".

United States forces eventually triumphed after a losing battle at Little Bighorn. Custer did not live to see his Seventh cavalry surround the Sioux camp to arrest the chief called Big Foot. On December 28, 1890, Chief Big Foot and his warriors were sitting with cavalry officers engaged in parley when a shot was fired. United States forces fired from the hills as Sioux warriors ran for their weapons. In the ensuing minutes, two hundred fifty Sioux men, women and children were killed by the Seventh Cavalry at the Wounded Knee massacre, and twenty-five United States soldiers were killed. Wounded Knee ended the Indian Wars forever. A stone monument now marks the site.

The Badlands and Black Hills now belonged to the United States. The Badlands did not receive their name because of hostile Indians or dangerous outlaws. Instead this was a translation of the Native American name meaning the land was bad to travel or live in due to the lack of vegetation and adequate water supply. Traveling through this area was difficult, thus–Badlands. The colorful strata of sediments mark the layers of time. Volcanoes in the west, possibly in the Yellowstone area, erupted some thirty-four million years ago and blanked the area in white ash. The ash is now evident in the white layer of material near the top of the plateaus of the Badlands. The Black Hills gleans its name from the thick forests of pine and spruce, which are dark in color when seen from a distance. The Sioux knew of gold in the hills, and it is likely that they used the metal the Europeans treasured at trading posts. The appearance of gold through these tribes likely stirred exploration into their territory.

By the turn-of-the-twentieth century, the Dakotas were well settled, placer gold was scarce, and the miners had moved underground.

In 1927 Gutzon Borglam selects the great granite sheet of igneous and metamorphic rock for his project because of the stone's strength and color. Harney Peak granite, composed of quartz, feldspar, biotite and muscovite, is the stuff of which Mount Rushmore National Monument is carved. The faces of George Washington, Thomas Jefferson, Theodore Roosevelt and Abraham Lincoln grace the top of a formation assumed to go at least eight miles into the earth. The surface is surprisingly free of cracks, which did occur when the molten rock cooled, but were filled by other molten magma of pegmatite dikes. Pegmatite is igneous rock similar to granite. These dikes are now seen as the white stripes on the foreheads of Washington and Lincoln.

South Dakota has many valuable resources including copper, silver, tin, mica and graphite mines as well as some nickel, iron and lead. But it is gold that brought this area national attention. South Dakota ranks third in the production of gold in the United Stated thanks in large part to the Homestake Mine. Over three hundred fifty thousand ounces of gold have been taken from this mine each year.

The most recent treasure unearthed in the badlands of South Dakota is a dinosaur unearthed by Sue Henderson, a paleontologist. The T-Rex she discovered is unusually complete, and the largest ever found. The head alone is five feet in length, and the dinosaur measures forty-two feet from nose to tail. If you want to visit Sue, as she is called, you will have to go to the Field Museum in Chicago, where she now resides.

But don't worry, visitors to South Dakota will find no shortage of digging opportunities. Who knows what you may discover?

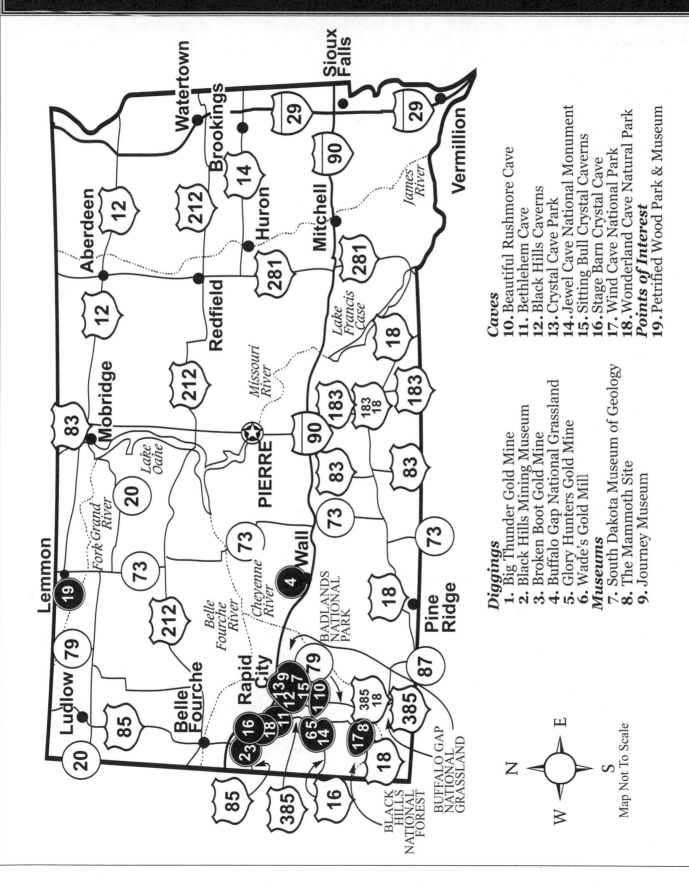

Diggings
1. Big Thunder Gold Mine
2. Black Hills Mining Museum
3. Broken Boot Gold Mine
4. Buffalo Gap National Grassland
5. Glory Hunters Gold Mine
6. Wade's Gold Mill

Museums
7. South Dakota Museum of Geology
8. The Mammoth Site
9. Journey Museum

Caves
10. Beautiful Rushmore Cave
11. Bethlehem Cave
12. Black Hills Caverns
13. Crystal Cave Park
14. Jewel Cave National Monument
15. Sitting Bull Crystal Caverns
16. Stage Barn Crystal Cave
17. Wind Cave National Park
18. Wonderland Cave Natural Park

Points of Interest
19. Petrified Wood Park & Museum

ADDRESS:
P.O. Box 459
Keystone, SD 57751
(605) 666-4847
(800) 843-1300 extension 774
strikegoldat@aol.com
http://www.bigthundermine.com/

DIRECTIONS:
Turn left at the stoplight in Keystone. Big Thunder Gold Mine is located just around the next corner about three blocks away.

SEASON:
May 1 through October 1
Off-season—By reservation

HOURS:
8:00 a.m. to 8:00 p.m.

COST:
$8.50–Adults tour fee
$5.50–Children's tour fee–ages 6-12
Free–Children ages 6 and under tour fee
$7.50 per pan–Fee for gold panning
$5.25 –Fee for panning with purchase of a tour ticket

WHAT TO BRING:
All supplies are provided by the mine.

INFORMATION:
The Big Thunder Gold Mine is in the Black Hills of South Dakota. The mine was claimed by two German immigrants in 1882. These men tunneled six hundred eighty feet into the mountain in their search for gold.

Visitors to the Big Thunder Gold Mine can enjoy the largest mining artifact collection in the Black Hills in the mining museum. Enjoy a mining tour along a one hundred thirty-foot tunnel, which is well lit and spacious. You will tour this underground mine with some knowledgeable and friendly people. At the tour's end you will be allowed to dig your own genuine gold ore. For an additional fee you can pan for gold beside the Battle Creek Stream. Wear a light jacket and comfortable shoes on the mine tour. The temperature underground is a constant 50°F.

ADDRESS:
Black Hills Mining Museum
323 West Main Street
Lead, SD 57754
(605) 584-1605
bhminmus@mato.com
http://www.mining-museum.blackhills.com/

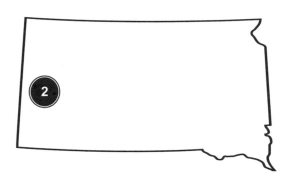

DIRECTIONS:
Located on Main Street in Lead, South Dakota.

SEASON:
Open all year round

HOURS:
10:00 a.m. to 5 p.m.–Last tour at 4:30 p.m. (summer hours)
9:45 a.m. to 4:30 p.m.–Tuesday to Saturday (winter hours)

COST:
   Mine Tour:
   $20–Fee for family package
   $6.00–Adult fee
   $5–Seniors & Students fee
   Free–Children ages 6 and under

   Gold Panning:
   $5– Fee per person

WHAT TO BRING:
No special equipment, clothing or gear is needed.

INFORMATION:
   This museum visit includes a fifty minute guided tour through a simulated underground level of the Homestake Gold Mine, giving a look at both early day and modern underground mining techniques. The Homestake mine was one of the world's largest, descending to depths of eight thousand feet below the city of Lead. Back above ground view historic photographs, working models, local history exhibits and mining equipment, explores mining in the Black Hills from 1876 to the present. The museum has hands-on gold panning displays where museum staff will teach greenhorns the techniques of panning for gold and you keep what you find.

ADDRESS:
Broken Boot Gold Mine
Upper Main Street
Deadwood, SD 57732
(605) 578-1876 or (605) 578-9997
info@brokenbootgoldmine.com
http://www.brokenbootgoldmine.com/

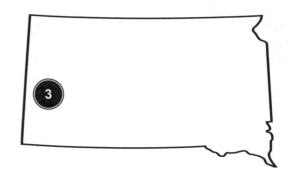

DIRECTIONS:
Located at the intersection of U.S. Highway 14A and Main Street.

SEASON:
Mid-May through mid-September

HOURS:
8:30 a.m. to 5:30 p.m.

COST:
$5–Adult fee for mine tour
$1–Children's fee for mine tour
$5–Fee for gold panning

WHAT TO BRING:
No special equipment needed.

INFORMATION:
    Broken Boot produced gold from 1878 to 1904 in one of the countries last gold rushes. A short video introduces you to local history and gold mining before visitors take a fifty-minute guided tour of the mine. Tours depart every thirty minutes. After your tour visitors can pan for gold at the mine. Experienced miners provide tips and instruction and you keep all the gold you find.

ADDRESS:
National Grasslands Visitor Center
708 Main Street
P.O. Box 425
Wall, SD 57790
(605) 279-2125
http://www.fs.fed.us/r2/nebraska/education/visitor_centers/ngvc.shtml

DIRECTIONS:
The Buffalo Gap National Grassland is located in south-west South Dakota, covering a territory of over five hundred ninety-one thousand acres, which borders and is intermingled with private, state, tribal and national park lands.

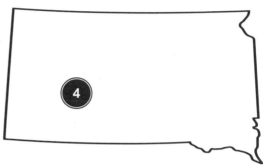

SEASON:
Open year-round

HOURS:
7:00 a.m. to 8:00 p.m. daily–Memorial Day to Labor Day
8:00 a.m. to 4:30 p.m. daily–Off-season

COST:
Free–Admission

WHAT TO BRING:
A collecting container, water and a snack. Hat and sunscreen are recommended.

INFORMATION:
    At first glance this place may seem vast and empty. The great open expanse and constant wind may seem desolate and lonely at first, but look closely about you and notice the richness of the plants and animals which make this place their homes. Camping, hiking, biking and bird watching are popular pastimes here.

    The Buffalo Gap National Grassland, in the southwest portion of South Dakota, is well-known to local rockhounds for the large agate beds. While you enjoy the grand expanse of undulating grass keep an eye out for brightly colored agates. Petrified wood is found here along with prairie agates. Some are found polished for you by the action of streams. Occasionally rose quartz, black tourmaline and muscovite mica is found.

    Check with the local USDA Forest Service office to see if permits are required for collecting.

ADDRESS:
Glory Hunters Gold Mine
P.O. Box 262
Hill City, SD 57745
(605) 574-2081
gloryhnt@rapidcity.com
http://www.angelfire.com/sd/gloryhunters/

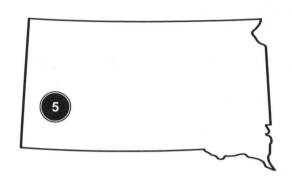

DIRECTIONS:
Glory Hunters is located sixteen miles from Hill City in the Old Time Mining District. From Hill City take the Deerfield Lake Road for nine miles until you come to the "Jay-Hook" curve. There you will see a sign for Mystic and Deerfield. Take the gravel road toward Mystic for seven miles to the owner's residence marked by a sign. From there the owners will take you to the claim.

SEASON:
May through September–Weather permitting

HOURS:
9:00 a.m. to 8:00 p.m.–Seven days a week
(CALL FIRST, so they know to expect you)

COST:
$45–Fee for instruction course
$20 per day–Fee for mining
$10–Fee for rental of sluice box or trommel
$150 per day–Fee for miner's kit (screener, washer system and pan)
Free–Fee for camping on site (RV campground and primitive campsites available nearby)

WHAT TO BRING:
You're are welcome to bring your own equipment or rent equipment at the mine.

INFORMATION:
This mine offers fun for beginners and experienced prospectors. The site is in the Black Hills on Rapid Creek in the Rochford Valley where the gold rush began in 1876.

Glory Hunters Gold Mine offers a placer mining instruction class that takes about one hour and teaches you how to study the land to find a promising place to mine through the process of mining and to the final stages of concentrating your material to extract the gold.

Camping on the claim is free with permission.

ADDRESS:
Box 312
Hill City, SD 57745
(605) 574-2680
wades@wadesgoldmill.com
http://www.wadesgoldmill.com/

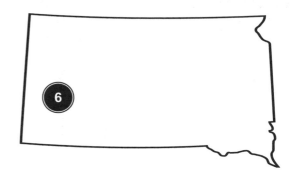

DIRECTIONS:
Take U.S. Highway 385 and U.S. Highway 16 to Hill City. In Hill City turn up the hill on Deerfield Road by the convenience store and the Super 8 Motel. Go three-fourths of a mile on the blacktop to the mine.

SEASON:
Memorial Day through Labor Day

HOURS:
9:00 a.m. to 6:00 p.m.–Starting times for the two-hour tours

COST:
$8–Adult fee for mill and museum tour
$4–Children's fee ages 6–11 for mill and museum tour
$6–Fee for gold panning lesson
$3–Fee for bucket or gold ore

WHAT TO BRING:
Wade's Gold Mill will supply you with all the equipment you need.

INFORMATION:
Wade's Gold Mill is an educational experience for the whole family. You will learn local mining history and see the working and processing of gold.

The museum tour gives visitors a good look at what mining was like during the South Dakota Gold Rush of 1874. Gold mining and mill processing equipment has been gathered and reconstructed into a working operation. There is a mining photo gallery of old time miners and area mill operations. This is a living history museum. The mill tour is a tour of a placer mill that shows how a mill operates.

A short panning lesson is offered which lasts about ten minutes. The long panning lesson goes into more detail and lasts about an hour. Both teach the basics of panning for gold.

MUSEUMS

Site 7.
South Dakota Museum of Geology
501 East St. Joseph Street
Rapid City, SD, 57701
(800) 544-8162 extension 2467
http://www.museum.sdsmt.edu/
• This museum has a collection of more than two hundred fifty thousand vertebrate fossils and six thousand minerals, with an emphasis on the fossils and minerals of the Dakotas.

Site 8.
The Mammoth Site
P.O. Box 692
1800 West Highway 18 Bypass
Hot Springs, SD 57747
(605) 745-6017
http://www.mammothsite.com/
• In 1974, a discovery was made, a twenty-six thousand-year-old fossil trove of Ice Age fossils excavated from a sinkhole where animals of another age went to drink and were trapped. A thirty-minute tour and ten minute video focuses on the Ice Age and this site. Over fifty-two mammoths have been identified here with bear, camel, prairie dog, dog and wolf.

Site 9.
Journey Museum
222 New York Street
Rapid City, SD 57701
(605) 394-6923
http://www.journeymuseum.org/english/
• This museum has a large collection of Sioux artifacts, and history collection from the western Plains. The geology collection emphasizes the rock formations and fossil remains of this region, including the gold of the Black Hills.

CAVES

Site 10.
Beautiful Rushmore Cave
13622 Highway 40
Keystone, SD 57751-6604
(605) 255-4384 or (605) 255-4467
http://www.beautifulrushmorecave.com
• A one-hour guided tour winds visitors through a series of chambers and passages. The tour highlight is the Big Room with extraordinary stalactites, columns and flowstone beside ribbons and draperies.

Site 11.
Bethlehem Cave
P.O. Box 592
Black Hawk, SD 57718
(605) 787-7500
• This limestone cave contains a crystal-lined shelter, which gives the site its name. Prospectors discovered the cave and local ranchers explored the cave in the winter months. Today visitors can take a guided tour on walkways that are well-lit and see the caves many secret treasures.

Site 12.
Black Hills Caverns

2600 Cavern Road
Rapid City, SD 57702
(605) 343-0542
http://www.blackhillscaverns.com
• Lakota warriors used calcite crystals from this cave to gain strength. Today visitors can see the glittering underground world with many fantastic formations.

Site 13.
Crystal Cave Park

7700 Nameless Cave Road
Rapid City, SD 57702
(605)-342-8008
• Eighty percent of this cavern's walls are lined with crystals, which cling to the ceilings and walls. Also known as "dogtooth spar" these crystals take hundreds of years to grow just one inch.

Site 14.
Jewel Cave National Monument

11149 U.S. Highway 16
Building B12
Custer, SD 57730
(605) 673-2288
http://www.nps.gov/jeca/
• This cave is the world's second longest. Cave tours take visitors past pristine cave systems with a wide variety of formations including; frostwork, flowstone, draperies, boxwork, stalactites and stalagmites. The cave is also home to several varieties of bats.

Site 15.
Sitting Bull Crystal Caverns

13745 South Highway 16
Rapid City, SD 57701
(605) 342-2777
http://www.sittingbullcrystalcave.com
• In the 1920s, the cave owners sponsored Sioux Indian pageants with the help of a friend and medicine man named Black Elk. It was Black Elk who chose the Cave's name. The cave owners also operated a trading post, trading Sioux crafts for needed hardware, clothing and other items. The cave itself contains a variety of limestone formations, chambers and passages.

Site 16.
Stage Barn Crystal Cave

10829 Stagebarn Road
Piedmont, SD 57769
(605) 787-4505
• This cave gets its name from the stagecoach barn, which was located at its mouth. A one-hour tour takes guests past rare and beautiful limestone formations following well-lit paths with a moderate to steep grade. The cave includes colorful crystal formations, and some of the largest limestone cliffs in the Black Hills.

Site 17.
Wind Cave National Park
   26611 U.S. Highway 385
   Hot Springs, SD 57747
   (605) 745-4600
   http://www.nps.gov/wica/
   • This cave system is well-known for unusual boxwork, unique limestone formations and fine calcite fins resembling honeycombs. Outside the cave bison, elk, pronghorn, mule deer, prairie dogs and coyotes make their homes.

Site 18.
Wonderland Cave Natural Park
   Box 83
   Nemo, SD 57759
   (605) 578-1728–summer only
   http://www.southdakotacaves.com/wonderland_cave.htm
   • Grottoes, caverns and passageways glimmer with crystals in Wonderland Cave. Limestone formations appear in abundance including stalactites and stalagmites.

POINTS OF INTEREST

Site 19.
Petrified Wood Park & Museum
   500 Main Street
   Lemmon, SD 57638
   (605) 374-3964
   http://www.lemmonsd.com/petrified.html
   • An abundance of petrified wood over fifty million years old is found in this area. A pioneer named O.S. Quammen enlisted government geologists to study the area, unearthing mammoth, fish, snails, grass, leaves and of course–trees. During the height of the Depression, Quammen secured federal funds to employ hundreds of men to gather the petrified wood and fashion them into unusual sculpture-like shapes. At a time when drought and depression crushed local economy, this project helped this town survive and left a strange and wonderful park for future visitors.

Lone star, yellow rose and topaz.

The state of Texas brings to mind cattle drives, cowboys and vast open plains. Few prospectors wandered beneath Texas skies because gold was never found here. But if you think for a minute that there is nothing mined in Texas, you'd be dead wrong (partner).

For nearly twelve thousand years Native Americans have known about the flint quarries six miles south of Fritch, Texas. The quartz in this flint makes it extremely hard. The ability of flint to cleave to a razor sharp edge makes it ideal for fashioning tools and weapons. The area where flint occurs is only ten miles across. The quarries themselves are merely shallow pits in the earth. There are petroglyphs and flint from this quarry has been found all over the Great Plains. Alibates Flint Quarries National Monument gives tours of this area daily. Local rock shops have flint for sale. Visitors can dig their own flint at Lake McClellan Recreation Area.

Another interesting find in Texas is petrified palm wood. Thirty million years ago, Texas was a lush tropical area and much of the land was under water. Fossilized corals, sponges and mollusks are all unearthed in what is now an arid landscape.

Rockhounds will be pleasantly surprised at the variety of minerals available in Texas. Opals, galena, agates, labradorite, jaspers of all description, and petrified wood are all found here. Two well-known collecting areas are the Stillwell Ranch and Woodward Ranch. Both are open to the public.

Selenite crystals are found at Lake Mackenzie Reservoir. These unusual gypsum crystal clusters are not a beautiful color, but their shape and formation makes them a welcome addition to a rock enthusiast's collection. Caution should be exercised while digging that crystals are not damaged.

The most sought after stone in this state is Topaz, the official gem of Texas. Topaz, aluminum silicate, takes second in hardness only to diamonds and occurs in nature in several colors including orange, yellow, red, pink, champagne, green and the most recognized, blue. Here in Texas, topaz is most commonly a clear crystal. Clear topaz is easily changed to blue by the addition of heat.

Topaz is found in separate crystals, crystal masses and in the granite outcroppings, along streambeds and in the ravines of Mason County. In the early days, locals and tourists hunted for topaz in the granite hills and sandy creeks. This area produced the largest-known topaz gems found in North America. Several of these hefty crystals now reside in the Smithsonian Institute in Washington, DC. At the turn-of-the-twentieth-century lucky treasure hunters occasionally found stones as big as coconuts. Unfortunately, those days are gone. Most Texas topaz is much smaller.

Topaz digging goes on year-round, but the months of November through January are by far the most pleasant for this type of work. Try your hand at Garner Seaquist Ranch or the Wayne Hofmann Ranch in Mason County. Maybe you'll find a topaz as blue as the Texas skies.

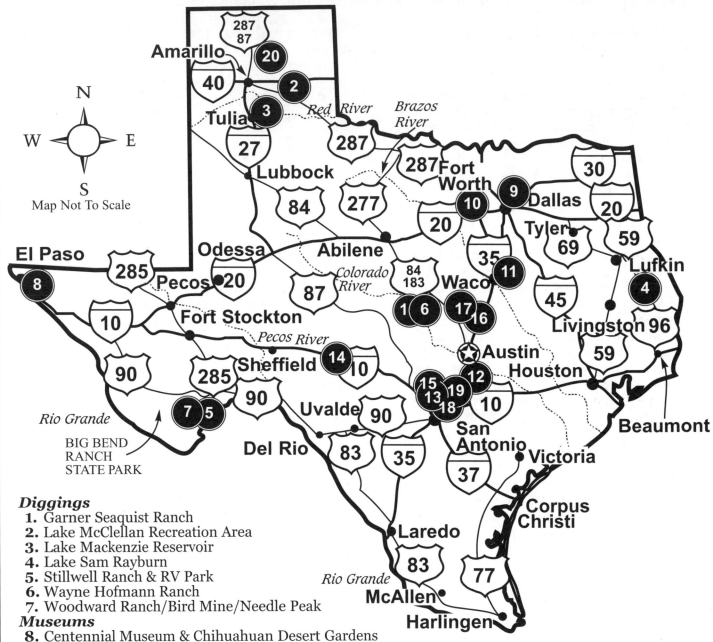

Diggings
1. Garner Seaquist Ranch
2. Lake McClellan Recreation Area
3. Lake Mackenzie Reservoir
4. Lake Sam Rayburn
5. Stillwell Ranch & RV Park
6. Wayne Hofmann Ranch
7. Woodward Ranch/Bird Mine/Needle Peak

Museums
8. Centennial Museum & Chihuahuan Desert Gardens
9. Museum of Nature & Science Dallas, Texas
10. Fort Worth Museum of Science and History
11. Mayborn Museum Complex
12. Texas Natural Science Center

Caves
13. Cascade Caverns
14. Caverns of Sonora
15. The Cave-Without-A-Name
16. Inner Space Caverns

17. Longhorn Cavern State Park
18. Natural Bridge Caverns
19. Wonder Cave

Points of Interest
20. Alibates Flint Quarries National Monument

ADDRESS:
P.O. Box 35
Mason, TX 76856
(915) 347-5413
(915) 347-5713 Nu-Way Grocery

DIRECTIONS:
Pick up keys and pay fees at the Nu-Way Grocery on the northwest corner of the square in Mason. To get to the mine take U.S. Highway 87 north. From the Mason Courthouse it is one and one-fourth miles to a blinking yellow light. Turn left at the light onto U.S. Highway 377/State Highway 29. Continue one and four-tenths miles to the fork in the road with a roadside park in the middle. Keep right (toward Menard) another half a mile.

SEASON:
Open year-round
(except October to December during hunting season)

HOURS:
Daylight

COST:
$15 per person per day—Fee
$5—Fee for camping in primitive sites
$10 per day—Fee for hookups to water and electricity with use of showers

WHAT TO BRING:
You will need a pick and shovel, spray bottle of water, container with a lid and a 1/4-inch mesh wire sifting screen.

INFORMATION:
Mason County is known for its topaz, which can be found in a range of colors including clear brown, yellow and sky blue. Searching for topaz is ideal after a few days of rain. Rain softens the ground and shows off the topaz. The mine will let you hunt all day, and keep all the stones you find. The terrain is rocky with little shade.

No reservations are needed. Pay fees and pick up the keys at the Nu-Way Grocery on the northwest corner of the square in Mason. The Loefflers also have the keys to the Garner Seaquist Ranch. The Loefflers live in the white house on the right side of the road in Grit, near this mine and the Wayne Hofmann Ranch.

ADDRESS:
Lake McClellan Recreation Area
c/o Texas Parks and Wildlife
4200 Smith School Road
Austin, TX 78744
(580) 497-2143 Forest Service
(806) 779-2092 Campground

DIRECTIONS:
Go three miles north of Interstate Highway 40. Get off at Exit 128. You can also go south from Pampa on State Highway 70 to FM 2477.

SEASON:
Open year-round

HOURS:
Park opens at 8:00 a.m.

COST:
$5–Fee per vehicle
$5–Fee per boat
$10–Fee for RV hookups per day
$3–Fee to obtain a collecting permit
For more information call the marina at (806) 633-4420

WHAT TO BRING:
Rock hammer, pick, eye protection, sun screen, shovel and gloves are recommended.

INFORMATION:
This lake was created and the surrounding area allowed to revert back to natural grasses and brush, which anchor the soil and help prevent erosion. The government purchased the land during the Great Depression, and eventually opened it to the public. Visitors will see flat terrain with some rolling hills.

The only quartz quarry in this part of the country is located near the reservoir.

Facilities include: picnicking, camping, fishing and boating. Some motorcycle trails are also available. There is a concession stand and grocery store on premises. Rock collectors can obtain a collecting permit and pay their collecting fee of $3 at the concession stand. Colorful flint can be found on the lakeshore. Good concentrations of flint are found throughout the park, especially along the creek banks. If you collect below the dam, be sure to check with the office to see if water is scheduled to be released during your visit.

The park has some interesting year-round residents including a prairie dog town on the north end of the lake.

ADDRESS:
Reservoir Controlling Authority
Mackenzie Municipal Water Authority
141 South Mackenzie Drive
Silverton, TX 79257
(806) 633-4318
(806) 633-4335 marina
questions@lakemackenzie.com
http://www.lakemackenzie.com/

DIRECTIONS:
Located east of Tulia, (located fifty miles south of Amarillo along U.S. Highway 87). Take State Highway 86 for twenty-three miles then turn left onto State Highway 207. At that point drive about six and two-tenths miles to the Lake Mackenzie Reservoir.

SEASON:
Open year-round

HOURS:
The reservoir opens at 9:00 a.m.

COST:
$3—Fee for park admission per day
Additional charge for camping

WHAT TO BRING:
Collecting bucket, rock hammer, pick and gloves.

INFORMATION:
Petrified palm wood, barite—desert rose, selenite crystals, small fossils and a variety of agates can be found north of Lake Mackenzie. The hills north of the lake and the lakeshore are potential collecting sites. Selenite sheets are easiest to find as they often stick out of the ground. Fossilized sharks teeth and fossilized bone are also found here.

You can walk the shore, boat to secret places pedestrian collectors can't reach, or scamper up the hills on the north to find your treasures.

Before doing any collecting, please be sure to obtain a use permit and ask about which areas are public and private.

ADDRESS:
Sam Rayburn Project Office
Pt. 3
Box 486
Jasper, TX 75951
(409) 384-5716
http://www.swf-wc.usace.army/mil/samray

DIRECTIONS:
To get to this site from Zavalla in eastern Texas, (about thirty-two miles northwest of Jasper along State Highway 63 or nineteen miles southeast of Lufkin along U.S. Highway 69) take State Highway 63 east about five miles to Farm Road 2743. From here, drive about four miles to the junction of Farm Road 3373. Route 3373 will take visitors to Brock's Landing or continue on Route 2743 to the Caney Creek Recreation Area.

SEASON:
Open year-round

HOURS:
8:00 a.m. to 4:30 p.m.–Monday to Friday
(reservoir office hours)

COST:
$3–Fee for day use
$6–Fee for camping

WHAT TO BRING:
No special tools are needed. Bring a bucket, sun screen, a hat, ohhh–and a boat if you have one.

INFORMATION:
Both Caney Creek Recreation and Brock's Landing are good places to search. If you have a boat, Caney Creek has a boat launch ramp, store and campsites. Fishing is a popular recreation here and the variety of fish includes: largemouth bass, crappie, catfish, striped bass and white bass. Having a boat allows you to reach sites not easily accessed by those approaching by land, and increases your chances of finding nice material.

The petrified wood found here is usually gray or brown and polishes well.

Some of the banks are steep, so searchers need to be careful of their footing and watch children closely.

ADDRESS:
Stillwell Ranch Store & RV Park
c/o Stillwell Store
H.C. 65, Box 430
Alpine, TX 79830
(436) 376-2244
stillwell@stillwellstore.com
http://www.freeranger.com/stillwell/

DIRECTIONS:
Located North of Big Ben National Park. From Marathon take U.S. Highway 385 south. After thirty-nine miles take a left onto Ranch Road (Route 2627) and drive six and four-tenths miles south to the entrance of the Stillwell Ranch.

SEASON: Open year-round
(but boy is it hot for collecting in the summer!)

HOURS:
Until you are tuckered out

COST:
There is a nominal rock collecting fee
$17.50–Fee for a full-hookup per night

WHAT TO BRING:
Collecting buckets, rock hammer, pick, chisel and eye protection.

INFORMATION:
A working cattle ranch of immense proportions, the Stillwell Ranch caters to rockhounds. This ranch, store and RV park have much to offer. For a nominal fee you gain access to the ranch and a remarkable variety of collecting sites and specimens including: petrified wood, beautiful flint, agates and jaspers in a variety of colors and fine quality picture rock that is highly prized.

A range of camping facilities from primitive to full-hookup is available along with gas, a laundry room, restrooms, a bathhouse and a general store. Pets are permitted.

ADDRESS:
Wesley Loeffler
4890 West State Highway 29
Mason, TX 76856
(915) 347-6415
http://geology.uprm.edu/Morelock/29Mas.htm

DIRECTIONS:
Take U.S. Highway 87 north from Mason Courthouse one and one-fourth miles to a blinking yellow light. Turn left at the light onto U.S. Highway 377/State Highway 29. Continue one and four-tenths miles to the fork in the road with a roadside park in the middle. Keep right (toward Menard) another half a mile. The Loefflers live in the white house (the Old Grit Store) on the right side of the road in Grit, Texas.

SEASON:
Open January through September
(October to December is hunting season)

HOURS:
Daylight

COST:
$10 per person per day–Children ages 10 to Adult
$5–Children ages 6 to 10
Free–Children ages 5 and under

WHAT TO BRING:
Bring standard mining equipment, a spray bottle of water, a container with a lid and a 1/4-inch mesh wire sifting screen.

INFORMATION:
Mason County is known for its topaz in colors ranging from clear brown to yellow to sky blue. Searching for topaz is ideal after a few days of rain. Rain softens the ground and shows off the topaz. The mine will let you hunt all day, and keep all the stones you find. The terrain is rocky with little shade.

The town of Mason has many shops that sell topaz and topaz jewelry, as well as guided topaz tours. Other area attractions include the Eckert James River Bat Cave with a large colony of Mexican free-tailed bats.

ADDRESS:
HC 65 Box 40
Terlingua Route
Alpine, TX 79830-9717
(432) 364-2271
http://www.woodwardranch.net/

DIRECTIONS:
Woodward Ranch is located sixteen and three-tenths miles south of Alpine on State Highway 118. At the sign turn right and follow the dirt road approximately two miles to the fork, then turn left and look for the rock shop.

SEASON:
Open year-round

HOURS:
Call for a reservation

COST:
Woodward Ranch:
$2 per person—Fee for collecting
Free—Fee for children 6 and under
Pay by what you decide to keep. Cost varies depending on the material you collect. Agate is sold by the pound, labradorite by the gram and opal by the piece.

Bird Mine:
$15—Fee for collecting

WHAT TO BRING:
Rock hammer, pick, collecting buckets and any other rock collecting equipment you use.

INFORMATION:
This cattle ranch is open to rockhounds. The variety of rocks and minerals found at Woodward Ranch is boggling, including agates of all varieties (moss, plume, banded and picture), geodes, amethyst, opal, fluorescent calcite and labradorite to name a few.

Though the ranch welcomes visitors year-round, the most pleasant seasons for searching are late fall and early spring when the weather is mild.

From Woodward Ranch you can receive directions and access to the other two collecting sites, the Bird Mine and Needle Peak.

Bird Mine contains minerals including wulfenite, hematite and galena, to name a few. At Needle Peak, collectors find florescent calcite and mercury ore in a variety of bright colors, carnelian and many lovely agate varieties.

If you don't have time to find the rocks yourself there is a great variety of specimens for sale at the rock shop.

Camping sites are available and for RVs, there are full-hookups, showers and restrooms. Rugged areas with no hookups are also available.

MUSEUMS

Site 8.

Centennial Museum & Chihuahuan Desert Gardens

   University of Texas at El Paso
   El Paso, TX 79968-0533
   (915) 747-5565
   http://museum.utep.edu/default.htm
   • Enjoy the Geology gallery's mineralogical specimens and discover the paleontology of the surrounding areas.

Site 9.

Museum of Nature & Science Dallas, Texas

   3535 Grand Avenue in Fair Park
   Dallas, TX 75210
   (214) 428-5555
   http://www.natureandscience.org.
   • The collection of rocks and minerals consists of over two thousand five hundred specimens including all major groups, but with an emphasis on silicates. There are also exhibits on Texas dinosaurs and Ice Age fossils.

Site 10.

Fort Worth Museum of Science and History

   1501 Montgomery Street
   Fort Worth, TX 76107
   (817) 255-9300 or (888) 255-9300
   http://www.fwmuseum.org/
   • This museum has several exhibits on fossils and dinosaurs.

Site 11.

Mayborn Museum Complex

   1300 S. University Parks
   Waco, TX 76706
   (254) 710-1100
   http://www.baylor.edu/mayborn
   • This is the oldest continuously operating museum in Texas and contains a collection of rocks and minerals, regional flora and fauna, and fossils.

Site 12.

Texas Natural Science Center

   Texas Memorial Museum
   2400 Trinity Street
   Austin, TX 78705
   (512) 471-1604
   http://www.utexas.edu/tmm
   • This museum has an extensive collection of rocks, minerals and crystals and an exhibit entitled "Waltz Across Time," which explores geologic time as recorded in the rocks of Texas.

Caves

Site 13.
Cascade Caverns

226 Cascade Caverns Road
Boerne, TX 78015
(830) 755-8080
http://www.cascadecaverns.com/
• This tour is about one hour, and takes visitors through well-lit walking trails. This cave has active formations and includes a one hundred-foot waterfall that goes dry seasonally. Camping is available on site.

Site 14
Caverns of Sonora

Interstate Highway 10
Exit 392
Sonora, TX 76950
(325) 387-3105
http://www.cavernsofsonora.com/
• This cave has an astonishing ninety percent of its formations still growing. Thirty-minute guided tours take visitors past the best of the cave's features.

Site 15
The Cave-Without-A-Name

325 Kreutzberg Road
Boerne, TX 78006
(930) 537-4212
http://www.cavewithoutaname.com/
• This natural, living cave has formations still growing and is filled with spectacular formations of stalactites, stalagmites, soda straws, drapery and flowstone and includes six major chambers. Walking trails are easy and well lit.

Site 16
Inner Space Caverns

P.O. Box 451
Georgetown, TX 78627
(512) 931-2283
• http://www.innerspace.com
This cave offers guided tours along well-lit walkways. Visitors will see beautiful limestone flowstone and underground formations. After your tour, visitors can pan for gold or gemstones.

Site 17
Longhorn Cavern State Park

P.O. Box 732
Burnet, TX 78611
(877) 441-2283
http://www.longhorncaverns.com
• Water and time created this lovely limestone cave. Fossil remains reveal that Ice Age animals once lived here. Comanche Indians also used the cavern over four hundred years ago. More recently this cavern was a Confederate stronghold where gunpowder was secretly made and stored during the Civil War.

Site 18
Natural Bridge Caverns
26495 Natural Bridge Cavern Road
Natural Bridge Caverns, TX 78266
(210) 651-6101
http://www.naturalbridgecaverns.com
• The entrance to this cave was once the largest chamber in the cave system, but erosion collapsed the rock. Now it is a sinkhole and it created a sixty-foot natural bridge which gives the cavern its name. The cavern contains two special chambers, the Bear Pit and Pluto's Anteroom. The Bear Pit gains its name from an eight thousand-year-old jawbone of a black bear found here. Pluto's Anteroom is the largest room and contains unique limestone formations.

Site 19
Wonder Cave
Wonder World Park
P.O. Box 1369
San Marcos, TX 78666
(512) 392-3760
http://www.wonderworldpark.com/
• This cave was not formed by water, and is not growing. It formed thirty million years ago during a great earthquake. The cave was discovered when a pioneer farmer drilled for water and lost his drill as it fell into an underground chamber. Visitors descend by elevator and view the magnitude of this prehistoric earthquake.

POINTS OF INTEREST

Site 20.
Alibates Flint Quarries National Monument
419 E. Broadway
Fritch, TX 79036
(806) 857-3151
http://www.nps.gov/alfl/
• Ancient people used this areas unusual rainbow colored flint to create tools strong enough to kill buffalo and woolly mammoths. Spear points and arrowheads are among the many artifacts recovered here.

The Golden Spike meets the Atomic Age.

There is evidence that Native Americans, Spaniards and Mexicans were the first miners in Utah. The influx of Mormon settlers changed this only temporarily. Though Brigham Young, the church's leader and Utah's first governor, disapproved of mining, he could not staunch the tide. At first he only encouraged mining the necessities for agriculture—lead for bullets, coal for heat and iron for tools. But he was eventually overwhelmed by "the evils of mining life." His nemesis, Colonel Patrick Connor, commander of the Third California Volunteers, was sent to Utah in 1862. He was sent to keep an eye on the Overland mail, but he found time to have his men scour the hills for precious metals, which he found. A determined anti-Mormon, he set about diminishing the Mormon Church's influence in Utah by making the discovery that was guaranteed to open the territory to non-Mormons. He sent word that precious metals abounded, and miners flooded in from California to search for gold and silver. Mining towns sprang up and life forever changed in Utah. The industry grew still larger when the transcontinental railroad was completed. In 1869, the Golden Spike was set in Promontory Summit, Utah. Mining now had an easy way to transport ore, metal and men around the country.

Utah did not confine their mining activities to copper, silver and gold. In 1889, the Inland Crystal Salt Company was formed. By the dawn of the next century, the industry of mining fell second only to agriculture in Utah. Silver mining was king but eventually abdicated to copper and coal mining.

Utah is famous for another mineral. Do you know what it is?

European settlers first mined this lesser mineral in 1871, but Native Americans had used it for centuries to make paints. The salts and oxides from this mineral were used as a colorant in ceramics, dyes and the manufacturing of glass. Added to steel, it increased the metal's tensile strength. In 1898, it was considered a wonder drug and added to baths salts, therapeutic muds and salves. During the World War I, this mineral illuminated watch faces and compasses. But it was not until the 1950s that the real financial boom occurred for this mineral, uranium, with the dawn of the atomic age.

Today, visitors will enjoy finding their own fossilized fish at either Lin Ottinger's Tour or U-Dig Fossils. Stop by one of Utah's museums to learn about dinosaurs, and this state's rich mining heritage.

Mining in Utah is not a historical footnote, but a continuing vital part in this state's economy. This industry continues today with lead, zinc, iron, silver, copper and gold. Digging is not limited to metals; uranium is still mined, as is limestone for mortar and red sandstone for building material. No one knows where or when the next bonanza will be, but whatever it is, it will certainly be found in Utah.

UTAH SITE MAP

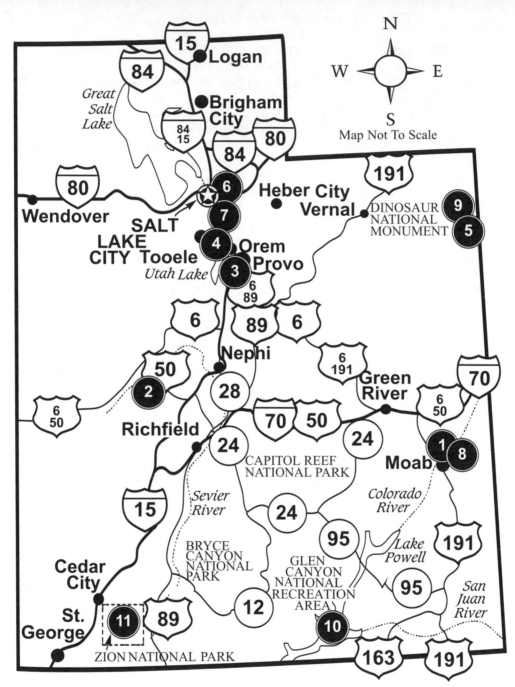

Diggings
1. Lin Ottinger's Tours
2. U-Dig Fossils

Museums
3. BYU Earth Science Museum
4. John Hutchings Museum of Natural History
5. Utah Field House of Natural History State Park Museum
6. Utah Museum of Natural History

Caves
7. Timpanogos Cave National Monument

Points of Interest
8. Arches National Park
9. Dinosaur National Monument
10. Natural Bridges National Monument
11. Zion National Park

ADDRESS:
Moab Rock Shop
600 North Main
Moab, UT 84532
(435) 259-7312

DIRECTIONS:
The Moab Rock Shop is located on U.S. Highway
191, which is Main Street in Moab.

SEASON:
Open year-round

HOURS:
9:00 a.m. to 8:00 p.m.–Season hours
9:00 a.m. to 5:00 p.m.–Winter hours

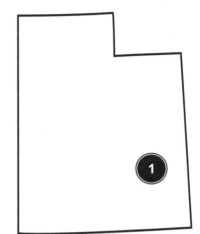

COST:
$129 per person per day–Fee which includes lunch
$75 per person per half-day–Fee

WHAT TO BRING:
All equipment is supplied by the outfitters, even your lunch and drinks.

INFORMATION:
   Lin Ottinger's Tours offer a wide variety of scenic tours and hiking. Photographer, geologist and naturalist, Lin Ottinger is known as the dinosaur man. Brigham Young University even named a dinosaur after him, Iguanodon ottingerei.
   The area around Moab, Utah is extraordinary with deep canyons, towering red cliffs, buttes and balanced rock and natural stone arches all carved by wind and time. Tours for fossils and rock hunting can be planned to fit your desires. Collecting is permitted on the tours except in the national parks. Lin Ottinger can assist you in shipping your specimens. Some fossils found on the tours include trilobites, coral, clams and petrified wood.
   Mr. Ottinger invites you to come early and browse around the museum and enjoy the collection of dinosaur bones, fossils, rare minerals and gemstones from the Moab area. Call to make reservations.

U-DIG FOSSILS

TRILOBITES & OTHER FOSSILS

SITE 2   *UTAH*

MAILING ADDRESS:
U-Dig Fossils
P.O. Box 1113
Delta, UT 84624
STREET ADDRESS:
350 East 300 South
Delta, UT 84624
(435) 864-3638
udig@xmission.com
http://www.u-digfossils.com

DIRECTIONS:
Drive thirty-two miles from Delta on U.S. Highways 6/50 south. At the Long Ridge Reservoir sign, travel twenty miles down a well-maintained gravel road to reach the mine. According to the owners, any type of vehicle can travel this road.

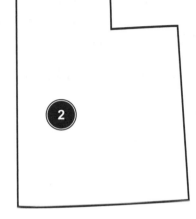

SEASON:
April 15 through October 15

HOURS:
9:00 a.m. to 6:00 p.m.–Monday to Saturday, closed Sunday

COST:
$20 per person–Fee for adults for two hours
$12–Fee for children ages 7 to 16 for two hours
$30 per person–Fee for adults for four hours
$20–Fee for children ages 7 to 16 for four hours
$50 per person–Fee for adults for eight hours
$30–Fee for children ages 7 to 16 for eight hours
Groups larger than ten are asked to call in advance

WHAT TO BRING:
Tools are provided. You will be provided with a hammer and buckets. Visitors should bring garden gloves or other work gloves, safety glasses, and warm clothing is suggested in case the weather changes. Bring plenty to drink and a lunch if you plan to stay the full four hours.

INFORMATION:
Trilobites are an extinct marine animal similar to a crab. They were the first known invertebrate life on earth. Their fossil remains are five hundred fifty million years old.

The mine site was once the ocean floor. The trilobites are now found in limestone shale. Visitors will be provided with a hammer. The shale can be easily split to search. Rock has been extracted or loosened for your convenience. If you prefer to dig your own unassisted, larger tools are available.

The average visitor finds ten to fifteen trilobites in a four-hour period. If you are having difficulty, assistance is available from U-DIG personnel. Toilet facilities are available.

MUSEUMS

Site 3.
BYU Earth Science Museum
1683 North Canyon Road
Provo UT 84602
(801) 422-3680
http://cpms.byu.edu/ESM/
• This university museum claims to have one of the world's best Jurassic dinosaur bone collections, including two fully mounted skeletons of Camptosaurus and Allosaurus, a dinosaur egg, and a window view of the preparation lab where fossils are prepared.

Site 4.
John Hutchings Museum of Natural History
55 North Center
Lehi, UT 84043
(801) 768 7180
http://www.hutchingsmuseum.org/
• Mormon pioneer heritage, minerals, fossils and Native American cultural artifacts are displayed here.

Site 5.
Utah Field House of Natural History State Park Museum
496 East Main Street
Vernal, UT 84078
(435) 789-3799
http://www.stateparks.utah.gov/park/index.php?id=UFSP
• This museum features reproductions of fossil dinosaurs, exhibits of fluorescent minerals and rocks and minerals of this region. Outside visit the dinosaur garden with seventeen life-sized prehistoric animals located along the garden paths.

Site 6.
Utah Museum of Natural History
1390 East Presidents Circle, University of Utah
Salt Lake City, UT 84112-0050
(801) 581-6927
http://www.umnh.utah.edu/
• This museum includes a collection of invertebrate and vertebrate fossils (over twenty-four thousand total), rocks and minerals including the Inglesby and Buranek Collections.

CAVES

Site 7.
Timpanogos Cave National Monument
Rural Route 3
Box 200
American Fork, UT 84003
(801) 756-5239
http://www.nps.gov/tica/index.htm
• Three spectacular caverns contain unique formations and color variations. The entrance to this cave requires an uphill hike of one thousand feet and provides visitors with incredible views of American Fork Canyon before heading underground.

POINTS OF INTEREST

Site 8.
Arches National Park
P.O. Box 907
Moab, UT 84532
(435) 719-2299
http://www.nps.gov/arch/index.htm
• Over two thousand spectacular sandstone arches carved by wind are located here, more than any other place on earth.

Site 9.
Dinosaur National Monument
4545 E. Highway 40
Dinosaur, CO 81610-9724
(435) 781-7700 or (970) 374-3000
http://www.nps.gov/dino/
• This monument sits on the Colorado-Utah border. The visitor's center in Vernal, Utah examines how scientists study fossils to uncover secrets of the past. The visitor center is closed indefinitely, check with the park for reopening date.

Site 10.
Natural Bridges National Monument
HC-60 Box 1
Lake Powell, UT 84533-0101
(435) 692-1234
http://www.nps.gov/nabr/
• Three colossal bridges formed by streams racing down ancient canyons now bear witness to the power of erosion.

Site 11.
Zion National Park
P.O. Box 168
Springdale, UT 84767
(435) 772-3256
http://www.nps.gov/zion/
• Zion has a majesty and sacred feeling. The red sandstone formations, once covered by a sea, now rise to the blue sky. Occasional fossilized fish and seashells prove what seems doubtful, that this park was once on the bottom of an ocean. One of the most spectacular places in the park is "the Narrows," where a stream cuts a narrow canyon between steeply rising cliffs. Rock enthusiasts will love this park.

Seattle–gateway to the Klondike.

Miners unsuccessful in California fanned north searching for better claims. Gold was discovered in Okanogan in the 1860s. Many of the seekers were emigrants who suffered greatly under California's unfair mining laws, which excluded them from any chance at a valuable claim. Some of these were Chinese miners who searched along the Columbia River sandbars and up tributaries. These men built the "China Ditch" in the 1860s, which was constructed to carry water three miles up the Methow River and allow them to sluice for gold. How much gold they recovered is not known, but hopefully enough to justify the effort of the ditch construction. Later settlers used this ditch to irrigate their crops and apple orchards.

Throughout the 1860s and to the 1880s, miners worked small claims in what is now Washington State. Copper was found along with silver, coal, magnesium, lead and zinc. The amount of gold recovered seemed to make the effort worthwhile, though no huge strikes were ever recorded. The effort of search and recovery succeeded in bringing many settlers north to this area. Prospectors searched for gold and found coal. Coal mining began in 1886 in the town of Roslyn by the Northern Pacific Coal Company.

Towns and villages became established, but people struggled to make ends meet. A nationwide depression gripped the country. The port city of Seattle was on the long downward slide of the back end of the boom and bust economy. The city could not meet its payroll and many men were without work. All that changed on July 17, 1897 when the steamer *Portland* arrived in the harbor carrying seventy men and over a ton of gold.

The city went crazy. Thousands of men immediately left for the Klondike goldfields. Some merchants with great foresight stayed behind to outfit "grubstakers" with supplies, and by doing so, became wealthy and powerful men. The news flashed over telegraph wires and soon the world beat a path to Seattle's door. Shipping merchants struggled to increase the size of their fleet to meet demand for passages north.

Miners struggling with questionable claims throughout the state journeyed north to the Klondike. Urban immigrants unable to find work made the arduous trip following their own gullibility and the chance at quick riches.

Unscrupulous men sold bogus maps and inferior supplies. Seattle's empty factories were hastily converted to card halls and saloons. As prospective miners waited for passage north, there was no shortage of ways to lose their stakes before the journey ever started. For good or bad, Seattle was now on the map. Klondike Gold Rush National Historic Park preserves this significant area of Seattle for guests to explore.

Travelers interested in more current events might like to visit Burke Museum of Natural History to learn about earthquakes, or witness the site of the most recent volcanic eruptions in the continental United States at the Mount Saint Helens National Volcanic Monument.

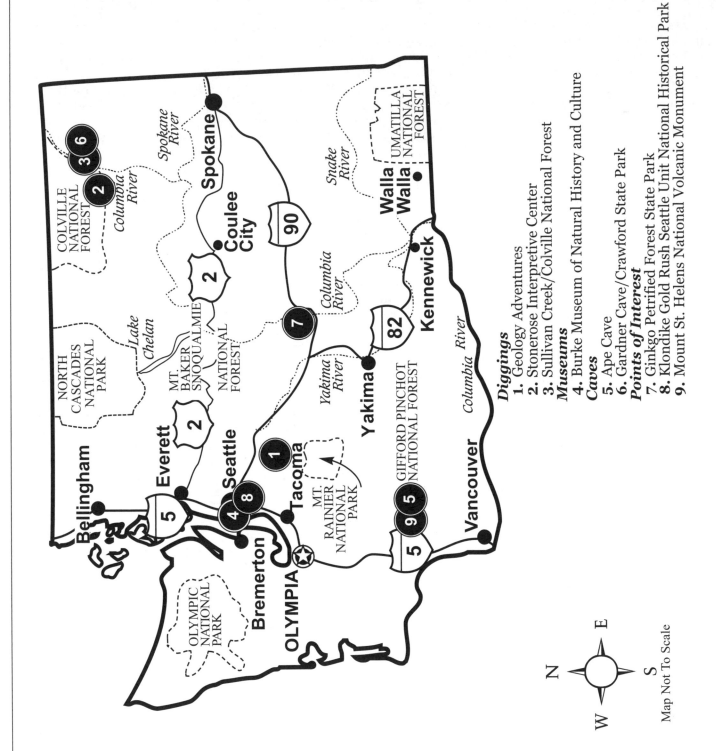

Diggings
1. Geology Adventures
2. Stonerose Interpretive Center
3. Sullivan Creek/Colville National Forest

Museums
4. Burke Museum of Natural History and Culture

Caves
5. Ape Cave
6. Gardner Cave/Crawford State Park

Points of Interest
7. Ginkgo Petrified Forest State Park
8. Klondike Gold Rush Seattle Unit National Historical Park
9. Mount St. Helens National Volcanic Monument

N
E
W
S

Map Not To Scale

ADDRESS:
Geology Adventures
P.O. Box 809
Ravensdale, WA 98051
(425) 413-1122
bob@geologyadventures.com
www.geologyadventures.com/
(When calling or e-mailing, be patient. They are
sometimes in the field for weeks at a time.)

DIRECTIONS:
You must call Geology Adventures because they run
field trips to different locations.

SEASON:
Open year-round

HOURS:
Daylight hours vary with each trip (two to four hours average, depending on the sight–some
trips take the entire day)

COST:
Varies–Fee (depends on the site and the type of minerals or fossils you are seeking–prices start
at $18)

WHAT TO BRING:
Call Geology Adventures for a complete list of what to bring. They supply you with all the tools
you need to search.

INFORMATION:
   Geology Adventures plans school trips, international trips and collector trips. They even do
children's birthday parties. They specialize in family trips.
   Want to try something really different? How about an evening field trip to search for
fluorescent minerals. They glow beneath the ultraviolet light provided for you.
   The Crystal Kid trip is located in a beautiful vista. Here you can find quartz crystals and five
other minerals.
   Geology Adventures will take you to find amber in three colors: yellow, orange and blue. Try
their website for more specifics or call for details on trips pending. You need to make reservations
seven days ahead of the trip date to confirm your field trip. Some trips fill quickly. The owner,
Bob Jackson, who describes himself as a fossil, collects specimens for museums and has
unearthed some wonderful collecting localities.

ADDRESS:
Stonerose Interpretive Center
P.O. Box 987
Republic, WA 99166
(509) 775-2295
srfossils@rcabletv.com
http://www.stonerosefossil.org

DIRECTIONS:
The Stonerose Interpretive Center is located in northeastern Washington State, in the town of Republic. Take Highway 20 to Republic. The center is at 15-1 North Kean Street on the corner of Kean Street and Highway 20 West, across from the park in Republic.

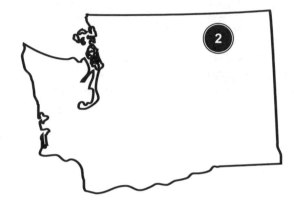

SEASON:
May to October

HOURS:
Wednesday through Sunday, call for hours

COST:
$5 per adult–Fee for admission
$3 per senior & children over 6 years of age–Fee for admission
Free children under 6 years of age

WHAT TO BRING:
Bring your own tools, including a cold chisel and hammer. Tools are available for rent at the center.

INFORMATION:
Visitors may want to begin in the Stonerose Interpretive Center, where they can see examples of local fossils and purchase their admission to hunt at the Stonerose Boot Hill Fossil Site.

All finds must be shown to the curator or staff personnel, and you may take home three fossil pieces per person, per day. The Interpretive Center reserves the right to retain any fossil that has scientific value or significance for their collection.

ADDRESS:
Sullivan Lake Ranger District
12641 Sullivan Lake Road
Metaline Falls, WA 99153
(509) 446-7500
http://www.fs.fed.us/r6/colville/index.html

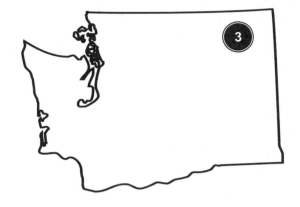

DIRECTIONS:
Metaline Falls is approximately ninety miles north of Spokane. From Metaline Falls, take Sullivan Lake Road eight miles to the prospecting area on Sullivan Creek. The creek is within the Sullivan Lake Ranger District in the Colville National Forest. Begin at the Sullivan Creek ranger station for directions and information on the creek.

SEASON:
Open year-round

HOURS:
Daylight

COST:
Free

WHAT TO BRING:
Bring standard mining and gold mining equipment. Sluice boxes and dredges (two and one half-inch to four-inch dredges, depending on area) are permitted. Bring your own food, camping supplies and drinking water. This is a national forest and camping is primitive.

INFORMATION:
There are two areas or reaches to be prospected and gold of all sizes can be found here. The upper reach extends from the creek's source to its junction with Outlet Creek near Sullivan Creek Ranger Station. This area is open for dredging and sluicing from July 1 to August 31. Dredges up to two and a half inches in diameter are permitted. The lower reach area is located between the junction of Outlet and Sullivan Creeks to Pend Oreille River, which is north of Metaline Falls. This area is open from June 1 to October 31 each year.

Dredges up to four inches in diameter are permitted in the lower reaches. Gold panning is permitted in both areas year-round. A permit is required to dredge. It can be obtained from the Washington State Department of Fisheries and Wildlife, Habitat Management, Olympia Headquarters Office, 600 North Capitol Way, Olympia, Washington 98501-1091. The phone number is (360) 902-2200.

MUSEUMS

Site 4.
Burke Museum of Natural History and Culture
University of Washington, Box 353010
Seattle, WA 98195
(206) 543-5590
http://www.washington.edu/burkemuseum/
• The geology division maintains a collection of fossils and minerals. Special exhibits include, "Life and Times of Washington State" is a hands on exhibit of the passage through time in geology and biology.

CAVES

Site 5.
Ape Cave
Mount St. Helens National Volcanic Monument
42218 NE Yale Bridge Road
Amboy, WA 98601
(360)-247-3900
http://www.fs.fed.us/gpnf/recreation/ape-cave/index.shtml
• The Boy Scout Troop known as the Mount Saint Helen Apes get credit for this cave's exploration and the name Ape Cave. The cave follows an existing streambed, which widened and deepened the channel. After the lava ceased the chambers filled with volcanic gasses that glazed and melted the rock walls and gave the cave its blue-black appearance. Encroaching mudflow later gave the lower cave the flat sandy floor. This cave formed by lava flow and consists of one main chamber and a few side channels.

Site 6.
Gardner Cave/Crawford State Park
General Delivery
Metaline Falls, WA 99153
(509) 446-4065
http://www.povn.com/byway/towns/Gardner%20Cave.html
• Gardner Cave slopes downward for over one-thousand feet and is the third longest limestone cave in Washington State. Metaline limestone formed from the shells of a long ago ocean. The mountains rose over seventy million years ago. Rainwater, carrying carbon dioxide, gradually seeped into the cracks in the limestone eating away the stone bit by bit until the caverns formed.

POINTS OF INTEREST

Site 7.
Ginkgo Petrified Forest State Park
Vantage, WA 98950
(509) 856-2700
http://www.parks.wa.gov/parkpage.asp?selectedpark=Ginkgo+Petrified+Forest%2FWanapumt+Recreational+Area
• This petrified forest formed when an ancient volcano erupted and covered the surrounding trees with thick layers of ash. This means that petrified material does not lie on the surface, but must be excavated with heavy equipment. The area was discovered only in the 1930s during a road construction project. The tree for which the park is named no longer grows in the wild. The park features activities including hiking, camping, water skiing and interpretive appreciation.

Site 8.
Klondike Gold Rush Seattle Unit National Historical Park
319 Second Avenue South
Seattle, WA 98104
(206) 220-4240
http://www.nps.gov/klse/
• Pioneer Square is the historic departure place of many "stampeders" headed for the Alaskan gold fields.

Site 9.
Mount St. Helens National Volcanic Monument
42218 NE Yale Bridge Road
Amboy, WA 98601
(360) 449-7800
http://www.fs.fed.us/gpnf/mshnvm/
• On a Sunday morning in May of 1980, Mount Saint Helens erupted with the force of an earthquake measuring 5.1 on the Richter scale and collapsing the mountain in moments. The resulting avalanche of rock and ice toppled trees over an area of one hundred fifty miles and blanketed the area with volcanic ash. The eruption continued for nine hours. Two years later this area became a National Monument. Visitors to the park can take part in interpretative walks, presentations and travel to the east, south and west sides of the mountain. The visitor's centers at Amboy, Castle Rock, Johnston Ridge and Coldwater Ridge provide education on the volcano, answer questions and offer many special programs.

The Cowboy State or the Mining State?

Wyoming has proved rich beyond all imagination. The riches were not apparent at first, many crossed above them unknowing–but they were there. When Wyoming was obtained as part of the Louisiana Purchase of 1803, the nation did not realize the magnitude of the bargain we made.

The Cowboy State has a long history of mining and may be misnamed. Gold prospectors began the biggest industry in Wyoming unknowingly, as they searched for gold and discovered it at South Pass. This was no major rush, but the birth of Wyoming mining had arrived. A few men found gold–but coal in Carbon County was the real gold mine.

Coal mining began in 1868. By 1869 the area had nine thousand employees involved in coal production. The transcontinental railroad's completion made it possible for quick migration. Unemployed Chinese laborers flooded into Rock Springs to work in the coal mine. At first, Chinese and Caucasian miners worked side by side, but when the Chinese laborer refused to join a strike for higher wages, unrest mounted. When local mine owners replaced the Caucasian workers with Chinese miners, racial tension exploded. On September 2, 1865, a well-armed mob of angry, unemployed Caucasians marched en masse toward the Chinese camp, blocked all the escape routes and fired on the unarmed men. The camp was burned to the ground; Chinese miners fled in terror and were shot while trying to escape. The bodies of the dead and wounded were thrown into the flames. Twenty-eight Chinese were killed and fifteen wounded. Over five hundred escaped because conductors on the nearby railroad rescued them. Four days later federal troops escorted the survivors back to work. The viciousness and ferocity of the attack prompted Chinese diplomats to protest, and the federal government to compensate the survivors of the massacre.

Coal production was halted a mere four days and has been going strong ever since. In 1920, mine shafts were abandoned in favor of surface mines. Currently coal is the second largest mining industry in Wyoming behind oil and natural gas. This is officially called drilling, but in any case, the oil and natural gas industry are number one industries here. The value of natural gas was not immediately apparent. In earlier days the lighter gas, which sits on top of oil reserves was burned off. Oil drilling may be a relatively recent development in America, but the presence of oil in Wyoming was well documented. Native Americans used oil as a healing salve. Early settlers used the oil found on the surface to grease harnesses, fuel lanterns and when mixed with flour, the oil made a good axle grease.

Another major mining industry is trona, raking third in Wyoming behind oil/natural gas and coal. Trona, known as soda ash in its refined form, is used in many manufacturing processes; most prominent is the production of glass and laundry soap. Wyoming leads the world in trona production. Trona, oil and coal are not as glamorous as gold, but they turn out to be much more profitable.

In 1949 "yellow cake" mining began. This is a common term for uranium and was very lucrative. Other substances mined include, copper, bentonite and shale.

If you are interested in more dramatic discoveries consider dinosaurs. Wyoming has got them and has had them for years. In 1888, the fossil of a Triceratops skull was discovered in this state. Since then many more prehistoric finds have been unearthed. Scientists from all over the world come to Wyoming to study fossils. They are not the only ones able to unearth fascinating finds. There are many sites open to the public for fossil digging. Individuals can find fossilized fish and other small sea creatures or join an expedition for larger quarry. Consider the mines and digging sites listed in Wyoming for more information on where you can find fossils, opals, garnets and of course–gold.

Mining is Wyoming's economy. This state is the top coal producers in the world, and has the largest reserve of trona. Wyoming might consider exchanging those cowboy hats for hard hats and changing their license plate to read, "The Mining State."

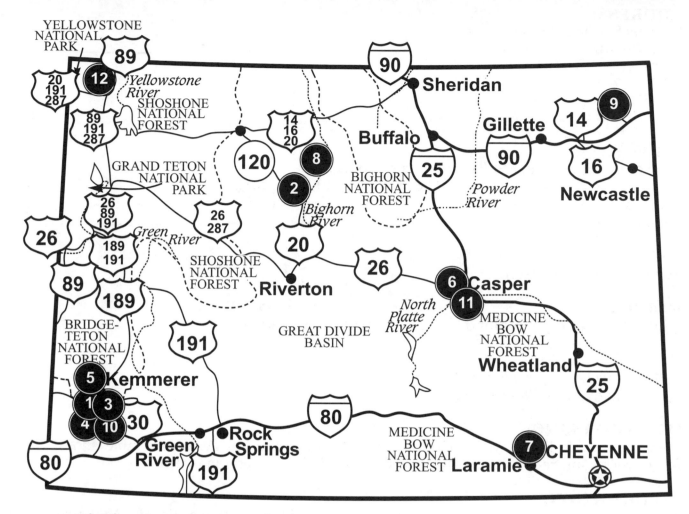

Diggings

1. Severns Studio & Fossil Company
2. The Wyoming Dinosaur Center
3. Tynsky's Fossil Fish Tours
4. Ulrich's Fossil Gallery
5. Warfield Fossil Quarries

Museums

6. Tate Geological Museum at Casper College
7. University of Wyoming Geological Museum
8. Washakie Museum of History, Art & Earth Sciences

Points of Interest

9. Devils Tower National Monument
10. Fossil Butte National Monument
11. Independence Rock State Historic Site
12. Yellowstone National Park

Map Not To Scale

ADDRESS:
Severns Studio & Fossil Quarry
P.O. Box 1347
Kemmerer, WY 83101
(307) 877-9402
FOSSIL@hughes.net
http://www.hamsfork.net/~fossil/

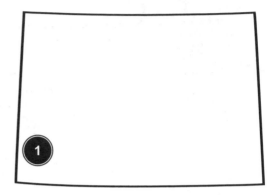

DIRECTIONS:
The Severns Studio and Fossil Quarry is approximately six miles west of Kemmerer, off U.S. Highway 30, Loma Vista Drive, and just east of Fossil Butte National Monument.

SEASON:
June 1 through August 31

HOURS:
8:30 a.m. to 4:00 p.m.–Monday to Friday (with a reservation)

COST:
$55 per five hours per digger–Adults
$35 per five hours–Children ages 7 to 18

WHAT TO BRING:
Wear adjustable light layered clothing, a hat, gloves and sturdy, comfortable shoes. Don't forget your sunscreen, camera and safety glasses. Bring something to drink.

INFORMATION:
This area resembled the Gulf Coast forty to sixty million years ago (Eocene Age). Crocodiles and alligators swam in the lakes and palm trees swayed. The fish, reptiles and mammals lived and died, eventually falling to the lake bottom and become fossils. The uplifting of the Rocky Mountains brought this shale and fossil treasure trove to the surface.

Severns Studio offers fossil hunting to you. All diggers must be at the transport site at 8:30 a.m. The number of diggers permitted is limited, so make a reservation. Your fee includes all the tools necessary, transportation to the dig site, and helpful instructions from a staff member. Proper collecting techniques will be covered before you begin. The amount of fossils you find will depend on how hard you work and how lucky you are. The owners compare fossil hunting to fishing. You'll get fossils, but some people do better than others.

You can keep all you find of common fish fossils, and some types of plants and insects. Rare specimens are the property of Severns Studio. You have about five hours to collect. Restroom facilities, water and a phone are available for use by visitors. Once you leave the dig site you can visit Severns Studio where fossils, jewelry, local art and more is offered for sale.

ADDRESS:
110 Carter Ranch Road/P.O. Box 868
Thermopolis, WY 82443
(800)455-DINO or (307)864-2997
wdinoc@wyodino.org
http://www.wyodino.org

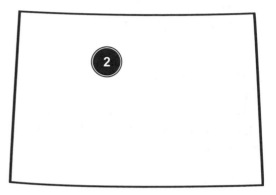

DIRECTIONS:
The Wyoming Dinosaur Center is located between Cody and Rock Springs off State Highway 20 in Thermopolis. From U.S. Highway 20 in Thermopolis take State Highway 120 north to Broadway. Drive past the Hot Springs Historic Museum and Town Hall. The road turns sharply right. Then turn left onto East Warren Street and Right onto Carter Ranch Road. The center is located on Carter Ranch Road.

SEASON:
Open year-round

HOURS:
8:00 a.m. to 6:00 p.m.–Monday to Sunday.
(Shuttle to the dig site leaves at 9:00 a.m. Last shuttle leaves the digs at 4:00 p.m.)
10:00 a.m. to 5:00 p.m.–September 15 to May 15
Winter season–Weather permitting (dig site open on a limited basis)

COST:
$8–Adult museum admission ($4.50–Fee for all others)
$12.50–Adult fee for dig site tour ($8.75–Fee for all others)
$16.50–Fee for combination dig site and museum tour ($10.75–Fee for all others)
$150 per day–Fee for Dig-For-A-Day program/$250 per day–Fee for a family of four

WHAT TO BRING:
Bring your own gear, hat, sunscreen and extra to drink if you plan on the Dig-For-A-Day program. Tools and lunch are provided.

INFORMATION:
    This museum and dig sites makes for a unique trip. You can see fossils of all sorts. There are nineteen full-size mounted skeletons including eight dinosaurs here. But you came here to dig for fossils, so let's get to it.
    The dig site tours allow you to go to the field by shuttle to watch what actually goes on at a dinosaur quarry. This is fascinating, but if you want to actually dig you'll need to join the Dig-For-A-Day trip, a full-day excursion. This begins with a brief orientation at the Wyoming Dinosaur Center at 8:00 a.m. A bus will bring you to the dig site where you begin your work under the supervision of scientists. The day's activities includes fossil discovery, stabilization, excavation, quarry mapping and documentation. At midday a lunch will be provided and then back to work. The day concludes at 4:00 p.m. The fossils uncovered belong to the museum, but fossil reproductions and real fossils are for sale at the gift shop.

ADDRESS:
Tynsky's Fossil Fish Tours
716 JC Penny Drive
Kemmerer, WY 83101
(307) 877-6885

DIRECTIONS:
Call first to make a reservation. From Kemmerer drive twelve miles along the Cokeville Highway. Approximately one-fourth of a mile before the Fossil Butte on the left. Take County Road 331 to the ranch.

SEASON:
June 1 through the end of August

HOURS:
8:00 a.m. to 5:00 p.m. (with a reservation)
8:00 a.m. to 1:00 p.m.–Tours

COST:
$55 per person–Fee
You are allowed to keep ten of the fish that you find

WHAT TO BRING:
The mine supplies all the tools you need. Just bring your personal belongings, food and plenty to drink.

INFORMATION:
    Your tour will begin at Lewis's Ranch House. A guide will meet you at the ranch and take you to the quarry for a short lesson on fossil hunting. Then you have about two hours to dig. At the end of your tour you will choose the ten fish you would like to keep. You will not be allowed to keep anything rare such as turtle, stingray or bat fossils.
    The owner says his customers always find fossils, and you will not go home empty-handed.
    There is no food available at the site, so bring your own. There is no running water at the quarry, just a portable toilet. Camping is not permitted on site.

ADDRESS:
Fossil Station #308
Kemmerer, WY 83101-0308
(307) 877-6466
csu/rich@onewest.net
http://www.ulrichsfossilgallery.com/

DIRECTIONS:
The Ulrich's Fossil Gallery is located on U.S. Highway 30, ten miles west of Kemmerer.

SEASON:
Open June through Labor Day

HOURS:
9:00 a.m. to 12:00 p.m. daily

COST:
$75 per person per day–Fee

WHAT TO BRING:
The Ulrich's Fossil Gallery supplies you with all tools and equipment you need for excavating and transporting your finds. Bring a camera, snack and plenty to drink.

INFORMATION:
This is a great opportunity to excavate fish fossils with a professional. Reservations are required so the owners may set you up with a staff member as a guide and instructor. The quarry is located at seven thousand two hundred feet in elevation. The gallery suggests that you wear layers of clothes. It is cool in the morning, and hot towards late morning. Sunglasses are highly recommended to reduce the glare.

You will be working on an ancient lake bed. Excavating is done seven days a week, weather permitting, so please call ahead. You are given three hours to quarry your fossils. You keep all specimens except those that are rare and unusual as designated by the state of Wyoming. These include, but are not limited to, garfish, stingrays and all mammals.

The quarry will transport you to the digging site from the quarry and furnish you with tools and equipment. Trips depart from the gallery at 9:00 a.m., unless other arrangements are made. This is an educational trip for all.

ADDRESS:
2072 Muddy String Road
Thayne, WY 83127
(307) 883-2445
warfosq@silverstar.com
http://home.silverstar.com/warfieldfossils/

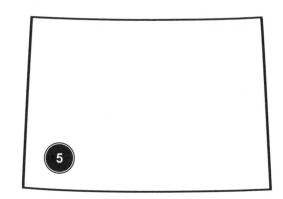

DIRECTIONS:
The Warfield Fossil Quarries are located north of
Kemmerer. From U.S. Highway 189 in Kemmerer, go
north to State Highway 233 and the turnoff is near the
Wyoming Highway Department building. From this
point, continue north until you find a fork in the road,
go right and continue on to BLM Road 4211. Take the
left fork onto this road and after passing four cattle
guards, continue one and one-half miles to another fork. Turn left and follow this road to the
quarry site. Visit their website to view a detailed map provided by the site.

SEASON:
Memorial Day through Labor Day

HOURS:
8:00 a.m. to 4:00 p.m.—Seven days a week. Call or write to make reservations. Reservations are
not needed for groups less than ten people.

COST:
$75 per person per day—Fee

WHAT TO BRING:
All supplies and instructions are included with your mining fee. Bring sunglasses, sunscreen,
hat and gloves, your lunch and drinks. It gets very hot at midday, so bring extra fluids.

INFORMATION:
    The fish fossils found here are over fifty million years old. You will have no trouble finding
fossils. They can be found in a few hours of work. You must work slowly so you don't ruin the
fossils that you reveal. Experts are on hand to instruct you. You may keep all the fossils you find,
except rare specimens such as stingrays, turtles or birds.
    The heavy overburden is removed by the quarry operators. You will be trying your hand at
splitting large, loose blocks of limestone to discover the fossils. Your patient searching will pay off
with beautiful undamaged fossils. It is highly recommended that you visit nearby Fossil Butte
National Monument Visitors Center before coming to the quarry. There you can educate
yourself to the mass potential that the entire Green River Formation has to offer.
    We suggest you start early. It is cool in the morning and a light jacket may be needed. It gets
very hot by midday, so wear clothes in layers so you can peel out of them. Remember you are going
to be digging in the Wyoming desert. The elevation here is approximately 7,200 feet, and you will
need to supply yourself with ALL the necessities like water, sunglasses, a hat and gloves to help
protect you from the elements. Please call or visit their website for more information on hotels
and campgrounds nearby.

Museums

Site 6.
Tate Geological Museum at Casper College
125 College Drive
Casper, WY 82601
(307) 268-2447
http://www.caspercollege.edu/community/campus/tate/index.html
• This is a small but fascinating museum at Casper College focusing on dinosaurs, paleontology and mineralogy.

Site 7.
University of Wyoming Geological Museum
Dept. 3006, 1000 E. University Avenue
University of Wyoming
Laramie, WY 82071
(307) 766-2646
http://www.uwyo.edu/geomuseum/
• Some of Wyoming's geologic riches are housed in this museum including fossils, rocks and mineral specimens numbering over fifty thousand.

Site 8. Washakie Museum of History, Art & Earth Science
1115 Obie Sue
Worland, WY 82401
(307) 347-4784 or (307) 347-4102
washakiemuseum@rtconnect.net
http://www.washakiemuseum.com/
• This museum blends art, science and history. There is a display of rocks and fossils and a rock shelter decorated with ancient petroglyphs.

Points of Interest

Site 9.
Devils Tower National Monument
P.O. Box 10
Devils Tower, WY 82714-0010
(307) 467-5283
http://www.nps.gov/deto/index.htm
• Our first National Monument is a molten magma plug of an extinct volcano rising skyward over one thousand feet.

Site 10.
Fossil Butte National Monument
P.O. Box 592
Kemmerer, WY 83101
(307) 877-4455
http://www.nps.gov/fobu/
• The former lake bed, now limestone, perfectly preserves the fossil remains of many extinct inhabitants including fish, stingrays, crocodiles, birds and snakes. See their fossils on exhibit at the visitors center.

Site 11.
Independence Rock State Historic Site

P.O. Box 1596
Evansville, WY 82636
(307) 577-5150
http://wyoparks.state.wy.us/IRslide.htm
• Wagon trains moving west all looked for Independence Rock. Since they usually arrived at this site around the fourth of July, the name seemed appropriate. Travelers carved their names on the rock or wrote messages in axle grease. Anxious travelers carefully checked for signs that friends and family traveling before them had safely reached this place. Today visitors can walk around the rock and even climb to the top for a look around. But unlike your ancestors, you are asked not to write on the rock.

Site 12.
Yellowstone National Park

National Park Service
P.O. Box 168
Yellowstone National Park, WY 82190
(307) 344-7381
http://www.nps.gov/yell/
• Yellowstone gets its name from the Native Americans who called the place "Rock Yellow River" for the yellow cliffs along the river. The unique geological features brought Yellowstone to national attention and congress made this place our first national park in 1872. Visitors can see more that two hundred active geysers, a waterfall over three hundred feet, the world's largest volcanic crater and of course, the most famous geyser–Old Faithful. Another huge draw at the park is the wildlife including bald eagles, buffalo, moose, elk, wolves and an occasional grizzly.

LOCATING GOLD DEPOSITS

The following steps will help you find a likely spot on a stream or river once you have found an area in which you would like to search. A little knowledge of how gold travels in water will assist you increase your chance of finding some color.

1. First find out as much as you can about the area in which you are going to prospect. Discover where gold was found in the past, how much was extracted and if the area is continuing to produce gold today

2. Prospectors need to learn the local regulations including where you may prospect, if dredges are allowed, and if you require a permit to search.

3. If possible approach the stream or river from a high vantage point which allows you to see how the water runs, where sandbanks are, where turns occur and how fast the water flows.

4. Gold is very heavy and does not like to travel in water. Look for places where water changes from fast to slow moving. This is a spot where the gold will drop.

5. Search on the inside bends of the stream which act as a catching point for gold and other heavy materials that get moved by the force of the water.

6. Check on the downstream side of large rocks and boulders. Gold will get trapped on the rear of the rocks in little whirlpools of water and collect there.

7. Don't pass up the areas that were once covered with water during the winter run-offs. These places that are now dry exposed rocks can contain some nice gold. These make an ideal area for highbanking, metal detecting or collecting material for a sluice box.

8. Cracks in exposed bedrock or slight gaps between large rocks make excellent collecting places for heavy material such as gold. These natural riffles can be searched with a crevice tool or screwdriver. This process is called "sniping."

9. The bottom of little waterfalls on a stream can trap gold and hold it. This is a good spot to do some dredging.

10. These are some tips can help you start your search, but don't forget the most important tip—gold is elusive and the best place to search is where you find it!

SAPPHIRES, RUBIES, TOPAZ, DIAMOND FROM A NON-SEEDED OR DIG-YOUR-OWN SITE

These tips and techniques are intended for those who will buy buckets of non-seeded dirt or dig their own dirt directly at a mine known to contain precious gems. Methods included here involve washing your concentrates. If no water supply is available, another method of recovery must be used.

1. Be prepared to get dirty. Dress in old clothing. Some miners wear rubber boots and rain pants to keep water and mud off their duds.

2. Know that heavy material, such as diamonds, sapphires, rubies, topaz, hematite and metals sink to the bottom of all other material. This principal is vital to the methods of recovery described here.

3. It is vital that you know what you are looking for IN THE ROUGH. So take the time and allow the proprietors to show you what the diamonds, sapphires and so on, look like in their natural state. Natural stones look very different than cut and prepared stones. You are better prepared to spot it in your screen if you have seen it before.

4. Know the indicators that you are in the right place. Diamonds are only found in kimberlite. Do you know what that looks like? If not find out. Gold and Montana sapphires are often found with hematite and black sands. The pink sapphires of North Carolina are often surrounded by bits of mica and a white mud called kaolin.

5. Realize that most precious stones are surrounded by look-alikes. For example, many first-timers mistake pyrite for gold. Diamonds are often surrounded by flashy bits of calcite. Sapphires and topaz often nestle beside worthless clear quartz. Know how to identify imposters and realize you will find many more of these than the elusive and valuable gemstones.

6. Bring the right equipment including: shovels, work gloves, heavy-duty rubber gloves, several five-gallon buckets, a washtub, boots and rain pants. In addition you will need several classifying screens including a grizzly (1/2-inch mesh), a 1/8-inch mesh, and a 1/16-inch mesh. Get a piece of foam cut to fit inside these standard screens and cut a piece of plywood to fit inside the screen as well. Finally you should bring a pocketknife, tweezers and a small closing container, such as a film container, to hold your gems.

7. Dig your material or purchase pre-classified buckets.

8. Fill your washtub half-full and stack your classifying screens from largest screen mesh on top to smallest on the bottom. Scoop the dirt you collected into the top of the stacked screens.

9. Separate clay, sand and dirt from the gravel by shaking it in water of your tub. Realize that the stones you find will be larger than the smallest screen you use. All others will collect in your washtub. If you want to catch the smallest stones you will have to later pan out your

waste dirt, and this takes a great deal of time. Some mines keep this excess or waste dirt, as in Montana, as it contains some gold. Continue shaking until only the gravel remains in the screens.

10. Check the grizzly and the 1/8-inch classifying screen by carefully fingering through the material and then discard the gravel in both. Remember that precious stones are very rare, and you will not find one very often.

11. Take the 1/16-inch classifying screen and hold it under the water with two hands. Vigorously shake the screen from side to side until all the material lines up from twelve to six o'clock in your screen. Then turn the screen a quarter turn so the material lines up from one hand to the other (three to nine o'clock) and repeat the shaking. This action makes all the heaviest material settle to the bottom center of the screen. Repeat the process at least once more. Then lift the material from the water and gently shake it vertically to settle the material and remove excess water.

12. Now add the foam cut out on top of the screen. Place the plywood on the foam, and then place your thumbs on the board and your fingers beneath the screen. In one smooth movement, flip the screen upside down and remove the screen. The gravel should sit on the foam and board with the heavy material forming a ring in the center. If you have trouble flipping the material or find no center, gather the gravel and try again. Some miners do not use foam or a board, but have a knack for flipping out the gravel like an omelet from a pan. You may see a series of gravel circles drying on a flat patch of earth.

13. Some material needs to dry before you can check it. This includes diamonds and topaz. The look-alikes fool the eye when wet. But when dry, clear quartz and topaz are hard to mistake. Diamonds never get cloudy, as calcite and no dirt sticks to them. Some stones, such as sapphires, do not require drying. They are easily plucked with tweezers from the surrounding hematite.

14. Once the material is dry, use the tip of your pocketknife to carefully sort through the center material. Place any keepers in the safety of a closed container.

15. Some miners keep the centers of all these turnings and re-run them for a final check. Go slow and be patient.

Many years ago when the forty-niners hit the streams searching for their fortunes, they carried with them their trusty metal gold pan. This pan was used to extract gold, and often to cook supper. Innovative Chinese miners even chiseled riffles in one side of the pan to catch more gold and speed the extraction process. Gold panning was and is backbreaking work. Today's pans are plastic with molded riffles so you won't have to bother chiseling your own, but you will find more gold and smaller flakes. Brand new pans need to be seasoned, so take your pan to the stream and ruff it up with dirt and rocks. This will help get any oils out of your pan. Oil attaches to gold and floats it away when you are panning. Don't eat your dinner out of your pan either, plastic makes a poor conductor so you'll have bring your camping supplies. But at least you won't be eating from the same pan you mixed mercury in to extract unseen gold from the black sands. Yup, prospectors did that, never knowing the risks of mercury hazards on your brain. It does explain all those silly dances that miners did when they found gold.

1. First find a good spot or area with a proven record for gold and dig yourself a few buckets of material.

2. Find a calm place in the river to do your test panning. Calm waters allow you to work your material and not have to fight with the river.

3. Fill your gold pan half-full with your material, including larger rocks, sticks clay and dirt.

4. Put your pan with material into the water. Break up clay and dirt with your hands. Wash off larger rocks and discard them. Gold sticks on a rock, gets caught in a clump of clay or dirt, so wash them in your pan.

5. With your pan still under the water slowly move the pan in a circular motion; this will get the material to move around in the pan. Allowing all of the lighter unwanted material to start to move out over the lip of your pan as the heaver material settles in the gold pan, (gold and black sand).

6. With the pan still in the water, tilt the material towards the riffles and slowly rock the pan back and forth. This helps to remove the lighter unwanted material. To avoid spilling heavy material, rock the material back by leveling your pan, then repeat the swirling motion to make sure that the heavy material again drops to the bottom of the pan. Repeat this step till you only see mostly black sand in your pan.

7. When you see mostly black sand slow down and keep a look out for those flakes of gold. A plastic sucker bottle and fine tweezers help you extract any visible gold from your pan. Don't worry about picking up some sand with the sucker bottle; you can always clean it more thoroughly later. Another useful tool is a magnet. In a plastic pan the magnet can draw hematite (black sands), which are magnetic, away from your fine gold.

Tip: Shoveling material into your gold pan through a 1/4-inch to 1/2-inch classifying screen will help you remove stones and other large material more quickly. Carefully check this material before discarding it for gold nuggets or river garnets. Good luck!

After you have found a likely place to dig for gold, collect some material and take it to a stream or river. There you can run a few test pans, and discover if the location shows some color. Then use a sluice and let the water do the classifying for you. All you need is a sluice box, shovel, gloves, buckets and you are ready to find some gold.

1. Find a spot on the river that has good depth and fast moving water. Digging is usually done near the river or stream and the concentrates brought to the sluice and fed into the upstream wider mouth of the sluice. Your digging site and sluicing site will not necessarily be beside each other, but try to keep them as close as possible so you will not have to carry your concentrates very far.

2. When digging, set an inch to a 1/2-inch mesh classifying screen over your five-gallon collecting bucket to screen out larger rocks. Check and discard the stones.

3. Place the sluice with the wide opening pointing upstream. The sluice should be almost level with the water with a slight downward pitch. Use river rocks to brace your sluice box. Place one long flat rock across the top of the sluice to keep the box in place in the current. Sometimes you need to use rocks from the river to help you change the flow of the water in the river. Such a dam can channel water toward your sluice if the current is slow or away from your sluice if the water is too fast and washing away nearly all the material.

4. Now you are ready to work some of your material through the sluice box. Slowly pour some dirt into the large opening at the top part of the sluice box. It is very important to go slowly and to regulate the amount of material that runs through the box. Give the water time to work the earth through of the box.

5. Remove large rocks from the riffles to help aid the flow of the water and increase the effectiveness of the sluice. Check all rocks before you discard them, so you don't toss away a nice nugget.

6. Use a shovel to remove the tailings pile that forms at the end of the sluice box to keep the current moving and prevent back-ups in the sluice.

7. After a while, check the material in the sluice box for a build up of black sand in the riffles. This indicates its time to clean out the sluice.

8. Place a large bucket under the end of your sluice box, then slowly lift the sluice up out of the water towards the bucket. This stops the flow of water and allows you to catch all loose material in the bucket.

9. Use a gold pan to pour water through the sluice as it still sits upright in the bucket. This washes more of your material into the pail.

10. With the sluice still in the bucket, unfasten the latch and lift the metal grate. Then remove and rinse the wire mesh in the bucket with the sluice still in the bucket. Let the carpet and miners moss slide into the bucket. When the metal parts of the sluice are rinsed and clean of black sands, set them aside on the bank.

11. Now clean the miners moss by turning it upside down and shaking it in the bucket of water. Finally turn the carpet upside down and tap the surface while the carpet is submerged so any gold trapped in the carpet will fall into the bucket of concentrates. Good Luck!

OFFICIAL STATE GEMS, MINERALS & ROCKS

States often choose a mineral, gem or rock that highlights the history, landscape or commerce. A lot can be learned about a place from the choice the legislature has made. Below is a listing in alphabetical order of our nations official gems, minerals and rocks.

STATE	GEM	MINERAL	ROCK
ALABAMA	STAR BLUE QUARTZ	HEMATITE	MARBLE
ALASKA	NEPHRITE JADE	GOLD	
ARIZONA	TURQUOISE	FIRE AGATE	PETRIFIED WOOD
ARKANSAS	DIAMOND	QUARTZ CRYSTAL	BAUXITE
CALIFORNIA	BENITOITE	GOLD	SERPENTINE
COLORADO	AQUAMARINE	RHODOCHROSITE	YULE MARBLE
CONNECTICUT	GARNET		
DELAWARE			SILLIMANITE
FLORIDA	MOONSTONE		AGATIZED CORAL
GEORGIA	QUARTZ	STAUROLITE	
HAWAII	BLACK CORAL		
IDAHO	STAR GARNET		
ILLINOIS	FLUORITE	FLUORITE	
INDIANA			LIMESTONE
IOWA			GEODE
KANSAS			
KENTUCKY	FRESHWATER PEARL	COAL	KENTUCKY AGATE
LOUISIANA	AGATE		PETRIFIED PALM
MAINE	TOURMALINE		
MARYLAND	PATUXENT RIVER STONE		
MASSACHUSETTS	RHODONITE	BABINGTONITE	ROXBURY PUDDINGSTONE GRANITE
MICHIGAN	GREENSTONE (CHLORASTROLITE)		PETOSKEY STONE
MINNESOTA	LAKE SUPERIOR AGATE		
MISSISSIPPI			PETRIFIED WOOD
MISSOURI		GALENA (LEAD)	MOZARKITE
MONTANA	YOGO SAPPHIRE	MOSS AGATE	
NEBRASKA	BLUE AGATE		PRAIRIE AGATE

STATE	GEM	MINERAL	ROCK
NEVADA	VIRGIN VALLEY BLACK FIRE OPAL, TURQUOISE	SILVER	SANDSTONE
NEW HAMPSHIRE	SMOKY QUARTZ	BERYL	CONWAY GRANITE
NEW JERSEY			
NEW MEXICO	TURQUOISE		
NEW YORK	GARNET, BLACK TOURMALINE, MOONSTONE	HEMATITE	
NORTH CAROLINA	EMERALD		GRANITE
NORTH DAKOTA			TEREDO WOOD
OHIO	OHIO FLINT		
OKLAHOMA			BARITE ROSE
OREGON	SUNSTONE		THUNDEREGGS
PENNSYLVANIA			TRILOBITE
RHODE ISLAND		BOWENITE	CUMBERLANDITE
SOUTH CAROLINA	AMETHYST		BLUE GRANITE
SOUTH DAKOTA	FAIRBURN AGATE	ROSE QUARTZ	
TENNESSEE	TENNESSEE PEARL	AGATE, TENNESSEE LIMESTONE	
TEXAS	BLUE TOPAZ		PETRIFIED PALMWOOD
UTAH	TOPAZ	COPPER	COAL
VERMONT	GROSSULAR GARNET	TALC	GRANITE, MARBLE, SLATE
VIRGINIA			CHESAPECTEN JEFFERSONIUS (FOSSIL)
WASHINGTON	PETRIFIED WOOD		
WEST VIRGINIA	LITHOSTROTIONELLA (WEST VIRGINIA FOSSIL CORAL)		
WISCONSIN	RUBY	GALENA (LEAD)	RED GRANITE
WYOMING	NEPHRITE JADE		

The association of stones to the month of a person's birth began about 400 AD. But birthstones were not commonly worn by those born in each month until the eighteenth century. There is some evidence that stones were not worn according to the month of your birth, but a set of all twelve stones might be obtained and worn in sequence according to the date in order to maintain one's health and for personal protection. If you consider this nothing but superstition and the working of an overactive imagination, consider how important a person's state of mind is to their health and well-being. The stones on the list below have changed only slightly through the ages, with some remaining unchanged.

JANUARY

Modern–Garnet
Ancient–Garnet
"No gems save garnets should be worn
By her who in this month is born;
They will insure her constancy,
True friendship and fidelity."[1]

The word garnet is derived from the Latin word for grain, and a Middle English and old French word for pomegranate, a fruit known for its deep red fruit. Because of their color, garnets were used in ancient time to cure conditions of the blood and are symbols of love and passion. Some garnets are such a deep red they are mistaken for rubies, although red is not the only color in which garnet occur. Garnets from Ceylon range from a cinnamon yellow to reddish orange. The most rare and valuable of all is the grossularite garnet known as the green garnet.

FEBRUARY

Modern–Amethyst
Ancient–Amethyst
"The February-born may find
Sincerity and peace of mind,
Freedom from passion and from care,
If she an amethyst will wear."[1]

The word amethyst comes from the Greek and roughly means "one who is not drunk." It was thought that water drunk from a goblet of purple glass resembled wine. Those who drank from such a cup did not get drunk, and therefore amethyst was believed to protect from drunkenness. During the Renaissance period, amethyst adorned religious objects including Bishop's rings. Amethysts are the most popular of the quartz family and range in color from red-violet to blue-violet and true purple.

MARCH

Modern–Aquamarine
Ancient–Bloodstone
"Who on this world of ours her eyes
In March first opens may be wise,
In days of peril firm and brave,
Wears she a bloodstone to her grave."[1]

Aquamarine derives its name from its resemblance to sea water. This stone is popular among many sailors who believed it protected them from the perils of the sea. Egyptians wore this stone in battle to protect and instill courage. In the Middle Ages, aquamarine earned another use, the guarantee of happy marriages and fidelity in newlyweds. The color of this blue beryl ranges from light blue to blue-green to dark blue.

APRIL

Modern–Diamond
Ancient–Diamond
"She who from April dates her years
Diamonds would wear, lest bitters
For vain repentance flow. This stone
Emblem of innocence is known."[2]

Diamond, pure crystallized carbon has become the most prized of gemstones. This gem wins the prize for hardness and comes in an astonishing variety of colors. Make sure to accept only the best. At one time, Hindus believed that wearing a flawed diamond could keep them from the highest level of heaven. Diamonds were used as an antidote for poison, though some believed the stone itself was poison, as it was said to be found in places guarded by a vile venomous beast that imbued its treasure with poison. It was noted in the Middle Ages that poor people more often succumbed to plague and the possession of diamonds by the rich became the likely reason. Diamonds were said to protect from plague and pestilence, cure numerous diseases including those of the bladder. How romantic.

MAY

Modern–Emerald
Ancient–Emerald
"Who first behold the light of day
In spring's sweet flow'ry month of May,
And wears an emerald all her life,
Shall be a loved and happy wife."[2]

The name emerald is Greek and means green stone. Emerald is believed to improve intelligence and cure diseases of the mind and heart. That makes it perfect to protect marriages, increase fertility and help in childbirth. This stone is softer and more fragile than sapphires, rubies and diamonds. Jewelers often cut it in the strong emerald cut to protect it from damage. Emeralds vary in hue from light to dark, and often have inclusions and black specks of carbon.

JUNE

Modern–Alexandrite
Ancient–Agate
"Who comes with summer to this earth,
And owes to June her hour of birth,
With ring of agate on her hand
Can health, long life and wealth command."[3]

Alexandrite is a newcomer to the gem market arriving in 1830. The stone derives its name from Prince Alexander as it was discovered on the day he came of age. This gem is unique as it changes in color. Light or dark green in sunlight it changes to red in candlelight or tungsten light. Most valued is brilliant green changing to fiery red. As it is a modern stone, there is no folklore or ancient superstition associated with this stone.

July

Modern–Ruby
Ancient–Turquoise
"The heav'n-blue turquoise should adorn
All those who in July are born;
For those they'll be exempt and free
From love's doubts and anxiety."[3]

From the Latin for red, ruby is symbolic of love, charity and victory. In ancient times, it was believed to sooth anger and bring courage. The red color caused early people to associate rubies with blood and fire. They were symbolic of war, battle, victory and therefore adorned by royalty, valued above diamonds. It was not until modern times that it was discovered that rubies have a twin. Sapphires are identical to rubies, both being corundums differing only in color. Sapphires come in numerous colors, while rubies are always red, varying only in shade.

August

Modern–Peridot
Ancient –Carnelian
"Wear a carnelian or for thee
No conjugal felicity;
The August-born without this stone,
'Tis' said, must live unloved, alone."[3]

Peridot is a variety of olivine. Peridot is purported to bring the wearer peace, luck and success. Peridot has never enjoyed the popularity of the big three, diamond, sapphire and ruby. But dark peridot may even have slipped into queen Cleopatra's emerald jewelry. In ancient times peridot was believed to derive its power from the sun, and thought to have strong medicinal powers. Peridot was believed to protect against enchantments, the evil eye and nightmares. Perhaps because of its soothing color, this stone was also believed to attract love and calm anger. Among its more mundane uses is the healing of insect bites. Peridot varies in color from bright yellow-green to green.

September

Modern–Sapphire
Ancient–Chrysolite (Peridot)
"A maid born when September leaves
Are rustling in the autumn breeze,
A chrysolite on brow should bind–
'Twill cure disease of the mind."[4]

The name sapphire comes from the Greek word for blue. This corundum actually comes in all varieties of color except red, which is reserved for rubies. Any other color of corundum is considered a sapphire. This stone has the celestial beauty of the heavens and has always been highly prized. It has been and still is considered a token of lasting love. Sapphires symbolize truth, tradition and sincerity. One thing is certain; they are tough, falling second only to diamond in hardness.

October

Modern–Rose Zircon, Opal
Ancient–Beryl
"October's child is born of woe,
And life's vicissitudes must know;
But lay a beryl on her breast,
And Hope will lull those woes to rest."[4]

The name may have come from the Roman word, opalus and the Greek word, opallios, meaning "to see a change of color." Of all the gemstones, opal is most unusual and has been described as having the fire of emeralds, sapphires and rubies. The amazing variety of colors in opals makes them highly prized. Opals were thought to improve eyesight and keep hair from turning white. This gem's most spectacular use is its ability to render the wearer invisible, though I wouldn't try this one at home. Opal is not a crystal, but a dehydrated silica jelly that cracks and thereby reflects light. The most valuable opals are dark gray or black. Since opals contain some water they are more fragile than other gemstones.

NOVEMBER

Modern–Topaz
Ancient–Topaz
"Who first comes to this world below
With drear November's fog and snow
Should prize the topaz's amber hue–
Emblem of friends and lovers true."[5]

The name topaz comes from Greek, and is derived from the location of the mines on the Island of Topazos. Topaz was used in ancient times to cure poor vision. During the black plague, topaz was pressed to sores to heal them. This gem is renowned for its curative powers. Topaz is a silicate of aluminum, and occurs in yellow, pink, blue, brown and colorless varieties.

DECEMBER

Modern–Blue Zircon
Ancient–Ruby
"If cold December gives you birth–
The month of snow and ice and mirth–
Place on your hand a ruby true;
Success with bless whate'er you do."[5]

The word zircon comes from the Persian language meaning golden, the original color of zircon when discovered. Blue zircon is a recent addition to the world of gemstones and became popular in the 1920s. For many years it was considered to possess mystic properties because it was noticed that stones occasionally changed color. Zircon is known to occasionally form in association with uranium and thorium, which over time could account for the color change. This magic transformation must have been quite disconcerting in ancient times. The most prized color is an electric blue. It is also occurs in pale blue, sky blue, greenish-blue. Zircon is often heated to enhance its natural color.

Footnote

---

[1] Kunz, *The Curious Lore of Precious Stones,* 1971, p.327
[2] Kunz, *The Curious Lore of Precious Stones,* 1971, p.328
[3] Kunz, *The Curious Lore of Precious Stones,* 1971, p.329
[4] Kunz, *The Curious Lore of Precious Stones,* 1971, p.330
[5] Kunz, *The Curious Lore of Precious Stones,* 1971, p.331

As you can see the marriage must survive eleven long years before the couple merits the gift of the most precious objects—gemstones.

YEAR	GIFT
1	Paper
2	Calico
3	Linen
4	Silk
5	Wood
6	Candy
7	Floral
8	Leather
9	Straw
10	Tin
12	Agate
13	Moonstone*
14	Moss-Agate
15	Rock Crystal/Glass
16	Topaz
17	Amethyst
18	Garnet
19	Rose Quartz
20	Jade
23	Sapphire
25	Silver
26	Star Sapphire, blue*
30	Pearl
35	Coral/Jade
39	Cats-eye*
40	Ruby
45	Alexandrite
50	Gold
52	Star Ruby*
55	Emerald
60	Diamond, yellow
65	Star Sapphire, gray*
75	Diamond

*All anniversaries, which are multiples of 13, have gems believed to counteract the bad influence of this unlucky number.[1]

Footnote
_____

[1]Kunz, *The Curious Lore of Precious Stones*, 1971, p.337

The biggest and brightest gems and nuggets capture our imagination. Some of these are old finds and come with long and strange histories. Some were found only in the last few years. Fantastic discoveries are made each year, but you have to get out there to make one. All of the minerals, gems and metals listed below are still being recovered. Best of all, there is a site somewhere in the U.S. open to the public that allows you the opportunity to find them. This listing is by no means a complete one. How could it be when new discoveries are being made? It is merely presented as a way to inspire you to your own discoveries.

GOLD

- The largest mass of gold ever found is the Holtermann Nugget. This monster nugget was discovered on October 19, 1872 in the Beyers & Holtermann Star of Hope Mine in Australia. It weighed 517 pounds and yielded 180 pounds of gold.

- The largest solid gold nugget is called "the Welcome Stranger" and was discovered in Australia 1869 in a wagon rut. The lustrous metal was as heavy as the mule driver who found the 210-pound nugget.

- The largest nugget found in America was unearthed in California during the Gold Rush. Found in the Morgan Mine in Carson Hill on November of 1854, it weighed an incredible 214 pounds.

- Alaska's biggest nugget proves that the best may still be out there. "The Alaska Centennial Nugget" was discovered in 1998 and weighed 24 pounds (294 Troy ounces). A miner in Ruby, Alaska noticed the massive nugget rolling before the bulldozer blade.

- In 1799, a child of twelve spotted the largest gold nugget found on the East Coast. The boy, Conrad Reed, found the 17-pound nugget in a local stream in Cabarrus County, North Carolina. He brought it home and for three years it served as a family doorstop. A local jeweler paid his father a week's wages for the gold, $3.50. This was less than one percent of the gold's value at the time.

- Colorado was home to a nugget weighing over 17 pounds. Discovered in 1887 by Tom Groves, the miner brought his precious find to the assayer's home wrapped in a blanket. "Tom's Baby," as it became known, can be seen at the Denver Museum of Nature & Science in Colorado.

- Georgia is also home to a number of large gold nuggets, many weighing over 2 pounds.

SILVER

- The largest single silver nugget, "the Smuggler Mine Nugget" was found in 1893 in a mine near Aspen, Colorado and weighed 2,350 pounds. Ironically it was not removed from the mine until 1894 because silver prices crashed the year of its discovery.

- In the same year, the Molly Gibson Mine yielded a silver nugget weighing a massive 1,840 pounds. Ironically, both of the largest silver nuggets ever found were discovered at the worst possible time, the year of the silver market crash.

PLATINUM

- The largest known platinum nugget was found in the Ural Mountains in Russia in 1843. This nugget weighed over 21 pounds, and was melted down almost immediately after its discovery.

- The second largest platinum nugget was also found in the Ural Mountains, and tipped the scales at over 17 pounds. This one survived the melting pot.
- In the U.S. you can see platinum at most major museums. The Natural History Museum of Los Angeles County has a 0.5 Troy ounce nugget recovered from a California stream.

DIAMONDS

- The largest known diamond in existence is "the Cullinan," discovered in January 1905 in South Africa and weighing 3,106 carats. This massive diamond yielded 106 cut stones including one weighing 530.20 carats. This stone called "the Star of Africa" was cut in a pear shape with 74 facets. It now graces the Royal Scepter of England, and is kept with the Crown Jewels in the Tower of London.
- The largest cut diamond is the "Golden Jubilee" diamond weighing 545.67 carats. It is currently set in the Thai Royal Scepter.
- The largest uncut diamond is owned by De Beers, of course, and weighs 1,462 carats.
- The largest mounted diamond currently resides in the Smithsonian Institution, weighs 127.01 carats and is called "the Portuguese Diamond." The owner, Mr. Harry Winston traded it for 2,400 carats of small diamonds in 1963. The gem is a flawless and octagonal cut white diamond. The history of this stone is sketchy. Efforts have been unsuccessful to discover its origins.
- Most unique diamond is the "Hope." The lovely blue diamond of 45.52 carats is believed by some to be cursed. It certainly was not lucky for a previous owner and former Queen of France, Marie-Antoinette, who was beheaded.
- The largest diamond discovered in North American is "the Uncle Sam," a 40.23 carat white diamond unearthed in a stream in Arkansas in 1924. This diamond was later emerald cut to a weight of 12.43 carats. This American treasure is on display at the Museum of Natural History in New York City.
- Smaller specimens are on display in most large museums. The Natural History Museum of Los Angeles County has a 1.95 carat uncut diamond recovered from the Smithflat area in 1896. The Crater of Diamonds State Park in Arkansas has a small museum that features many uncut diamonds. This museum also has castings of the largest gems recovered from this area, including the "Uncle Sam."

RUBIES

- One of the world's most famous rubies is the "Timur Ruby" weighing 352.50 carats. It was thought to be the largest ruby in existence but it isn't a ruby at all, but rather a rare red spinel. The spinel is part of a necklace belonging to Elizabeth II, the Queen of England, and worn on state occasions.
- The largest star ruby is the "Eminent Star Ruby," an oval cabochon with a six-ray star. This stone has a carat weight of 6,465 and is believed to come from India.
- The "Burma Hixon Ruby" was unearthed in one a renowned mine in Mogok, Myanmar. It weighs 196 carats and is owned by the Natural History Museum of Los Angeles County.
- The Black Prince's Ruby is as large as a hen's egg, and weighs approximately 170 carats. This gem found its way to England and is set in the state crown. Unfortunately it is also not a ruby but another red spinel.
- Closer to home, a star ruby resides at the Natural History Museum of Los Angeles County. This gem really is a ruby, weighs 18.29 carats and is on display in the Hixon Gem Vault.

EMERALDS

- The largest carved emerald in the world was found in Brazil in August 1974. It weighed 86,136 carats and was carved by an artisan named Richard Chan from Hong Kong.

- Another famous emerald is "the Hooker Emerald," once owned by the sultan of the Ottoman Empire and reportedly was worn as a belt buckle. This gem was acquired by Tiffany & Co. and set with 901 diamonds in a tiara. This setting changed again in the 1950s to a brooch, and was donated to the Smithsonian Institution in 1977. It is currently on display in Washington, DC.

- The largest emerald found in North Carolina was unearthed in 1998 and weighed 858 carats. Originally named "the Jolly Green Giant," this uncut gem is now on display in the North Carolina Museum of Natural Science and renamed the more dignified "the Empress Caroline."

- The largest cut emerald found in North America comes from Hiddenite, North Carolina. Found in 1980, the gem weighs 15.46 carats and has two names "the Kite Emerald" or "the June Culp Zeitner Emerald."

SAPPHIRE

- The largest star sapphire is called "the Lone Star" and weighed 9,719.5 carats. The stone was cut in London in 1989.

- "The Star of Asia" is another beautiful star sapphire on display in the Smithsonian Institution. This 330 carat gem is royal blue in color.

- "The Logan Sapphire" is a faceted gem of 423 carats. This gem was mined in Sri Lanka, and is roughly the size of a chicken's egg.

- An uncut sapphire from Sri Lanka that was 3,965 carats may be the largest uncut specimen known in existence. It is the size of a fist, and is expected to yield somewhere between fifty and one hundred cut gems.

OPAL

- The largest opal is a single piece of white opal weighing 26,350 carats. Found in 1989 in Australia it is called "Jupiter Five."

- The largest-known opal-bearing rock is the seven-ton "Painted Lady" found in the Andamooka Opal Fields in South Australia. This monster rock is over nine feet long, four feet wide, and contains veins of opal up to an inch thick.

- The largest black opal was also found in Australia in 1972, and produced a finished gem weighing 1,520 carats called "Empress of Glengarry."

JADE

- Largest piece of Jade was found in Canada in 1992 and weighed 577 tons or 1,154,000 pounds.

- The Emerald Buddha is a 30-inch statue carved of jadeite and housed in its own sacred temple in Bangkok, Thailand. The statue was discovered in 1434 when lightning struck a pagoda and revealed an unimpressive stucco Buddha. Over time the plaster fell away, and the beautiful jade Buddha was revealed. The Emerald Buddha is thought to bring good fortune, and several miracles are attributed to it. Want more? Well, this little Buddha has a golden wardrobe that changes with the season. In winter he wears a golden shawl, and when it rains he has a golden hat and seven golden umbrellas above his head.

AMBER

- The largest piece of amber weighed in at over 33 pounds. It was discovered in Burma and now resides in the Natural History Museum in London, England.

TOPAZ

- Two of the largest topaz crystals ever unearthed were discovered in Brazil and now reside in the Smithsonian Institution in Washington, DC. They weigh 111 pounds and 70 pounds respectively, and still exist in their natural state because of the nearby discovery of a large 10-pound topaz crystal more suitable for cutting. The result is the "American Golden Topaz" which has a carat weight of 22,892.5 and contains 172 facets. This rare gem is nearly 17-inches tall and over 14 inches wide.

FOSSILS

- Do you know Sue? Sue is the largest Tyrannosaurus rex skeleton ever recovered. There are only seven skeletons more than half complete known to exist, and she's the biggest. This fossil is named for her discoverer, Sue Hendrickson, who found it in 1990 in the badlands of South Dakota. Sue is an extraordinary ninety percent complete, and now lives in Chicago in The Field Museum.

- The Carcharodon megalodon was a prehistoric ancestor of the great white shark. This swimming monster was as large as a city bus, and shed hundreds, perhaps thousands of teeth in a lifetime. These teeth are recovered today by divers in rivers in South Carolina and off the coast of Venice, Florida. Teeth over five-inches long are rare, but not unheard of.

SHIPWRECK TREASURE

- The most spectacular shipwreck recovery is the wreck of the *Central America*. This ship sank in a hurricane in 1857 off the coast of the Carolinas in very deep water (eight thousand feet). The *Central America* was a side-wheel steamer carrying bounty of the California gold fields. The ingots, nuggets and gold dust and freshly minted coins measured many tons. Tommy Thompson discovered the wreck in 1989. This project was the first ship ever to be salvaged from such a depth and used robots to recover the treasure.

- A wreck of spectacular wealth salvaged in shallow water is the Nuestra Señora de Atocha found in fifty feet of water by Mel Fisher after a staggering sixteen-year search. Somewhere in the warm water off Key West this ship sank in a hurricane in 1622. One of twenty-eight treasure ships, it was laden with New World wealth. The recovered treasure is estimated to be worth over four hundred million. Some of the booty is on display in Key West at the Mel Fisher Maritime Heritage Museum, including a twelve-foot gold chain weighing six pounds, and a bishop's cross set with seven magnificent emeralds from Columbia. The search continues today for the back-half of the ship.

- If fifty-feet is still too deep, how about the 1715 fleet? This armada of twelve ships sank off the barbarous coast of Florida, now Vero Beach, in a hurricane. In 1997, a gold butterfly brooch set with 161 diamonds, a second brooch set with 170 diamonds and two earrings each containing 53 diamonds were found only seventy-five feet from the beach. The jewelry's value was estimated at $1.2 million. Although water searching is prohibited by salvage claims, beach hunting is permitted. A lucky metal detector enthusiast recovered a gold whistle in the shape of a dragon on the beach after a storm.

Admiralty Claim: A specific type of claim leased to salvaging companies to guarantee their exclusive use of a certain area of ocean bottom. This means you may not use a metal detector in the area of the wreck sites.

Backhoe: Large machine similar to a bulldozer, which moves dirt and uncovers new material.

Black Sand: Black grains of sand made of hematite. This is a very heavy metal that is often associated with gold. Seeing it in your gold pan is a good sign.

Bureau of Land Management (BLM): National organization created to protect, preserve and manage public land. Some mining and rock collecting is permitted on BLM land in designated areas. Permits are often required.

Carat: Unit used to express the weight of gemstones. One carat is equal to two hundred milligrams.

Claim: A tract of land staked out by an individual to mine. This means it is not open to you and is protected by law.

Concentrates: Dirt that has been reduced by removing all large rocks, light soil and organic material. This leaves concentrated, heavy dirt that is likely to contain heavy gold or gemstones.

Discriminator: A function of a metal detector, used to tune out junk metal such as flip tops and tin foil. It is also used to tune out mineralized soil or rocks (hot rocks).

Dredge: Mining equipment used in a stream to find gold. It works like a powerful water vacuum on the streambed. It sucks up the bottom soil. Heavy material including gold falls onto a ridged mat, while light material washes through and falls back to the stream floor.

Dump: Where the non-valuable rock and debris is discarded at a mine site.

Escudo: Spanish coin made of gold. An escudo weighs one ounce. They are also commonly called a doubloon. They were minted in South America by the Spanish conquistadors from the 1600s to the 1700s. Gold was then shipped to Spain. Some treasure galleons carrying escudos were lost in storms along the U.S. coast.

Gold Dust: Fine particles of gold found in rivers, streams, oceans, soil and, hopefully, your gold pan. Finding gold dust indicates you have a found a good place to search more thoroughly.

Hand-Operated Tools: Tools used by hand. Some examples include shovels, picks, garden trowels, garden rakes and pry bars.

Highbanker: This is a desert sluice box. It is used where water is unavailable or inconvenient. It has its own supply of recycled water that wets dirt and sends it into a sluice box. Some highbankers use hot air instead of water.

Hot Rocks: Rocks with a concentration of metal or salt that cause metal detectors to give a false signal. This signal leads metal detectors to think they have found something of value. Hot rocks should be checked. If quartz is found you may have hope that gold may be present.

Mesh Screens: Mesh screens are used to remove larger rocks and organic material from dirt in an effort to concentrate it. Mesh screens are commercially produced and easily fit into five-gallon buckets. Many miners make their own with chicken wire and wood. Sizes describe the size of the mesh openings. The most common sizes are 1/4-inch and 1/2-inch mesh screens.

Mine Run: A large quantity of mined material offered for sale. It may include as much material as is produced in a half day or full day of mining. The quantity of material included varies from mine to mine, so get specifics before you buy.

Mineralization: Soil that has a concentration of minerals, metals or salts. This plays havoc with metal detectors which read it as valuable material such as gold or silver. Rocks may also be mineralized and are called hot rocks. Wet ocean sand is highly mineralized. A metal detector with a good discriminator is needed in cases of mineralized material.

Mini Jig: A mining tool that washes dirt and removes light waste rock and organic material. The condensed material containing heavier metal is collected for more careful inspection. It is used to find such materials as garnets, gold, rubies and sapphires.

Native Rock: The rock most prevalent to a specific area. The rock surrounding or being penetrated by mineral veins and deposits.

Placer Gold: Gold found in its natural state without any host rock. Examples include gold dust and gold nuggets. Placer gold is commonly found in streams and rivers where it has washed away from its source.

Pry Bar: A tool made of steel that is used to move a heavy rock or to turn over a rock to expose material underneath. A crow bar is a large pry bar. They come in a variety of sizes.

Reales: A Spanish coin made of silver. A one-ounce coin was called an eight reale. This is where the term "pieces of eight" came from. They were minted in South America by the Spanish from the 1600s to the 1700s.

Seeded: This is dirt offered to you by a mine that has had objects added to it to ensure that you are not disappointed. Material added is not always indigenous to the area. Gemstones added are usually of inferior quality.

Sluice Box: This piece of mining equipment is used in combination with a running stream. The water runs through one end of the box and out the other. Material from the streambed is added to the top of the box. Light material runs off with the water, while the gold and heavy materials fall to the mat in the sluice box for closer examination.

Snuffer Bottle: A plastic bottle used to suck up fine gold dust from your gold pan.

Tailings: Term referring to mining material that has been discarded during the mining process, also called waste rock. This is not usually the best material to search, but can contain fine specimens and is much easier than digging your own.

Ultraviolet Light: A type of light bulb that is long or short wave. It is also called a black light. This light is used to spot rocks that fluoresce, or glow in a variety of colors as the ultraviolet light is shone upon them.

Under Claim: Area of land that has been claimed by an individual or company to mine. This means it is not open to you and is protected by law. Claim markers mean keep off and should be respected.

Annual Buyers' Guide, *Lapidary Journal*. Boulder: Primedia, Inc., 2000.

Bauer, Jaroslav & Vladimir Vouska. *A Guide in Color to Precious & Semiprecious Stones*. Chartwell Books, Inc., 1992.

Cipriani, Curzio. *Simon & Schuster's Guide to Gems and Precious Stones*. New York: Simon & Schuster, 1986.

Cunningham, Scott. *Cunningham's Encyclopedia of Crystal, Gem and Metal Magic*. St. Paul: Llewellyn's Publications, 1995.

Cross, Brad. *Gem Trails of Texas*. Baldwin Park: Gem Guides Book Co., 2001

Gold Prospectors Association of America. *1994 Gold Prospector's Mining Guide*. Temecula: Gold Prospectors Association of America, 1994.

Kunz, George Frederick. *The Curious Lore of Precious Stones*. New York: Dover Publications, 1971.

Lawless, Chuck. *The Old West Sourcebook, A Traveler's Guide*. Crown Publishers, 1994.

Mitchell, James R. *Gem Trails of Arizona*. Baldwin Park: Gem Guides Book Co., 2001.

Mitchell, James R. *Gem Trails of Colorado*. Baldwin Park: Gem Guides Book Co., 1997.

Mitchell, James R. *Gem Trails of Nevada*. Baldwin Park: Gem Guides Book Co., 2002.

Mitchell, James R. *Gem Trails of New Mexico*. Baldwin Park: Gem Guides Book Co., 2001.

Mitchell, James R. *Gem Trails of Northern California*. Baldwin Park: Gem Guides Book Co., 1995.

Mitchell, James R. *Gem Trails of Southern California*. Baldwin Park: Gem Guides Book Co., 1996.

Moore, Barry. Herkimer Diamonds, *A Complete Guide for the Prospector and Collector*. New York: Herkimer Diamond Development Corp., 1989.

Petralia, Joseph, F. *GOLD!, GOLD!, A Beginner's Handbook and Recreational Guide*. San Francisco: Sierra Trading Post, 1999.

Post, Jeffrey E. *The National Gem Collection*. New York: Harry Abrams, Inc., 1997.

Reader's Digest: Off the Beaten Path. Reader's Digest Inc., 1997.

Reilly, Kevin; Rowe, Gary T; and Marnville, Kevin. *Hurricane Treasure, 1715 Beach Sites, Locations Revealed*. Pompano Beach: Pirate Express Publishing, 1990.

Symes, R.F. & R.R. Harding. *DK Smithsonian Eyewitness Book: Crystal and Gem*. London: Dorling Kindersley, 1991.

Ward, Fred. *Diamonds*. Bethesda: Gem Book Publishers, 1993.

Ward, Fred. *Emeralds*. Bethesda: Gem Book Publishers, 1993.

Ward, Fred. *Rubies & Sapphires*. Bethesda: Gem Book Publishers, 1995.

White, John Sampson. *The Smithsonian Treasury Minerals and Gems*. Washington, DC: Smithsonian Institution Press, 1991.

http://www.ucmp.berkeley.edu/index.php, The University of California Museum of Paleontology, Berkeley & the Regents of the University of California, 2002.

http://www.goodearthgraphics.com/showcave.html, The United States Show Cave Directory, 1996.

http://cavern.com/, National Cave Association, Park City, Kentucky, 2001.

http://www.jewelrymall.com/stategems.html, Jewelry Mall, 1999.

http://www2.fi.edu/, The Franklin Institute Online, Philadelphia, Pennsylvania, 2001.

http://www.sfmuseum.org/hist7/tencom.html, Gladys Hansen, Museum of the City of San Francisco, 2001.

SUGGESTED READING

MAGAZINES

The American Mineralogist
Mineralogical Society of America
1015 18th Street NW, Suite 601
Washington, DC 20006

Gems and Gemology
GIA, Mail Stop 38
Robert Moulawad Campus
5345 Armada Drive
Carlsbad, CA 92008

Lapidary Journal/Jewelry Arts
300 Chesterfield Parkway, Suite 100
Malvern, PA 19355

Mineralogical Record
P.O. Box 35565
Tucson, AZ 85740

Rock & Gem
290 Maple Court, Suite 232
Ventura, CA 93003

Rocks & Minerals
Heldref Publications
1319 18th Street, NW
Washington, DC 20036-1802

BOOKS

IDENTIFYING ROCKS & MINERALS

Chesterman, Charles W. *Audubon Field Guide to North American Rocks and Minerals*. Alfred A. Knopf, Inc., New York, New York, 1979.

Fejer, Eva & Cecelia Fitzsimons. *An Instant Guide to Rocks and Minerals*. Gramercy Books, New York, New York, 1988.

Arduini, Paolo and Giorgio Teruzzi. *Simon & Schuster's Guide to Fossils*. Simon & Schuster Inc., New York, New York, 1986.

Maley, Terry S. *Field Geology Illustrated*. Mineral Land Publications, Boise, Idaho, 2005.

Pellant, Chris. *DK Smithsonian Handbook: Rocks and Minerals*. Dorling Kindersley, Inc., New York, New York, 2002.

Pough, Frederick H. *Petersen Field Guides® Rocks and Minerals*, 5th ed. Houghton Mifflin Co., New York, New York, 1996.

Pough, Frederick H. *Petersen First Guide® Rocks and Minerals*. Houghton Mifflin Co., New York, New York, 1991.

Prinz, Martin, George Harlow, and Joseph Peters, editors. *Simon & Schuster's Guide to Rocks and Minerals*. Simon & Schuster Inc., New York, 1977.

Zim, Herbert S. and Paul R. Shaffer. *Rocks and Minerals*. St. Martin's Press, Racine, Wisconsin, 2001.

FIELD COLLECTING

Blair, Gerry. *Rockhounding Arizona*. Falcon Press, Helena, Montana, 1992.

Butler, Gail A. *Rockhounding California*. Falcon Press, Helena, Montana, 1995.

Cross, Brad. *Gem Trails of Texas*. Gem Guides Book Co., Baldwin Park, California, 2001.

Feldman, Robert. *Rockhounding Montana*. Falcon Press, Helena, Montana, 2006.

Girard, Roselle M. *Texas Rocks and Minerals: An Amateur's Guide*, rev. ed. Bureau of Economic Geology, University of Texas, Austin, Texas, 1964.

Johnson, H. Cyril and Robert N. Johnson. *Coast to Coast Gem Atlas*, 5th ed. Cy Johnson & Son, Susanville, California, 1987.

Kelty, David. *The GPS Guide to Western States*. Gem Guides Book Co., 2007

Kimbler, Frank S., and Robert J. Narsavage, Jr. *New Mexico Rocks and Minerals*. Sunstone Press, Santa Fe, New Mexico, 1981.

Krause, Barry. *Mineral Collector's Handbook*. Sterling Publishing Co., Inc., New York, New York, 1996.

Mitchell, James R. *Gem Trails of Arizona*. Gem Guides Book Co., Baldwin Park, California, 2001.

Mitchell, James R. *Gem Trails of Colorado*. Gem Guides Book Co., Baldwin Park, California, 2007.

Mitchell, James R. *Gem Trails of Nevada*. Gem Guides Book Co., Baldwin Park, California, 2002.

Mitchell, James R. *Gem Trails of New Mexico*. Gem Guides Book Co., Baldwin Park, California, 2001.

Mitchell, James R. *Gem Trails of Northern California*. Gem Guides Book Co., Baldwin Park, California, 2005.

Mitchell, James R. *Gem Trails of Oregon*. Gem Guides Book Co., Baldwin Park, California, 1998.

Mitchell, James R. *Gem Trails of Southern California*. Gem Guides Book Co., Baldwin Park, California, 2003.

Mitchell, James R. *Gem Trails of Utah*. Gem Guides Book Co., Baldwin Park, California, 2006.

Mitchell, James R. *The Rockhound's Handbook*. Gem Guides Book Co., Baldwin Park, California, 1997.

Ream, Lanny R. *Idaho Minerals*. Museum of North Idaho, Coeur d'Alene, Idaho, 2004.

Ream, Lanny R. *Gem & Mineral Collector's Guide to Idaho*. Gem Guides Book Co., Baldwin Park, California, 2000.

Stepanski, Scott, and Karenne Snow. *Gem Trails of Pennsylvania and New Jersey*. Gem Guides Book Co., Baldwin Park, California, 2000.

Voynick, Stephen M. *Colorado Rockhounding*. Mountain Press Publishing Company, Missoula, Montana, 1994.

Wilson, James R. *A Collector's Guide to Rock, Mineral & Fossil Localities of Utah*. Utah Geological Survey, Salt Lake City, Utah, 1995.

Zeitner, June Culp. *Midwest Gem, Fossil and Mineral Trails: Great Lakes States*. Gem Guides Book Co., Baldwin Park, California, 1999.

Zeitner, June Culp. *Midwest Gem, Fossil and Mineral Trails: Prairie States*. Gem Guides Book Co., Baldwin Park, California, 1998.

GOLD PROSPECTING

Black, Jack. *Gold Prospector's Handbook*. Gem Guides Book Co., Baldwin Park, California, 1978.

Butler, Gail A. *Recreational Gold Prospecting for Fun and Profit*. Gem Guides Book Co., Baldwin Park, California, 1998.

de Lorenzo, Lois. *Gold Fever: The Art of Panning and Sluicing*. Gem Guides Book Co., Baldwin Park, California, 1978.

Garrett, Charles L. *Modern Metal Detectors*, Rev. ed. Ram Publishing Company, Dallas, Texas, 1998.

Klein, James and Jerry Keene. *How to Find Gold*. Keene Engineering Co., Northridge, California, 1996.

Klein, James. *Where to Find Gold in Northern California*. Gem Guides Book Co., Baldwin Park, California, 2000.

Klein, James. *Where to Find Gold in Southern California*. Gem Guides Book Co., Baldwin Park, California, 1994.

Lagal, Roy. *The New Gold Panning is Easy*. Ram Publishing Company, Dallas, Texas, 2001.

McCracken, Dave. *Gold Mining in the 21st Century*. Keene Industries, Northridge, California, 2005.

McPherson, Roger. *Modern Prospecting*. Gem Guides Co., Baldwin Park, California, 2002.

Ryan, A. H. *The Weekend Gold Miner*. Gem Guides Book Co., Baldwin Park, California, 1991.

Silva, Mark S. *Stake Your Claim: A Step-by-Step Guide*. Mark S. Silva, Santa Cruz, California, 2007.

Here are some websites of interest to rockhounds, treasure hunters and fossil buffs. You can't spend every day searching for interesting collectibles, so for those down days you can search the Internet for virtual finds and interesting information. Please note that websites change and expire. This list was accurate when we went to press. Enjoy the ride.

GOLD SITES

THE NEW '49ERS
http://www.goldgold.com/
- This recreational gold prospecting club helps hobby prospectors learn tips and techniques, provides opportunities for trips to their claims on the Klamath River in California and the creek near Happy Camp. The group also maintains claims in Arizona.

ORIGINAL SIXTEEN TO ONE MINE
http://www.origsix.com/
- This California gold mine is famous for the crystalline deposited in snowy white quartz. This commercial operation offers tours to the public and sells specimens and jewelry.

49ER MIKE'S PROSPECTORS CACHE
http://www.tomashworth.com/
- This site has a plethora of information on gold mining, metal detecting and treasure hunting, including tips, how-to information, forums, chats and treasure hunting equipment for sale.

PROSPECTOR'S GOLD & GEMS
http://users.frii.com/gold/gold.html
- This site sells gold nuggets, dust, platinum, emeralds and other precious things.

SHIPWRECK TREASURE SITES

MEL FISHER'S TREASURE SITE
http://www.melfisher.com/
- Explore Spanish treasure recovered from the coast of Florida by legendary treasure hunter Mel Fisher and his crew.

SPANISH MAIN TREASURE COMPANY
http://www.nvo.com/treasure/faqaboutus/
- This salvage company, founded by Captain Carl Fismer, recovers artifacts and sunken treasure from shipwrecks around the world. They sell treasure, coins, artifacts and other items of interest to those who want to own a piece of history or a piece of eight.

EXPEDITION *WHYDAH*
http://www.whydah.com/
- The pirate ship *Whydah* captained by infamous Sam Bellamy, sunk in 1717 off the coast of Cape Cod taking one hundred forty-four men and booty from over fifty ships to the bottom. Treasure salvager Barry Clifford found the wreck and the salvaged artifacts can be seen online or at his museum in Providence town. The site has a ship's store.

INSTITUTE OF MARINE ARCHAEOLOGICAL CONSERVATION
http://www.imacdigest.com/
- Visitors can keep abreast of the current events and issues in treasure salvage here.

QUARTZ CRYSTALS SITES

STARFIRE QUARTZ CRYSTALS MINES
http://www.starfirecrystals.com/
- This is a crystal mine that sells all types of rock specimens, and operates a crystal mine where you can dig your own crystals.

WEGNER QUARTZ CRYSTAL MINES
http://www.wegnercrystalmines.com/
- This is a crystal mine that sells all types of rock specimens and operates a crystal mine where you can dig your own crystals.

WORLD CHAMPIONSHIP CRYSTAL DIG ARKANSAS
http://www.mtidachamber.com/crystal_dig_info.htm
- Annual contest offering prizes to the winner, crystal trophies and of course, you keep all the crystals you dig.

QUARTZ, QUILTZ AND CRAFTZ FESTIVAL ARKANSAS
http://www.mtidachamber.com/quartz_festival.htm
- This is an annual crafts festival focusing on gems, minerals and oddly enough—quilts!

CRYSTAL HEAVEN MINING CO. INC.
http://www.crystalheaven.com/
- This site has much information on the digging, cleaning and sale of quartz crystals and metaphysics.

ROCK SHOPS SITES

WRIGHT'S ROCK SHOP
http://www.wrightsrockshop.com/
- This Arkansas rock shop specializes in quartz crystals and clusters.

THE SILVER ARMADILLO
http://www.silverarmadillo.com/silverarmadillo/index2.html
- This North Carolina store is a showroom of jewelry, minerals and fossils from around the world.

THE ROCKHOUND SHOP
http://www.rockhoundshop.com/index.htm
- Located in Victoria, British Columbia, this family-owned shop carries a wide range of supplies, equipment and books for collectors, prospectors, stone-polishers, soft-stone carvers and jewelry makers.

THE ROCK SHED
http://www.therockshed.com/
- This South Dakota store carries a large variety of rocks, gemstones, minerals and fossil specimens; as well as books, lapidary equipment and jewelry making supplies.

MAMA'S MINERALS
http://www.mamasminerals.com/index.html
- This New Mexico shop has everything for the rockhound, mineral or fossil collector, meteorite enthusiast or metaphysician.

FACETS GEM & MINERAL GALLERY
http://www.4facets.com/index.html
- This Oregon shop has everything carries everything a budding rockhound would want from specimens, books, lapidary supplies and tools.

DAVE'S DOWN TO EARTH ROCK SHOP
http://www.davesdowntoearthrockshop.com/
- This Illinois rock shop and museum is a haven for all who love fossils, minerals and just plain cool stuff!

CALDRON CRAFTS
http://www.CaldronCrafts.com
- This Maryland shop is a treasure trove for the rock, mineral, or crystal collector with information and supplies for displaying your finds, creating jewelry, or learning about the metaphysical properties of your finds.

BOB'S ROCK SHOP
http://www.rockhounds.com/rockshop/table.html
- A non-commercial site that displays mineral specimens and provides topical information on locating gems and minerals.

ARIZONA ROCKSHOP
http://www.arizona-rockshop.com/
- This Arizona rock shop offers information on rocks and specimens for sale.

Gems and Mineral Sites

CHRYSOPASE MINES OF AUSTRALIA

http://www.australianjade.com.au/index.html
- This Australian site tells you everything you want to know about chrysopase, including how to buy it.

FABRE MINERALS

http://www.fabre-minerals.com/
- This site sells high quality mineral specimens from around the world.

MYSTIC MERCHANT

http://www.mysticmerchant.com/
- Gem and jewelry enthusiasts will find gems, crystals, cabochons, faceted and one of a kind jewelry for sale at this site. Metaphysical books and information are also available.

TRINITY MINERAL COMPANY

http://www.trinityminerals.com/index.htm
- This shop has an interesting variety of gold and mineral specimens for sale.

THE ARKENSTONE

http://www.irocks.com/
- This company supplies a variety of specimen rocks and minerals.

MINERAL MINERS.COM

http://www.mineralminers.com/
- This virtual gallery displays thousands of photographs of mineral specimens, crystals, gemstones, hand crafted jewelry, rough material and gift items.

HERKIMER DIAMONDS MINE

http://www.herkimerdiamond.com/
- These world-famous double-terminated quartz crystals are faceted by natural forces. The Herkimer Diamond Mine site includes information on the crystals, tips on how to mine, recent finds and specimens, jewelry and books for sale.

JOHN BETTS FINE MINERALS

http://www.johnbetts-fineminerals.com/
- New minerals are added every week to this site, so customers will be pleased with the variety and constant arrival of new specimens.

Prospecting and Metal Detector Sites

KEENE ENGINEERING

http://www.keeneengineering.com/
- At this site you can find virtually all your prospecting and mining needs all in one place.

KELLYCO METAL DETECTORS SUPER STORE

http://www.kellycodetectors.com/
- This distributor supplies all brands of metal detectors and other tools for the metal detector hobbyists.

THE LIFESTYLE STORE

http://www.lifestylestore.com/
- The most complete gold prospecting and outdoor equipment supplier on the Internet with affiliated stores throughout the West.

MINELAB, INC.

http://www.minelab.com.au/
- This Australian manufacturer created the broadband system of metal detectors, and has many models from which to choose.

TREASURE NET

http://www.treasurenet.com/
- This site keeps hobbyists up-to-date on what is being found, places to go, and is a good addition to any metal detector's links.

WHITES ELECTRONICS, INC.
http://www.whiteselectronics.com/
• Whites metal detectors are tried and true–a well-known brand.

FOSSIL SITES

COLLECTING FOSSILS IN CALIFORNIA
http://www.gtlsys.com/
• This site provides information on fossil sites in California, and instructions on how to collect, prepare and display your finds.

AMBERICA WEST
http://www.ambericawest.com/index2.html
• Amber of all sorts is sold at this site. Many of the specimens have insects, plants, spiders and an occasional lizard encased in amber.

TWO GUYS FOSSILS
http://www.twoguysfossils.com/
• Fossils from all over the world for sale.

STEVE'S FOSSIL SHARK TEETH
http://www.megalodonteeth.com/
• This site offers a wide variety of fossilized shark teeth for sale including, great white teeth, megalodon teeth and prints, books and other items.

LAPIDARY AND GEMOLOGY SITES

JOHN MILLER'S GEMOLOGY & LAPIDARY PAGES
http://www.tradeshop.com/gems/index.html
• This site has much information on faceting, as well as tips and techniques on gem cutting and lapidary arts. It is a comprehensive introduction to the jewelry trade.

MSI MULTISTONE INTERNATIONAL INC.
http://www.multistoneintl.com/rough/
• From meteors to incense burners, this place has it for sale.

GEMOLOGICAL INSTITUTE OF AMERICA
http://www.gia.edu/
• This association is an educational institute which certifies gemologists and offers various correspondence courses in the area of gemology.

INTERNATIONAL COLORED GEMSTONE ASSOCIATION
http://www.gemstone.org/
• This association is a colored gemstone information resource, which includes gem lore, gems of the rich and famous, gemstone characteristics and more.

MAGAZINE SITES

LAPIDARY JOURNAL/JEWELRY ARTS
http://www.lapidaryjournal.com/
• *The Lapidary Journal* now *Jewelry Arts,* is a well-known trade magazine for gold and silversmiths, lapidary and gem cutters.

ROCK & GEM MAGAZINE
http://www.rockngem.com/
• *Rock & Gem Magazine* specializes in stories to fascinate gem trail readers, and contains the latest lapidary news.

COLORED STONE MAGAZINE
http://www.colored-stone.com/
• *Colored Stone Magazine* informs readers of who, what, where and when gemstones surface around the world.

ROCKS & MINERALS
http://www.rocksandminerals.org/
• Published by the Heldref Publications Group, this is a magazine for everyone interested in rocks and minerals.

PHOTO GALLERY

Photo Gallery

A copper nugget specimen.

Mining concentrates.

Selenite from Oklahoma.

Thunderegg agates.

Jasper and agate found in the Pacific northwest.

Using a metal detector in the field.

Screening and classifying sapphires.

Gathering water for classifying concentrates.

Using a gold sluice.

Dredging

Screening topaz.

In the field, using a rock pick to free a specimen.

In Montana screening through sapphires.

The Gem Trails Series

Desert Gem Trails, *Strong*.
80 pgs., ISBN 0-910652-15-5, $5.00

Gem Trails of Arizona, *Mitchell*.
272 pgs., ISBN 978-1-889786-47-6, $14.95

Gem Trails of Colorado, *Mitchell*.
224 pgs., ISBN 978-1-889786-41-4, $12.95

Gem Trails of Northern California, *Mitchell*.
192 pgs., ISBN 1-889786-28-4, $12.95

Gem Trails of Southern California, *Mitchell*.
224 pgs., ISBN 1-889786-25-X, $12.95

Gem Trails of Nevada, *Mitchell*.
192 pgs., ISBN 1-889786-15-2, $12.95

Gem Trails of New Mexico, *Mitchell*.
240 pgs., ISBN 1-889786-12-8, $14.95

Gem Trails of Oregon, *Romaine*.
272 pgs., ISBN 978-1-889786-44-5, $14.95

Gem Trails of Pennsylvania & New Jersey,
Stepanski and Snow.
160 pgs., ISBN 1-889786-09-8, $12.95

Gem Trails of Texas, *Cross*.
160 pgs., ISBN 1-889786-11-X, $12.95

Gem Trails of Utah, *Mitchell*.
168 pgs., ISBN 1-889786-37-3, $12.95

Gem Trails of Washington, *Romaine*.
200 pgs., ISBN 1-889786-40-3, $12.95

The GPS Guide to Western Gem Trails, *Kelty*.
240 pgs., ISBN 1-889786-35-7, $17.95

Midwest Gem, Fossil & Mineral Trails:
Great Lakes States, *Zeitner*.
128 pgs., ISBN 1-889786-06-3, $10.95

Midwest Gem, Fossil & Mineral Trails:
Prairie States, *Zeitner*.
128 pgs., ISBN 0-935182-94-2, $10.95

Rocks, Minerals and Geology

Florida's Geological Treasures, *Comfort*.
160 pgs., ISBN 0-935182-95-0, $11.95

Geodes: Nature's Treasures, *Cross & Zeitner*.
304 pgs., ISBN 1-889786-32-3, $18.95

The Rockhound's Handbook, *Mitchell*.
304 pgs., ISBN 978-1-889786-43-8, $15.95

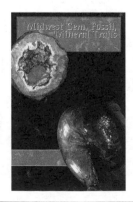

Prospecting & Treasure Hunting

Fee Mining and Mineral Adventures in the
Eastern U.S., *Monaco*.
  264 pgs., ISBN 978-1-889786-49-0, $15.95
Gold Digger's Atlas, *Johnson*.
  64 pgs., ISBN 1-889786-08-X, $7.50
Gold Fever: The Art of Panning and Sluicing,
  de Lorenzo. 80 pgs., ISBN 0-935182-00-4, $6.95
Gold Prospector's Handbook, *Black*.
  176 pgs., ISBN 0-935182-32-2, $10.95
Modern Prospecting, *McPherson*.
  300 pgs., ISBN 1-889786-16-0, $14.95
Placer Gold Deposits of Arizona, *Johnson*.
  103 pgs., ISBN 0-935182-33-0, $9.95
Placer Gold Deposits of Nevada, *Johnson*.
  118 pgs., ISBN 0-89632-010-3, $9.95
Placer Gold Deposits of New Mexico, *Johnson*.
  46 pgs., ISBN 0-89632-004-9, $7.95
Recreational Gold Prospecting for
  Fun and Profit, *Butler*.
  206 pgs., ISBN 0-935182-98-5, $12.95
Sterling Legend: Story of the
  Lost Dutchman Mine, *Conatser*.
  94 pgs., ISBN 1-889786-23-3, $9.95
The Weekend Gold Miner, Ryan.
  80 pgs., ISBN 0-935182-46-2, $5.50
Where to Find Gold & Gems in Nevada, *Klein*.
  109 pgs., ISBN 0-935182-15-2, $8.95
Where to Find Gold in Northern California,
  Klein. 125 pgs., ISBN 1-889786-05-5, $10.95
Where to Find Gold in Southern California,
  Klein. 112 pgs., ISBN 0-935182-68-3, $9.95
Where to Find Gold in the Desert, *Klein*.
  144 pgs., ISBN 0-935182-81-0, $9.95

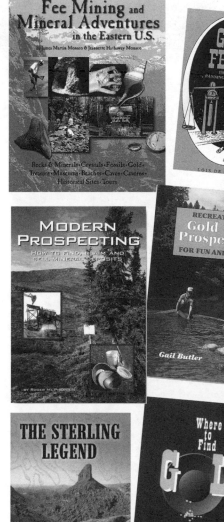

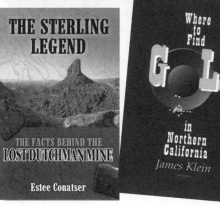

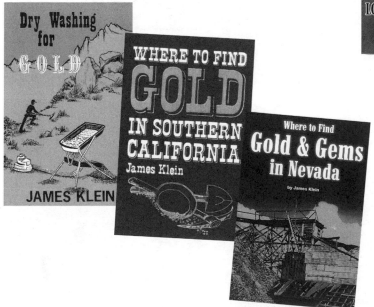

**Available at your local
rock shop, outdoor store,
or bookseller.**

NOTES

NOTES

HAVE WE MISSED A MINE OR COLLECTING SITE?

   If you know of a mine or collecting site that should be included in future editions of this book, please bring it to our attention. Just fill out the bottom half of this sheet and return it to the address listed below. If your location is added to the next edition, we will send you a copy of the next edition free. Thank you for your help.

NAME OF MINE: ─────────────────────────

ADDRESS: ─────────────────────────
─────────────────────────
─────────────────────────

PHONE: ─────────────────────────

TYPE OF MATERIAL FOUND AT MINE: ─────────────
─────────────────────────

METHOD OF COLLECTING: ─────────────────
(EQUIPMENT USED) ─────────────────────

COST: ───────   **SEASON OF OPERATION:** ─────────

ADDITIONAL INFORMATION: ─────────────────
─────────────────────────
─────────────────────────

YOUR NAME & ADDRESS: ───────────────────
─────────────────────────
─────────────────────────

RETURN TO: Attn: Editor
Gem Guides Book Co.
1275 W. 9th Street
Upland, CA 91786